Influence
&
Communication

How to use Influence and Communication to Achieve Success in Your Business and Personal Life

By
Hellen Davis, CLU

The growth of the human mind is still high adventure,

in many ways the highest adventure on Earth.

Norman Cousins

Influence & Communication

Published by Indaba Press
18 Ridgewood Road, Suite 201
Malvern, PA 19355

ISBN: 1-58570-063-0

Printed in the United States of America

Distributed in the United States by Indaba Press

For general information contact:
Indaba, Inc.
info@indaba1.com
www.Indaba1.com

Disclaimer: This manual is a collection of white papers written by master influencer and sales maven, Hellen Davis, over the past twelve years. Throughout the book, Hellen adds examples, comments, experiences, and stories from various industries for managers, entrepreneurs and sales people. Different audiences will relate better to different exercises and examples. The book is primarily targeted for people who must influence and communicate well in order to succeed. When different audiences are targeted, we identify the target audience within the text, saving us the awkward attempt of trying to write three or four different books. This way we also avoid the risk of the reader translating management lessons into the sales arena and vice versa. Wherever possible we will attempt to guide the reader to the best examples and stories for their field or industry. While great care was taken to edit this manual, if you do find any errors or typos we welcome your feedback! Your assistance is greatly appreciated. We do revisions and reprinting on a regular basis to provide you with the highest quality product possible. This is not so much a manual to be read, as it is a manual to be used. The reader does not have to read it from cover to cover to understand the peak performance concepts for influence, language and communication. The compilation of materials is such as to allow the reader to look at most sections as individual modules; and to apply the concepts they need to become better in their field. Because this format was adopted, some repetition (but not so much as to become irritating!) of concepts may be encountered. **We like to think that you can open the manual to any page and get ideas to make your influencing, communication, and language skills better.**

TABLE OF CONTENTS

Introduction to the Impact of Language

In speaking or writing, weak language reduces the impact of our words. It undermines our ability to get our point across.

Weak, ineffective language can hinder our growth. Weak language sabotages our message and robs us of our ability to succeed. It tears at the thread of the cloth that holds our messages and thoughts together. It undermines the very structure of our success and power.

Fortunately, most of us use English with ease and a great degree of effectiveness in situations where we feel comfortable. But, what happens to our stress level when we feel 'out of our league' in verbal or written communication?

When situations arise in which we are forced to give a presentation, write an important letter, or produce something that may be printed for others to read, we often become acutely conscious of how we are speaking or writing. Many times, we feel frustrated and inadequate—even if our words are 'okay' for every day situations.

After studying grammar at school, you may perceive grammar to be a set of boring rules that squabble over petty points. However, throughout your life you will be judged on your command of language. Therefore, it is imperative to understand that the better you communicate, the more successful you will become. Your success may simply become enhanced because your confidence level is higher due to your ease with spoken and written language.

Powerful communicators and leaders understand that correct language usage is vital for peak performance. Effective language usage and grammar are the master keys to persuasion, influence, clarity, and control of your world.

Learn to reason forward and backward on both sides of a question.

Thomas Blandi

Science & Influence

The study of language and communication is a dynamic science. With increased research, the field is consistently changing. New ideas are constantly emerging. Branches of the sciences have evolved because so many people understand that effective communication in a business environment is often judged by whether the person exhibited effective influencing skills. Neuroscience, linguistic research, and behavioral analysis studies have traditionally remained separate, rarely combining efforts with the synergy necessary to tackle the task of fully studying the effects that language geared toward influencing techniques have on the psyche.

Scientists (as well as laymen) have become more conscious of people's desire to communicate and influence efficiently and effectively. With this in mind, I have borrowed models and theories from several sciences. Some of the models I have translated directly, others I have expanded upon and created a new entity—one that fits today's business world. Take the models in this book and adapt them to your personal style, understanding that not all of the techniques will work for you.

Time and time again, research has shown that each of our goals are shaped and formulated by our ability to communicate. People who are perceived as weak often struggle with powerful language. They are overcome by the grammar of weakness. Powerful, strong communicators willingly embrace, command and control the language of power and success.

Powerful language helps us take control of our lives. Commanding verbiage positively impacts our self-confidence. Positive, powerful language leads to our success throughout our life. Effective command of the English language strengthens us and forges bonds with others.

With powerful communication comes the ability to transform yourself into a peak performer. When you shed the language of weakness and fear, and acquire the language of success and courage, you transform yourself from follower to leader.

Your command of the English language and your skill in conveying messages sends a message to those around you. When you communicate clearly, effectively, and confidently others look to you for guidance. When you don't, people discount your ideas and suggestions.

Many people are reluctant to learn and then use powerful language. They think they might appear too pushy if they speak eloquently. Or they have the false belief that by using powerful language they will "take something away" from others during the communication loop. These beliefs are limiting. Powerful language is not arrogant, confrontational, or belittling. The language of power strives to enhance relationships. It seeks to create empathy, clarity, and trust.

Throughout history, those with excellent language usage have inspired, led, and challenged us to become the very best we possibly can.

This book was created in response to the hundreds of seminars I have led in which people have described their frustration with being unable to communicate clearly, concisely, and effectively on every occasion. Their feelings of disappointment frequently stem from lost opportunities. Some people recant details of losing business to a salesperson that communicated better than they did even when the other person's product was not as good. Others speak of not being taken seriously by management and peers. Company representatives expound about their competitor's literature in glowing, envious terms when comparing their own corporation's marketing literature.

Many tell sad tales of how weak language and poor communication planning has consistently sabotaged them or worked against them politically in the workplace. Legions have described social situations in which they felt inferior just because they felt others were better at using language than they were.

Throughout this book, stories have been added to illustrate how to communicate effectively. I also have added analogies of ineffective communication to highlight how not to present yourself. To ensure privacy I have usually altered people's names.

Thank you to contributors

To everyone who has shared their stories and given insight into weak and strong communication during my seminars, I send my heart-felt thanks and appreciation.

INFLUENCE, LANGUAGE, & COMMUNICATION

To truly gain mastery of influence and communication, you must understand and perfect the nuances of language's behavior patterns. Many are easy to understand and using them will require little more than grasping the concept and thinking about previous conversations. These patterns occur everywhere. We use them every day to persuade and influence people. My goal is for you to be able to recognize them and use them for maximum impact. How do you become a master influencer? The same way you become a master at anything – by practicing persuasion and influencing techniques that work. Many are described in this **book.** Listen for one or two language patterns during conversations. Analyze patterns in your business. Pick out some patterns from print advertisements, letters or from e-mail messages. Then, after you recognize them and understand their usage, begin using them yourself. Repetition and practice over time will ensure mastery.

Language is terribly complex. Not all words and phrases in this book are subject to hard and fast rules. I wish they were! This book and the lessons contained in it deal with *general* influencing rules. The information has a solid foundation based on extensive behavioral and psychological research and decades of personal sales and management experience.

It is for precisely this reason that there are (unfortunately) no simple answers for what to say and what not to say. Is every rule in this manual always going to work as planned? No, but most of the time the strategies will move you closer to your influencing goal. Of course there are always exceptions to any rule. This is one of the reasons canned presentations rarely fit all situations and precisely why salespeople so strongly detest them. The reason most companies and sales managers still teach scripted presentations is that *most* of the time they *do* work – *if they are delivered properly.* They are usually based in strong language patterns that are well grounded in behavioral science. I believe that if salespeople and managers *understand why* they work, they could *tailor their presentations* to their personality (and personal value system) and that of their target audience. That is why one of the goals of this book is to help readers to understand the how's and the why's of the influencing process. Ideally, this knowledge will help you to become a master of influence while keeping your personality and style intact.

My advice -- Take the lessons and mold them to your style.

Never try to adopt an influencing technique that does not work with your personal style of communication or selling. If you attempt to do this, those you are trying to influence will sense incongruency. When incongruency exists, trust deteriorates; and you will fail. The majority of the lessons in this manual can be adapted to any person's style. Use the lessons individually or group them together to increase your effectiveness as a master persuader. Use your common sense and hone your skills. Enjoy the influencing process!

This book was written to assist you in positively influencing clients, client/customer prospects, employees, family members, and upper level management. I wrote it specifically for anyone who wants a better command of the English language in a clear, concise format.

Some of the ideas and skill sets in this book will not be new to you. They will simply serve as a refresher course. However, most of the convincer techniques, psychological models, language patterns, and influencing strategies, I am sure, you have never seen before.

Good luck in your quest for reaching peak performance influencing and communication skills!

PERCEPTION & REALITY

Analyzing Perception versus Reality

The starting point for communication and understanding influencing rules and language patterns is being able to analyze perception versus reality.

In an ideal world, perception and reality would always be equal. People often say, "Perception equals reality." Actually, nothing could possibly be further from the truth! Think about it. Perception is how people view reality. Perception is not reality – people just think it is! What is important about perception and reality? The influencing process is controlled by perception. People base their behavior and actions on their perceptions. For example, if I think you are telling the truth, I will base my decisions about my interactions with you on this view. If I think you are lying to me, I will have another set of reactions to you. In dealing with people's behavior, it really doesn't matter whether I am factual if you think I'm not!

When Christopher Columbus was trying to obtain financing for his voyage across the Atlantic, he told people that he could travel to the Far East faster by sailing westward. At that time, travel to the Far East included a trip around the treacherous Cape of Good Hope—the Cape of Storms. Columbus said he could avoid the Cape and its perils. No one before him had suggested this bold venture. He said he could save time and money with his western route.

At the time, the common perception was that the Earth was flat. People believed that if you sailed far enough, you would come to the end of the Earth and simply fall off. It was deemed foolhardy and dangerous to take a vessel and her crew to their sure death by sailing west.

For nearly a decade, Columbus tried to attain financing for his quest. He held onto his dream and eventually procured financing from Queen Isabella of Spain. In 1492, although he did not sail to the Far East, he discovered the New World and debunked many of the myths of his time. His perception was at odds with the perception of others. Neither perception was in fact reality based. Columbus's perception of what reality had to be played a major role in his discovery of the New World and assured him a place in history. Other peoples' perception caused substantial stress for Columbus and resulted in many years' delay before he was able to alter a backer's perception, enabling him to begin his voyage.

The lesson here is simple, the quicker you are able to control perception, the faster you will achieve your influencing goals.

Have you ever found it curious that sometimes people base their actions on things that you know are definitely false—rather than on the truth? Why is that?

Scam artists make their living swindling money and possessions from innocent victims. These criminals completely understand that humans tend to base decisions, behavior, and actions—not on the truth—but on *that which we perceive to be true.*

Attorney Generals in every state can recant endless stories of people buying swamp land in Florida, 'insider' information used to make (or lose) millions, $4,000 19" color TV sets in 'sweepstakes', miracle pills, Ponzi schemes and other grand plans designed to have people part with their cash quickly. These schemes are fixed on baseless promises and happen largely due to perception.

Why do people participate in crazy schemes? How do intelligent people get roped into believing scam artists? Why do individuals save their whole life and get conned out of their life savings by a smooth-talking criminal? It is all about perception versus reality.

People tend to think positively. They believe the world is a bright place – full of hope. People who hope to immigrate to the United States often dream of streets paved with gold. Folks venture into the rainforest seeking miracle cures and adventurers seek out Shangri-La, Atlantis and the Wonders of the Ancient World. Human beings think about their dreams and goals and aspirations. If a person has been unsuccessful in achieving their goals and someone else comes along promising to help—they tend to believe the other person first—then perhaps doubt them later. We have become very good at overlooking warning signs when our minds fixate on a dream. This is basic human behavior – and scam artists take full advantage of the way our minds work.

Since childhood, we have been trained to believe that people are to be trusted—until they do something to jeopardize that trust. Our legal system operates on first giving a person the benefit of the doubt. Innocent until proven guilty is our mantra.

With this mentality – with this pattern of behavior—innocents are quickly roped in with pledges of easy money, good health, quick weight loss, and other things their hearts desire. This is especially true whenever scam artists use excellent communication and psychological tactics. The more trusting the victims are—the less dishonesty and deception they have experienced throughout their life—the more likely they are to suffer a loss through perception.

Key Point

Your goal should always be to:
Make certain your view of reality (your perception) is as close to reality as possible.

Language and Perception

In any communication loop there is a sender and a receiver. During communication, the roles of sender and receiver constantly shift. As soon as you send a message to another person there is an expectation that they will send a message back to you based on their response to your communication.

What is often misunderstood about the sender/receiver relationship is that there are no fine lines of distinction between when you stop sending and begin receiving—and vice versa. In fact, you continue receiving communication information from other parties even when you are sending out messages. Your senses are constantly picking up signals sent from others even while you speak. When you are listening, your body signals responses through conscious or unconscious body language.

Sender's Responsibility

As the sender, you must take 100% responsibility to:

1. Create your message
2. Deliver it
3. Make sure your message is understood.

Receiver's Responsibility

The receiver has no responsibility in making sure that your message is delivered or that they have received and understand it as you wanted it to be relayed.

Let's look at some examples of how this works.

If I sent you an email and expect a response, it is **my job** to confirm that the email was delivered to you. I must also verify that my message is written in language that you comprehend, with a clear understanding of the action steps that I expect from you.

Miscommunication happens all the time. Luckily, in the first months of my marriage I learned to take 100% responsibility for the messages I delivered to my husband. Unfortunately, I learned the hard way. But, sometimes learning the hard way helps the lesson to stick!

During the first years of our marriage, my husband and I were each starting our own companies. The days were full. We worked hard preparing to meet clients, selling, prospecting, and scrambling to get everything done. Most workdays were high-stress and at least 12-hours long. Typically, when Friday came, we were ready to stay home and eat whatever was handy. One Sunday, I casually mentioned to my husband that I missed cooking for him on Friday nights. When we were dating, I lived in California and he lived in Philadelphia. Usually when Jack flew across the country to visit, he arrived tired on Friday night. I got into the habit of preparing a wonderful home-cooked meal. That particular Sunday, Jack said he missed that, too. After our conversation, I decided to surprise him by preparing a lovely meal the following Friday. Throughout the week I gathered everything I needed for my surprise -- ingredients, candles, and our favorite wine.

On Friday morning, I kissed Jack goodbye and told him I would see him for dinner that evening. I could see he was preoccupied and asked what was on his schedule for the day. He said that he had been preparing for nearly two months for an appointment he had scheduled with a client that afternoon. I wished him good luck and said, "You'll do fine! I'll see you at dinnertime. We'll relax and you can tell me how well it went." I then asked what time he thought he'd be home. As he was running out the door he said, "Around 6 o'clock." “Perfect timing!” I thought, as I mentally went through my plans.

At about noon, I stopped working and went shopping for the final ingredients. At one, I was in the beauty salon getting my hair and nails done. By 3 o'clock, I was cleaning and preparing our romantic dinner. At 6 o'clock, the food was in the oven, the candles were lit, I had put on a special outfit, and the wine was breathing. At 6:15, precisely the moment I was calling Jack, he was leaving the message that he would be home before seven -- with pizza! Boy, was I angry! Then, I thought, "It doesn't matter – we’ll heat up the pizza and eat it tomorrow."

At 6:45 PM, my husband walked in the door carrying a pizza box. I looked at his face as he took in the scene and I knew my plans were in trouble. His first words were, "What's that I smell? Did you cook dinner? I didn't know! I already bought pizza and have eaten two slices.” By the look on his face, I had made a mistake in not telling him of my dinner plans!

Unfortunately, my disappointment (that the evening was turning into disaster!) made me defensive. He also tried to justify his ‘not knowing’ -- in other words -- that he was right and I was wrong because I hadn’t told him what was in my head. Listen to the conversation we had that evening.

Hellen: Why did you buy pizza? I told you I would see you for dinner.

Jack: I didn't know you were cooking. I told you I'd see you at dinnertime. It's dinnertime and I'm here. You didn't say anything about food.

Hellen: But why did you eat the pizza before you got home? Couldn't you have waited? Wouldn't it have been nice if we had eaten together for a change? Didn't we have this conversation on Sunday?

Jack: You didn't say anything about making dinner on Sunday!

Hellen: Yes we did! Don't you remember? We talked about how much we both missed eating together on Fridays.

Jack: We were talking about dating in California!

Hellen: Well, times have changed! When we were dating you would've waited to eat with me! You would always be starving on Friday nights then too, but would always wait to eat with me.

Jack: For crying out loud, it's just pizza! Not a gourmet meal! It's not my fault that you didn't tell me your plans! I thought you would like not having to cook tonight. I know how busy you are. This morning, you said we were just going to relax tonight. This doesn't look like you're relaxing. When we were dating, you told me your whole agenda for the weekend when I was visiting you -- starting with dinner on Friday. That's why I would wait! I haven't eaten anything since breakfast this morning. I was getting a headache and that's why I ate. I didn't know you had this whole thing planned. You didn't tell me!

Hellen: You're right. **(Suddenly realizing it was entirely my fault!)** I'm sorry. But now the whole evening's ruined! (Thank goodness my husband picked up that I really was sorry and he tried to help me put the evening back on the right track.)

Jack: No, it's not! I'm still hungry. Let's pretend this didn't happen and that I just walked in the door. I'll trash this pizza outside and we'll start again. I'll pretend I'm hungry...

Hellen: (laughing) Okay, but you'd better give me a minute to put my happy face back on!

Needless to say, after we both started laughing, it was a lovely evening and we both (but I especially) learned a valuable lesson. Now I take 100% responsibility in my role as the sender in communication. I know that it is my responsibility to be clear about my intentions and to ensure that the other person understands them. I also have to ascertain that any expectations I have are clearly outlined and comprehended by the receiver of the message. I expected Jack to come home and be hungry. Jack expected me to be hungry and not want to cook. It's amazing how quickly miscommunication, even between two well-intentioned people, can make negative emotions rise!

> Key Point #1
> Your senses take in information and translate it into mental images so that your mind can process thoughts, store information, react during communication, create innovative solutions, and a variety of other brain functions.
>
> Key Point #2
> As soon as reality is translated by your senses, reality turns into perception.

In most communication loops, perception overrides reality. A person's experiences, beliefs and values provide the building blocks of their perception. Perception is how you filter reality through your senses.

Perceptual Prisms & Positions: The Basis of Communication Analysis

Different people have different views of the world based on their experiences, values, and beliefs throughout their life. Just imagine that all communication between people is transferred through the senses by way of images, thoughts, and energy.

Sensory input is processed by a prism that filters reality. As soon as the sensory input reaches the prism, reality is turned into perception Perceptual prisms are the gateway to your mind. No images of the outside world can enter your mind unless they are filtered through your prism. Since communication is an event, all communication must enter your mind through your perceptual prism. Perceptual prisms are like snowflakes. No two perceptual prisms are identical. Every individual has a unique perceptual prism through which they filter reality.

Every individual in the communication loop processes incoming and outgoing messages through their perceptual prism. To get a clear picture of how people interact in any communication loop, visualize each individual as if they are speaking to you through their individual perceptual prism. The other persons' words, thoughts, and images only come to you after they have passed through the other person's prism. After they flow through their perceptual prism, the communication then passes through your perceptual prism. Perceptual prisms can positively influence communication or taint it negatively.

perceptual positions

THREE SIDES OF THE PERCEPTUAL PRISM

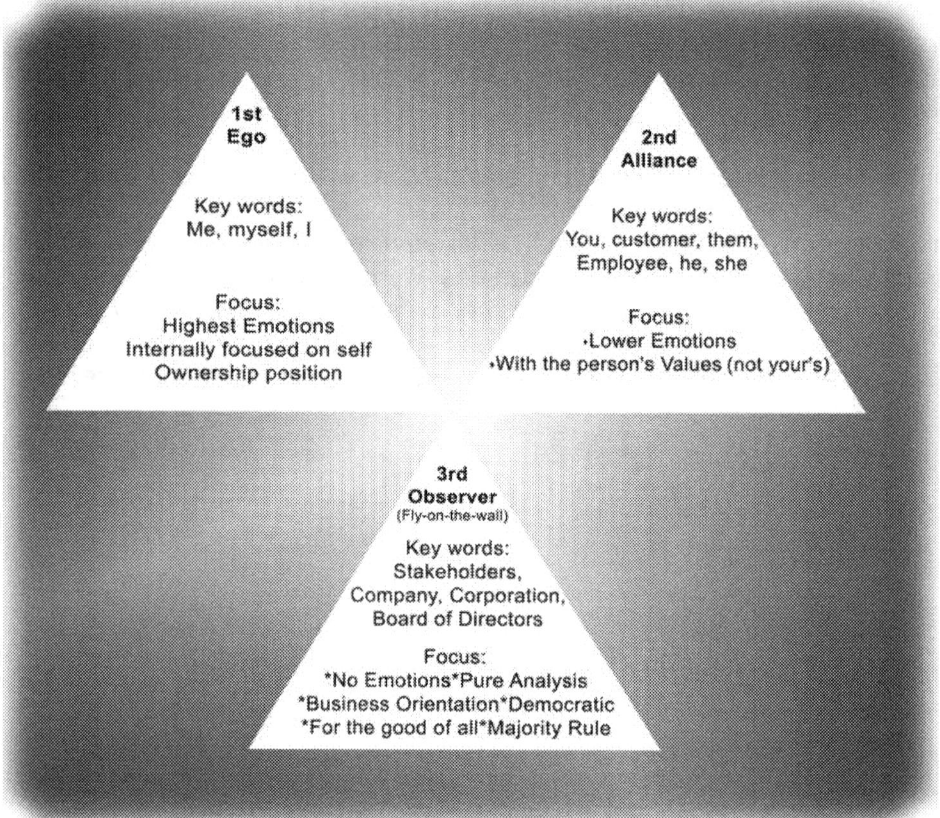

Peak performance communication uses all three perceptual positions.

You can only look through one side of the prism at a time. Planning is best!

Note: 2nd & 3rd perceptual positions may have more than one viewpoint (e.g., customer & employee).

[1] The Perceptual Prism Model is explained in greater detail in the book The 21 Laws of Influence.

Perceptual Position Communication Goal

The goal is to use **all** the perceptual prisms during interactions. To operate in all three perceptual positions for peak performance communication, you have to consciously make the decision to analyze interactions from the other perceptual prisms. You should consciously jump between all three perceptual positions. Perceptual flexibility & versatility are the keys to peak performance communication.

EXERCISE PERCEPTUAL POSITION COMMUNICATION GOAL

What is the value of analyzing perceptual positions?

____

____

____

____

____

____

What are the risks if you do not analyze communication from all three perceptual positions before trying to influence someone?

____

____

____

____

____

____

COMPONENTS OF COMMUNICATION

The influencing process has sometimes been referred to as the martial art of communication. A fundamental goal of learning the techniques of the influencing process is mastering the art of verbal and non-verbal communication on the conscious and subconscious levels. If you have knowledge of the patterns and models, the influencing process becomes easy to learn and very effective. Often, this knowledge is simply a natural progression of the skill sets we already possess.

The way we communicate with others and with ourselves
ultimately determines the quality of our lives.
—Anthony Robbins, Unlimited Power

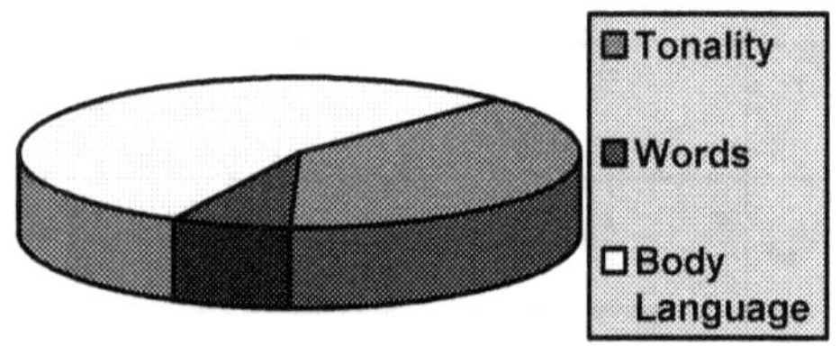

Communication is very detailed and involves so much more than the words we say. We are very expressive as human beings. A well-known research study[2] has shown that more than 55% of the impact of the message that you convey is determined by your body language; this includes your posture, gestures, facial expressions, and eye contact. More than 38% is delivered by the tonality of your voice and only 7% is sent by the content of your presentation. The content comprises the actual words you have chosen to use while communicating. When quoting this research, the actual percentages may change given differing messages, but the concept remains solid. Clearly, body language and tonality make an enormous impact on the meaning of what we say. **It is not what we say, but how we say it that makes the difference**.

> **Key Point**
> Research indicates that 55% of the message of your presentation will come from your body language: posture, gestures, eye contact, and facial expressions. 38% will be conveyed by your voice tonality and only 7% will be relayed by the content (actual words).

---

[2] *Mehrabian and Ferris, 'Inference of Attitudes from Non-verbal Communication in Two Channels' in the Journal of Counseling Psychology Vol. 31, 1967, pp. 248-252.*

Key point—It is dangerous to assume that certain body language means the same thing to everyone. You should pay close attention to the messages you are sending. Awareness that you may be misjudging other people's body language is critical. You may incorrectly receive the messages they wish to send because of your history in reading another person's body language signals.

Albert Mehrabian's studies on communication put forth the theory that when listeners judge the emotional content of a speech, they give the most weight to the speaker's facial expressions and body movement—their overall body language. Exactly how much weight? We can clearly see from the chart that 55% of the communication loop's messages are based on body language—posture, gestures, eye contact and facial expressions. When you are sending or receiving messages, parties involved in the communication dance continue to process and receive information from each other. Peoples' judgment calls about communication messages are based upon their individual perception and interpretation of body language. This is based on their experiences. Cultural differences will play a role in how people read body language.

The chart also makes clear that the next most important aspect in the communication loop is the vocal quality of the message. This particular study says that 38% of your message will be conveyed through voice tonality—total voice, voice pitch, and the speed (pace or tempo) of the delivery.

If you add the first two components of communication together—55% from body language and 38% from vocal quality—you will see that these two factors provide the majority of communication—93%.

Later, we will discuss body language and its impact on the influencing process in more depth. Several studies have attempted to provide insight into how people relate to each other specifically with regard to body language and vocal qualities. Some research reports that the premise for building a large degree of trust and rapport revolves around the theory of using your body and vocal qualities in harmony with others in the communication loop. In other words, you should mirror and match other people's body language and vocal qualities in order to create a high degree of trust.

To illustrate this point, imagine traveling from city to city in the United States as a regional sales director. It is your job to make the employees believe that you have the ability to lead the sales force towards a positive future. In this situation, trust is a necessary element in your success. Let's see how you could build trust by adjusting your tempo (vocal quality) to your audience:

Tempo Adjustments

You are on the first leg of a multi-city journey. The first city you stop in is New York City. You hop in a taxicab and immediately notice that the cabdriver speaks quickly. His words seem to be at a rapid fire pace. You feel them coming at you far more quickly than you can process them. Fortunately, in the 45 minutes it takes to get to the office building, you have settled into the pace. In fact, you notice that your speech pattern has stepped up a notch or two. Your team meets you and escorts you to the conference room. Everyone around you talks and walks more quickly than you are accustomed to here in the city that never sleeps. You are surprised to realize that, just by being in that atmosphere, your pace has increased and the pace of your words is very close to theirs. The meeting begins and your speech goes well. Everyone seems pumped up and ready to take on the task of bringing in new customers. The positive afterglow of the meeting is what you feel when you jump into a cab and head to the airport.

The next city on your agenda is Richmond, VA. On the plane, people going home from a sightseeing trip to New York surround you. By the time you land in Richmond, you have settled back to your normal pace. At the airport, you notice that the frantic pace of New York City has been left far behind. You hail a taxi. The driver gets out to help you with your luggage. On the way into the city, your driver points out interesting buildings and tells you the name of the river you have just crossed. He drives below the posted speed limit. By the time you reach the company's offices, the speed your body was running at in New York City has slowed dramatically.

> **According to behavioral and communication studies, the majority of communication's effect is channeled through body language and vocal qualities—ostensibly your verbal presentation—and very little is left for the meaning of the words. Major impact in the communication loop centers on <u>how people hear you, the speed at which they listen,</u> and <u>the way people see (perceive) you</u>.**

By the time the local manager greets you, your gestures and speech pattern have automatically slowed to the tempo of the people in Richmond. In the conference room, a late lunch has been set out and the salespeople start to arrive. You notice they don't get down to business right away. They talk about friends, family, and business freely. Many people ask about your flight and hope that your trip is going well. The session begins after lunch with each person in turn quoting a motivational snippet. As you listen, you jot one down of your own.

Finally, it is your turn to speak. The speech that took 15 minutes in New York City expands to 30 minutes here. As you are about to leave, you suddenly become consciously aware that your overall actions in both New York City and Richmond paralleled the pace of the people surrounding you. Funny that you hadn't noticed this before! You smile as you head for the airport.

Key point: Any communicator who ignores body language and vocal quality does so at his or her own peril. Gestures, movement, expressions, tonality, and the tempo of your delivery speak volumes—regardless of the words you use. Hone your skills—especially with regard to 93 percent of your message!

By now, you probably recognize that full understanding of this communication component will very often trigger thoughts in your mind regarding the messages you send—consciously or unconsciously, verbally and non-verbally – during your influencing attempts. That is the goal – you should be able to recognize and analyze the tempo of communication from an influencing standpoint, and adjust your tempo to that of the other person (people) in the communication loop.

Remember -- Only seven percent of your message is composed of the actual content—the meaning of the words—in your message.

What do successful influencers focus on?

All powerful influencers, including politicians, sales people, corporate leaders and ministers, are highly skilled and always accomplish four things when influencing people:

1. **Determine the desired outcome**.
2. **Tune your sensory acuity** so that you immediately realize the EXACT MOMENT you reach your outcome and can act or close efficiently. Note: Too many people talk too long!
3. **Evaluate and benchmark** consistently to ensure your goal track progress.
4. Have the **behavioral flexibility** to vary or change what you are doing if what you are currently doing is not working.

Some basic rules to help you develop communication skills are:

Smile

People tend to do business with people with a positive attitude. A positive attitude is reflected best by a smile! Caution—do not give the impression that you are a grinning idiot. Appropriate timing and awareness of smiling is important. People who smile too much can give the impression that others can take advantage of them or that they are not serious about tasks or opportunities presented.

Posture

Walk tall and send the clear message that you are in command—that you take pride in your appearance—that you are confident and purposeful. When you enter a room, plan to make an entrance that communicates who you are and what you think about yourself.

Eye contact

Eye contact instantly transmits energy. Appropriate eye contact is the key. Do not 'stare the other person down'. Eye contact is not a power struggle—it is a way to build trust.

Appropriate energy

Putting your best foot forward means going forth with positive energy. Appropriate is the key word. Ascertain what energy level is expected of you in any given situation. To become memorable in others' eyes, you might want to develop a strategy whereby you keep your energy level just a little above that which is expected of you. People's energy levels are contagious. Energy levels translate into attitude and behavior. Realize that your energy level has a direct impact on those around you. Are you emitting positive energy or are you beaming out negative rays?

> Remember this quote:
> "Attitudes—are contagious. Is yours worth catching?"

Get a grip

Deliver a great handshake. Have you ever been taught to shake hands effectively? Once upon a time, fathers took their sons aside in a rite of passage. Fathers explained the importance of a good, solid handshake. This rite of passage might seem unnecessary now to some. Rarely, when I ask women and men if they were taught to shake hands properly, do I get an affirmative answer in my seminars. The right kind of handshake is often a key to business and social success.

Learning to shake hands properly is very similar to the process used when learning to play a racket sport. When you learned to play tennis, your coach told to keep your eye on the ball until it hit the racket and then to follow through. When shaking hands, keep your eye on the web (the soft skin found between the thumb and index finger). As you see the other person's hand extent towards yours, keep your eye on the web until you have made contact with the web of their hand. The moment you feel contact, lift your eyes immediately. When you feel the connection, then, and only then, lift your eyes to theirs and smile. By doing this, your palm and theirs will automatically connect. Use a moderate, firm grip. Do not squeeze. Start talking before you let go of the other person's hand. Say, "It's wonderful to meet you", "I'm glad to meet you", or "How do you do?"

When you make contact web-to-web, you avoid a myriad of problems associated with handshakes. Some of these problems are:

- Lack of confidence
- Delivering a "wet fish" weak handshake
- Squishing people's hands [especially if they have rings on] and thereby appearing too rough.

The benefits of shaking hands correctly, with authority and confidence, are:

- We appear confident, at ease, and in charge.
- We look poised.
- We exude physical warmth.
- People remember touch and physical contact. They are more willing to trust someone who exhibits a powerful, confident air through their handshake.

Body language and non-verbal communication that kill trust are often signals that are sent out unconsciously by the sender but picked up consciously – sometimes with a great deal of irritation—by the receiver. The bottom line: Avoid sending gestures that limit or destroy trust. Consciously eliminate all verbal and non-verbal communication[3] that signals uncertainty, general nervousness, or fear.

---

[3] See the section titled -- Tendencies that Break Down the Influencing Process – later in the book.

Emulate Relaxed Energy

Energy can be perceived as a positive or negative quality. As we now know, most of the message we send is portrayed through our body language and vocal qualities. It would be wonderful to have everyone we meet think of us as enthusiastic, poised, confident, and content in our environment. Fortunately, exhibiting an air of relaxed energy is fairly easy to accomplish.

The place to start is with your breathing pattern. Think back to a time when you noticed someone was out of breath and appeared flustered. Often people assume that people who are out of breath are so because they are anxious, scared, upset, worried, nervous or stressed. If you ever notice that your breathing pattern is shorter, more shallow, or faster than normal, immediately adjust your pattern to the people around you. If you are able to quickly and consciously adjust your breathing rate to match that of other people, you will tend to stay in sync with them and they will feel more comfortable with you.

> People who are in sync with others (when communicating) tend to be viewed (perceived) as being trustworthier than those who are not in physiological harmony.

If you do find that you breathing rate has sped up, that you are in a negative emotional state, consciously adjusting your breathing pattern—slowing it down—will automatically result in a more positive, focused emotional state. Note: Do not pace your breathing with others if their breathing reflects a negative emotional state like frustration or anger. Also never match the breathing of someone who is ill.

Many studies have shown that emotional states are reflected in physiological sensations and symptoms. Often, we first notice that we're becoming anxious or negatively influenced by physical sensations, such as flushed cheeks, tight fists, sweaty palms, etc. Being aware of these negative signs causes us to become even more negatively influenced. For example: If you notice that you're scared and try to analyze your fear, this often results in an intensification of that fear—not a reduction of that negative emotion. If you find yourself in a situation in which you are blushing – asking yourself "Why am I blushing?" often only results in a redder face!

Key Point

The mind and body are completely linked. If you want to calm your mind, calm your body first.

Command Your Voice

Ferris' and Mehrabian's research shows that 38 percent of your communication message is conveyed through vocal qualities. Other studies have shown that people with deeper voices are generally perceived as more persuasive than those whose voices are more high-pitched. The study shows that this is true of women as well as men. Broadcast journalists are trained to lower the timber of their voices to become more clear and pleasing to the ear of their listening audience. If it is necessary for you to influence others, adjusting the pitch of your voice to a lower level has several benefits.

These include being able to:

- Make certain you are not straining your vocal cords.
- Minimize any nasal vocal quality (many listeners find 'nasal whining' annoying).
- Slow down your words to speak more clearly.
- Produce a more pleasing voice tonality.
- Increase your volume. A full, resonant sound carries better than a thin, tinny voice.
- Ensure that you articulate your words correctly.

Visual Impact

In today's corporate environment, many people are reluctant to address the issue of attire and image. A visually appealing image—one that conveys the message you wish to send—is vital as a communication channel. Whether you like it or not, judgment calls will be made on your appearance and attire. I'm not saying that it's right or fair—I'm simply stating, "It is what it is!"

Different situations require different attire. A suit may not be appropriate if you are calling on a client on a Friday 'casual day'. The other side of the coin is that casual clothing, which might be perfectly acceptable at your company, may not be appropriate for your client's environment. Always remember, gauge what type of attire is appropriate for the event or circumstance. You can balance what is comfortable for you and what is expected of you from those you will be communicating with. I had seen many people in corporate America sabotage themselves—consciously or unconsciously—by disregarding their visual impact. The bottom line: when in doubt err to the conservative side – dress up rather than down for any influencing event.

Image Counts --- Susan's Story

Several years ago, I was asked to assess a woman who was downsized because her department had been eliminated. Prior to meeting Susan, I had asked her manager to fax me a copy of her resume. Her credentials were impressive to say the least! What I had been told about her job search did not match what I was reading on her resume nor what I had previously reviewed from her performance reviews of the past few years.

Her manager stated that the company wanted to retain her. In fact, they had gone out of their way to arrange for numerous interviews in other departments. She had been with the company twenty years and her breadth and depth of knowledge was extensive.

The manager stated that Susan was also extremely pleasant, easy to work with and a wonderful team leader. The manager told me that the department had been downsized nearly five months ago. During that time, Susan had been on many first interviews but had never been asked back for a second interview. She had not received any job offers.

From Susan's credentials and from my conversation with her manager, I was stumped for a reason why this woman was unsuccessful in her job search. Any department would surely love to have her. What was going on?

I asked Susan's manager if he had any insight at all into why Susan had not yet found a position. He responded that he didn't have a clue.

A few days later I met with Susan. Even before I shook her hand I knew precisely why she was not being asked back for any second interviews.

Susan had on lipstick the color of a bright orange Jack-o-lantern. This in and of itself was not a crime. What was killing her chances of success was that the lipstick covered much more than just her lips. It was fully a quarter of an inch outside her lips onto her face!

Just by looking at her, I realized that many people would have a tough time getting past her appearance. They might find it difficult to imagine her in the role of a professional manager with those lips. I imagined the interviewer trying to concentrate on what Susan was saying while trying to ignore those bright orange lips. I know I would have found it difficult to disregard! If I were the interviewer, I would have been too embarrassed to deal with it at all. I would have quickly realized that I did not have to deal with it if I did not ask Susan back for another interview. It is easy to see why any manager would take the easy way out of this dilemma. I also understood that her male manager would have found it difficult to broach the makeup issue with Susan.

As a coach and consultant I have had to use many strange approaches—though I'll admit, you would have to go pretty far to top the approach I used with Susan.

"I've been looking forward to meeting you Susan", I said with a warm smile. I knew she was nervous. Her hands were sweaty as she delivered a wet fish handshake and mumbled hello. Strike two for Susan with that handshake and strike three for her tonality!

My impression of her was deteriorating rapidly. I struggled to remember the good things the manager had said about Susan. I was struggling as I desperately tried to recall the points on the impressive resume that I had re-read only half an hour previously. It was difficult to keep an open mind and was nearly impossible to think great thoughts about this wonderful woman because of the impressions she was sending out.

"Susan, you're going to think this very odd but would you come with me to the ladies room?" I asked. She didn't know what to think of me when I said those words. She looked at me as if I was a crazy woman! Nevertheless, we went to the ladies room. We stood in front of the mirror and I asked, "Have you ever heard of the book 'All I Really Need to Know I Learned in Kindergarten'?" Susan nodded her head.

"I've always found that books like that have some very valuable lessons," I continued. "In fact, the basic premise of that book about what we learned in kindergarten is rock solid information that helps us be successful throughout our lives. Don't you think so?" I needed her agreement about how valuable kindergarten's lessons were in her life before I continued.

Susan looked at me with an even more perplexed look on her face as she again nodded. I went on speaking. "I particularly remember my coloring lessons. You know the ones—the lines are our friends—keep in the lines. Susan, you may not like what I'm going to say next. But, it's my job to make sure that you are never at a disadvantage during an interview. I can help you help yourself by simply bringing your attention to what other people will perceive about you – especially from their first impressions.

I cannot in good conscience allow you to walk out of this room without telling you the impact your lipstick has on your non-verbal communication. Unfortunately, other people may never tell you what you need to hear because they are afraid to offend you about your appearance. My sole objective is to make you aware of the issues that may hold you back in your career."

By this time, Susan was in tears. I handed her a tissue and continued speaking, "Let's get that lipstick off your face. I am going downstairs to the store to buy another color of lipstick while you clean up. What color suits do you usually wear for interviewing?"

"Usually gray or navy," she sniffled, "But I like my lipstick. I've worn it for years. It's the only color that looks nice with my skin tone. I had my colors done and I'm warm. I don't wear pinks. You don't need to get me another color – you say I should stay in the lines but my lips are too thin! Look at them!"

I ignored her, smiled and said, "I won't buy pink. I don't care if you wear your orange lipstick at home or when you have a new position. But when you are interviewing – leave it at home and wear the one I'm going to buy you and stay in the lines. You'd be wise to try this before you discount my council. That is, if you want a job. I'll be right back."

Key Point

If you want to make a great impression, dress appropriately. Harmonize with the other person's perception of appropriate image and attire. A good rule is to dress just a 'notch above' those you are trying to impress if you are showing respect for their position (e.g. during an interview or when in a sales environment). With this simple rule, you'll make a positive impression through your image with regard to non-verbal communication.

This story has a great ending. On Susan's next interview, she shook hands properly (after practicing for only five minutes) and wore her new subtle lipstick. Within two weeks she had landed a position with the same company with a promotion and a salary increase. About a month after our meeting I received a tube of orange lipstick in the mail with a note to throw it away!

Tendencies that Break Down the Influencing Process

In behavioral studies it has been found that people tend <u>not</u> to do business with people who:

- Have bad non-verbal habits[4] —unconscious tapping, repeated shrugging, nervous tics
- End declarative sentences on a high tonality note (note: more common in women than men)
- Avoid eye contact
- Dress inappropriately for the situation or event
- Hesitate or use avoidance movements
- Cover their mouth or nose when talking (or listening)
- Make noise (by tapping, coughing, etc.)
- Play with their hair or earlobes
- Rub their eyes
- Scratch themselves
- Bite or lick their lips
- Bite their fingernails or skin
- Shift weight from side to side when standing or sitting
- Unconsciously tap their foot, pen or finger
- Move around too much
- Have 'shifty' eyes
- Have a weak handshake
- Interrupt them physically by pointing or shaking their head 'no'
- Swing, pump, or waggle their legs when sitting

---

[4] These can also perceived as nervousness, excitability, and erratic behavior.

COMMUNICATION & BEHAVIOR PATTERNS

An important aspect of peak performance is the study of communication behavior patterns. In order to excel, one must study what makes the difference between average results and excellent results. Our specific goal is to study the techniques of highly effective people and to transfer those skills to others. This is fairly simple to do if you break down communication into its components. After doing this you can analyze behavior and discern patterns. You can then methodically transfer these patterns by a process of comprehension and substitution.

Pattern transfer has been referred to as the new technology of achievement. It is also a powerful and practical approach to personal and business change.

The technology of pattern transfer is very practical. It is a set of models, skills, and techniques for thinking effectively and communicating efficiently. The specific purpose of the influencing process is to enable people to analyze, create, and increase choices that will directly enhance their quality of life while they are working towards goals and objectives. The patterns we use are composed of psychological models that form the basis of how people access and interpret reality as they experience it. It is based on the perceptions and expectations that are formed in the mind as we experience the world around us.

To truly comprehend communication, it is vital to grasp the concept that people take in and interpret information based on their individual experiences in life. For example, five people watching the same movie will have five very different reference points upon which they base their emotional involvement and therefore their judgment of the film. Each will view and remember reality differently. No two peoples' perception and interpretation of a situation can ever be the same. Different people perceive life differently, even if they have the same experiences.

Models deal specifically with the basis of peoples' beliefs, communication, and the impact of the stimuli that they received from the outside world. Models of excellence in communication give us a starting point from which to examine and analyze behavior and performance, as well as learning and education. The approach to all models is practical and has achieved proven results in many industries. By studying the models you can become increasingly influential by learning how to communicate at peak performance levels.

Communication and Interaction

Communication is a multi-faceted word that covers many aspects of how we interact with others. Communication should be thought of as a cycle or a loop that involves at least two people – it is an interaction with others. When interacting, you perceive the response and react with your own thoughts and feelings. Your reaction depends on your beliefs and values and is based to a large extent on your perceptual map of the world.

During communication, it is extremely important to pay attention to what the other person is saying and to have a clear, concise view of the context of the conversation. In relating to the other person, you will have an idea about what to say or what to do next. Whatever your behavior or whatever your aspect in the loop is, the other person will in turn respond to it—either in a positive or negative fashion.

> Communication happens on many levels.

You communicate with your words, tonality, vocal quality, and your body language. Body language encompasses postures, gestures, shrugs, and facial expressions. The body conveys messages even when you say nothing and remain extremely still. The other person will pick up some nuance or intuitively feel some form of response from you based on whatever their perception happens to be. Communication is basically a message that passes between individuals. Often the message you wish to relay is <u>not</u> the same as the message received by others.

Sometimes the other person misreads the message. Think back to a time when you said something innocently and then were amazed by the response from the other party. They responded to your words in the incorrect way.

EXERCISE — COMMUNICATION AND INTERACTION

How can you be certain the message you wish to convey is received? What can you do to help avoid misunderstandings?

____
____
____
____
____
____
____
____
____

EXERCISE VOCAL QUALITIES

Choose a partner and relay this sentence: It's a nice day today, isn't it?

Choose and write down three different messages in order (happy, menacing, sarcastic, etc.) to relay from this sentence without adding additional words. Do not tell the other person what emotional state or message you are trying to convey. Have the other person write down the emotions they thought that you were trying to convey. Now, compare notes. Does the message that you intended to relay match what they received? If the message does not match, explore the changes you would need to make. Let your partner give you positive feedback about what you do well and what you need to focus on to enhance your communication ability.

Politician and former Prime Minister of Britain, Margaret Thatcher, spent a great deal of time and expended a large amount of effort altering her vocal quality. She realized that her delivery and the relaying of her message were extremely important. Her voice was the one quality that needed improvement because of peoples' perceptions.

Example: Voice tonality and body language determine whether the word 'hello' is perceived as a simple greeting, a put-down, a threat, a message of satisfied longing of a lover or a hearty salutation from a long lost friend. Actors pay particular attention to body language and tonality. The words they speak only convey a very small part of their craft. Most actors need to be able to convey dozens of varying shades of meaning from simple expressions and phrases. Imagine for a moment all the messages that can be conveyed by the word 'no'. **Discuss!**

Most often we do not think consciously about the words we choose to use. Our habit patterns of word usage are ingrained in our body language and tonality.

What are the consequences of not aligning your body language and tonality?

____

____

____

____

____

How can you help deliver an effective message by aligning your body language to be in harmony with the communication you send out? What are some techniques you can use to accomplish this goal?

____

____

____

____

The Communication Loop

Communication is a loop. *Just as you are influencing others, they in turn are influencing you.* You can only take responsibility for your part in the loop. Your can choose to be consciously aware of the effects you create in others or not.

Integrity is very important in communication. You must keep within your value structure as you influence others during the communication loop. When influencing others you should be completely congruent in your values, message, and belief system. The communication techniques you have learned or will learn are neutral; it is up to you to use them ethically.

Language is terribly complex. Even during simple communication, you must always be aware of the critical aspects that are at work within communication loops. Some miscommunication is due to the fact that the same words may represent power in one context and weakness in another. Words often mean one thing in one sentence and something entirely different in another. Think about the word "post". How many meanings does this word have?

It is for precisely this reason that there are no simple answers for what to say and what not to say.

Loops and Systems/Cause and Effect

Loops and Systems are interrelated. Communication has often been thought of as a simple cause and effect relationship. The laws of cause and effect work for inanimate objects. It has been stated in physics that for every action there is an equal reaction. If one ball collides with another, you can predict with a fair amount of accuracy that the other ball will also move. But, after the initial collision of the balls, they no longer influence each other.

Cause and effect can be analyzed individually, as well as the patterns and paths of differing effects. If you look at cause and effect patterns during a game of pool you will notice that specific calculations and approximations can be made based on the experience of the pool player, the physics of the game itself, and the skill level of the players.

If you are watching a basketball game, you will see that living systems are an entirely different matter for cause and effect analysis. Example: If a person was playing basketball and drives to the net, there will probably be two or three defenders in his path. The player would need to determine how far to go and how many players were in his way. Additionally, the player with the ball has his goal, whereas, the defenders have an entirely different goal. A very savvy defender may hold, trip, elbow, or even knee the opposing player to distract him from achieving his goal. In reality, I would imagine that many other variables would come into play. The game is dynamic, ever changing, and difficult to predict.

The reality of human relationships is very complex. Many things happen simultaneously. It is a challenge (and nearly impossible) to understand and predict exactly what will occur and when it will occur. The future is based on a number of factors. Always remember that one person will influence another during the communication loop. We are continuously responding to the other person's influencing factors during the communication loop itself. It is a dance of one with another, where we continually respond to feedback in order to next respond and therefore continue the loop.

It is impossible to focus on only one side (your own) of the conversation loop and to have your outcome affect the other person in a positive light 100% of the time. You could spend a lifetime figuring out components of each individual conversation within the loop process. Our conscious mind is extremely limited—especially during the communication loop. This problem is further compounded by the fact that we can never see the whole communication loop at one time, only small parts of it.

THE THREE COMPONENTS OF THE COMMUNICATION LOOP

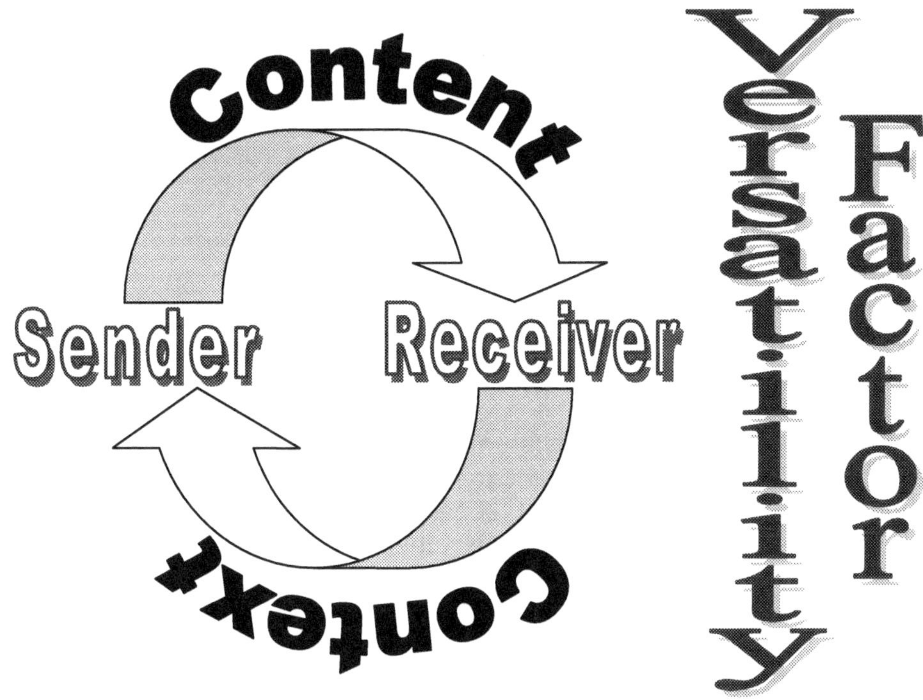

The communication loop has three integral parts. These form the whole meaning of communication in its basic sense.

1. **Content—***the words themselves.* The content is the *information and data that is imparted* during the communication loop.
2. **Context—**the total setting of the communication loop within whole systems.
3. **Versatility Factor—**the positive or negative reaction/s of the parties to introduced stimuli. How the parties respond.

Content

Content=Mutual agreement (comprehension) of the information/data transferred between parties in the communication loop. The parties should agree on the meaning of the words.

External Context of Communication

Context—the interrelated conditions in which something exists or occurs; the environment.

It is important for people to understand that all changes they experience happen within a much larger **external context**.

Understand that people react differently during the communication loop based on the context from which they gauge the exchange. It helps to considerably lessen the tension associated with communication if you consider what the other person is experiencing based on their views of the communication loop within a much larger, **external context**.

Examples of External versus Internal Context Focus

When Presidents change office in the United States, often a very large impact is felt within the political community of the United States itself. But, in the rest of the world the impact is often much smaller.

Consider a violent tornado. In the global context its impact is very, very small indeed. But the tornado's devastation has an extremely profound effect on the land and people where that tornado actually touched down and destroyed everything in its path.

Context Changes Emotional Impact during the Communication Loop

From individual to individual the context will change. **When context changes, an individual's feelings and emotional involvement often changes.**

Emotional involvement and impact differs from person to person based on a number of factors:

1). Historical stress tolerance for changes and communication
2) Current stress level
3) Stress and tolerance level immediately prior to engaging in the communication loop in question
4) Physical health
5) Ability to communicate effectively about their role within the context of the communication loop
6) Emotional well-being
7) Relationship to others affected by and/or experiencing/involved in the communication loop
8) Feelings of trust for the current environment (peers, management, etc.)
9) Personal financial situation
10) Personal emotional contentment
11) Level of self-confidence
12) Level of support from peers and management, etc.

It is important for both parties to put the change into the context that is appropriate for the current situation. **Remember**: You only control one side of the communication loop. It sometimes helps to diffuse stress during the communication loop by explaining and expanding the subject you are talking about into a very large range (e.g. into a regional or global context). Or into the business context that is appropriate for your business marketplace.

Current Context— Positive versus Negative

It is important to recognize that the context is never neutral—it always has negative or positive implications. This depends to a large extent on which viewpoint is used to define and examine the context of the communication loop, change or transition. If you look at the downsizing initiative of corporate America it is interesting to note that ten years ago a downsizing would result in a plummeting of the stock of the company.

Nowadays, the context of a downsizing is extremely positive for business analysts and often results in the immediate increase of a company's stock price. Even long after the downsizing has occurred; the stock's price has a tendency to be elevated. However, from the employee's standpoint the threat of a reduction in force is highly negative – especially if their job is on the line.

Keep these concepts and facts in mind during the communication loop. Each individual will view change in a different context. Bearing this in mind, it is prudent to put forward the context of the subject during the communication loop in a positive light to all involved.

EXERCISE CONTEXT

1. Write down three different contexts in which a specific subject may be viewed.

2. Establish who would be involved in each of the context viewpoints.

4. List the positive and negative aspects of a specific communication loop in a corporate and/or sales viewpoint.

5. Pinpoint who might view each aspect positively or negatively and the reason for their viewpoint.

5. Establish - What is important to you and to the other people in the communication loop?

Context = Relationship Factor

Context is also known as the relationship factor. What is the relationship factor as a whole? How does the context of the subject relate to others? And how does it fit into this system or other systems, as a whole?

When we think of the communication loop, it is also necessary to understand that our innermost thoughts, our world of beliefs, representational systems, and sub-modalities also form a system. The context of this system is extremely important because it changes our views on what we think about and how we influence others.

Changing one context of the inner thoughts system can have a widespread effect and will generate other changes, especially if the change of context is based on other core beliefs or values. You can relate this to the changing of a person' sub-modalities (subtle nuances and details) for feelings and emotions.

By changing just a small detail of the context of the event in the person's memory, you can change they way they feel and react to the memory. For example, if you are able to change the memory of a remark that was insulting to you into a memory that has you take pity on the speaker for their lack of intelligence, or simply attributing it to hatred or prejudice of your ethnicity, and not as a barb directly aimed at your heart and soul, the memory of the hurt caused might substantially lessen. Even remembering the old saying, "Sticks and stones can break my bones, but names can never hurt me!" can go a long way in changing the contextual memory of an insult.

It has often been said that a few well-chosen or poorly chosen words, at just the right moment in a person's life, can transform their views, their beliefs, their goals, and their outcomes for the rest of their life. Why then, wouldn't it make sense that if you change one small piece of a memory, that it could alter your entire state of mind? This is a powerful concept. This is what happens when you deal with the context and content within systems.

Content and Context of Communication as a Whole

If words are the content of the message, then postures, gestures, expressions, and tonality **are the context in which the message is embedded**. Together these two components (verbal and nonverbal messages) create the meaning of communication. It is necessary to understand that there is no guarantee that others will completely comprehend your message, as you would like to relay it.

How do you know whether they are receiving the correct message? The one you wish to deliver on every occasion? It is necessary to go back to the basics of the influencing process.

Communication = Response

Understand this—the meaning of communication is the response you receive from the people you are communicating with. Both in our business and personal lives we constantly utilize our communication skills and techniques to influence a wide range of people. It is an interesting paradox that, while no one would be interested in learning skills that are not effective or efficient, effective communication skills are sometimes denigrated and/or labeled as manipulative. In our society, manipulation carries with it an extremely negative connotation. Somehow it portrays the message that you are trying to force someone to do something that is against his or her best interests. This is certainly not true of most people when we communicate. To attain goals we must influence others effectively.

Most humans communicate and try to form situations in which all parties feel comfortable. Compromise is vital. This concept is of paramount importance during the influencing process.

People wish to attain balance and harmony with those around them. Using influencing techniques, you are able to have choices: to create harmony, wisdom, and to have the ecology/context frame built in at a very deep level. By using the influencing process you have the ability to respond efficiently and effectively to people around you. But more important, you will learn to understand their viewpoint.

Butterfly Effect

The Butterfly Effect from the Theory of Chaos (also known as the Ripple Effect) contends that the fluttering of butterfly wings has the potential to sufficiently disturb the air pressure at a critical time and place causing a major impact on the weather system as a whole—perhaps even creating a typhoon. In a complex system such as the weather system, a small change can potentially have a huge effect. Within the laws of physics, for example, one small push in the right direction can generate a profound change—if you know exactly where to push. By correctly planning a system of dominos, one small push has the potential of toppling thousands of other dominos that perhaps took hours or even weeks to set up.

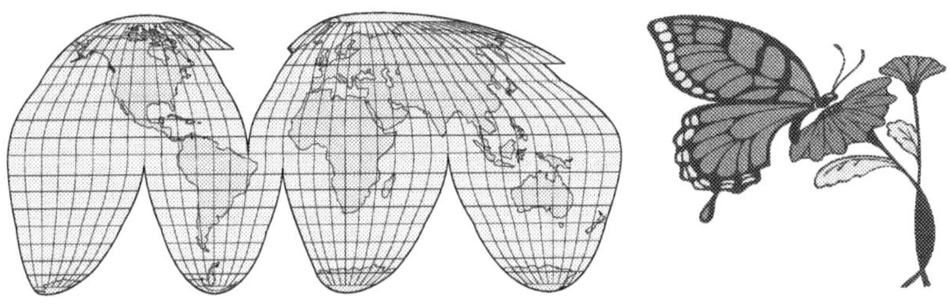

Note: Not all elements in a system have equal importance. Some elements have very little effect and can be changed at random or at will. Others have either a profound or devastating effect -- either positive or negative with widespread influence.

Used with permission

EXERCISE — THE BUTTERFLY EFFECT

1. Choose five different systems

2. Explain their content and context.

3. What encompasses a system in your profession?

4. Write examples of the context of the system as it moves from small to larger terms.

5. Now, include changes that are subtle and drastic.

6. How would these changes, whether small or large, affect the system as a whole?

7. What would the results of the consequences of these changes be?

Balancing Systems and Relationships

Part of the influencing process is the **study of elements within a system** and the **effects of change** within the system. Note: The Transitional Time Line[5] and the influencing process are integrally linked. When you try to influence others, you are really trying to change their current views to be in line with your way of thinking. Most of the psychological theories we share in this book can be examined simultaneously when determining how best to accomplish your objectives.

The goal for the influencing process is to balance systems and relationships, keeping each integral part in harmony with the rest, so that these pieces of the puzzle can act together to create a positive, beneficial outcome for the good of the entire system.

As an example, often the fear of success is a result of not examining the relationship between risk and reward when we strive toward goals. If the cost of becoming an Executive Vice President is that you will have to travel 80% of the month, you might postpone doing your MBA for years because you don't really want to succeed. By starting your MBA, it would mean that you have chosen to actively seek promotion. But at what price? If it means you will miss your children's best years – you might not want it at this stage of your life. If we have doubts about the cost of achieving the goal, we might sabotage our efforts – consciously or subconsciously.

We should pay attention to our self-talk. Appreciate that our goals will only be realized if our reservations and self-doubts are conquered within the wider system of our value hierarchy (how we make decisions) and our personal and professional relationships.

The communication loop is an element within a relationship system. Building relationships and communicating effectively is not a one-way process. You build trust with two-way communication. You rarely complete a sale when you don't have a relationship with a client.

---

[5] Discussed in detail in the Change Manual and later in this manual.

Behavior and Systems as a Whole

In behavioral science, it is important to think in terms of content and context—in terms of systems as a whole. Gregory Bateson was one of the most influential figures in the development of Neuro Linguistic Programming (NLP). He applied cybernetic, or "systems thinking" to biology, evolution and psychology. Virginia Satir, a world-renowned family therapist, established one of the original models for NLP behavior patterns for use in family therapy sessions. Her theory was to treat the family as a balanced system of relationships; not as a collection of individuals with individual experiences, but as a system of people's perceptions of their past experiences.

Virginia Satir helps families achieve a better and healthier balance by improving the model of family relationships. Her model for family therapy focuses specifically on where to intervene within the family as a system. The family therapy model she developed deals with relationships as a whole and with pinpointing what person/s within the system would need to make changes in their behavior so that all of the relationships in the family system improve.

You, Systems and Change

As with a kaleidoscope, you cannot move one rotation without changing the whole pattern. The best way to change others is to understand the impact that transition has on you. When you change, you change your relationships with other people. They must change as well. Because communication is a loop, your effect on the loop will change other people's responses and their feedback, which in turn will again change your response and your feedback, and so the loop goes on.

Versatility Factor

Versatility factor = the range of conscious and/or unconscious behavioral reaction/s of individuals during the communication loop to introduced stimuli.

Translation – Your versatility factor is your propensity and ability to change your actions and behavior based on what is happening around you.

EXERCISE — VISUAL SUCCESS

Imagine yourself as a chameleon in a box full of M&M's. Imagine yourself with many choices and options.

1. Would you be/feel comfortable with many options? Or is it better to have just a few?

2. How would you adjust?

3. How would you determine/evaluate what is important to you?

4. How did you prioritize and finally make the decision?

5. How is your decision making process pertinent to your life? Personal? Business?

Body Language & Communication

People interpret body language primarily based on their experiences, perceptions, personal biases, and prejudices. As you can imagine, we are not always correct in our interpretations. Often we make mistakes (erroneous judgment calls) based on our perception of the communication loop we are watching.

Many of us simply do not have a high level of skill in reading body language correctly. To read body language you must fine tune your ability to ascertain what various postures and gestures mean. This skill requires using your primary senses and is called tuning your sensory acuity. To complicate matters, many courses—especially sales training sessions—have erroneously taught us that body language can be categorized and recognized and acted upon the same way. For example, teaching that 'crossed arms' is always a sure way to recognize that a person is being negative simply isn't true. Many people cross their arms to keep warm. I sometimes cross my arms when I process information or when I ponder an interesting thought. Some people like to cross their arms simply because it's comfortable for them.

Body Language and Rapport

We *trust* people who are <u>like ourselves</u>.

We emulate people we respect and trust.
We act in a similar manner to people we like to do business with and expect certain behavior patterns to be adhered to in business situations. Body language and rapport are predominant factors in decision making in most business situations.

<u>RAPPORT = TRUST</u>

*"Studies show that the first person to be hired in a company is the one **most** like the boss and the first one that will be terminated is the one **least** like the boss."*

—Harvard Business Journal

Building trust and rapport is of paramount importance during the communication loop.

Individual Models of the World

To build rapport it is necessary to understand that people have their own model of the world. It is essential to establish an environment of trust and confidence and mutual participation during the influencing process. If this occurs, all parties will feel they can express their ideas and beliefs freely. This will ensure that the communication channels will remain open and that information will be exchanged freely.

Most people gain trust and rapport naturally. During the influencing process, it is important to gain conscious awareness of when trust and rapport have been established and how they are maintained.

We have already discussed sensory acuity. As you look around the room or notice people in restaurants, offices, or in meetings, how do you know that people trust one another and/or have created a sense of rapport during dialog? Communication seems to flow effortlessly when two people are in rapport. They seem to be in harmony. It is interesting to note that their bodies as well as their words match each other. This is true in almost every culture across the globe. It is also interesting to note that we can either create or destroy rapport extremely quickly and easily with the content or words we choose during communication. Fortunately, only 7% of our communication is comprised of actual words or content. Body language and tonality are much more important than the words spoken when initiating, building and maintaining rapport.

Note: Body language and tonality, eye contact and gestures are usually complimentary.

In most cultures, we discuss general topics: the weather, sports, children and families, current events, etc. when establishing rapport. Once rapport has been established we move onto more important or pertinent topics. Before addressing sensitive issues, make sure you have gained and are able to maintain rapport.

Think of a positive communication loop as a dance where the parties respond positively to each other's changes (versatility). The individuals respond by mirroring and matching each other's movements, gestures (body language), voice tonality, and pitch. The dance is based on mutual positive responsiveness to each other.

How Do You Feel When You Have Rapport?

Can you remember a time when you felt completely *comfortable* with someone? Take yourself back to that moment in time and try to remember what it was that made you feel so at ease. Was it the person's mannerisms, background, or beliefs? Whatever you felt about the encounter, you probably experienced strong rapport with the person in question. Rapport is the ability to make another person feel that you understand them and that you share some degree of commonality. Rapport is the **essence of effective communication.**

Non-verbal Rapport is the **unconscious agreement of trust** between people based upon body language, tonality, posture and gestures.

Most things that you are unconscious of happen **automatically** (habits, body responses, and pre-taught responses that are done without thinking).

Now that we have a definition of rapport, we need to know how to establish it in any situation—quickly and effectively.

On What Is Rapport Based?

The mind and body are totally **LINKED**. The way you use your physiology—the way you breathe, your posture, facial expressions, the nature and quality of your movements—actually determines what emotional state you are in at any time. Therefore, you can understand the power of tuning your sensory acuity with regard to your **own physiology** and how it affects everyone around you. Are you sending out the appropriate message to others?

Genetics and Rapport

Have you ever found yourself enjoying a conversation with somebody and noticing that both your bodies have adopted the same or a similar posture? If you think back you will find that the deeper the trust and rapport created with someone is the more your body will be in harmony with the other person.

The best teachers in the world are those who establish a high degree of rapport with their students. They enter the world of the learner. In this way they make it easier for the student to obtain a greater understanding of the subject matter or the skill set to be taught. Great teachers have wonderful relationships with their students. They get on well with their students and both parties have a high degree of trust with each other. Having a fabulous relationship between teacher and learner enables the task at hand—learning—to seem much easier. The information flow between the parties occurs smoothly and efficiently. When this occurs, it frees the learner's conscious mind so that it can then be used for learning faculties instead of normal rapport processing.

It has been theorized that rapport building is a genetic trait. In other words, the skill set would seem to be inbred. Studies have shown that newborn babies move in rhythm with the voices of the people around them. When people are not in rapport or they do not trust another person, or the communication link has been broken, their body language and their gestures reflect this fact. Whatever they are saying their bodies will not be matching. Whenever somebody does not have rapport or trust with the other person you can see it in their body language, their tonality, or their gestures. You can recognize it immediately by the mismatch created and the resulting feeling of discord.

How Do We Create Rapport?

The more you think about the statistics of influencing effectiveness, the more you will realize the power you will attain if you are able to establish strong rapport quickly and effectively. The higher the degree of rapport, the better you will be able to influence the other person. Rapport is based on **mirroring and matching** a person's behavior, both verbally and non-verbally. In order to gain the strongest rapport possible, one should act like the other person, speak like they do, breathe simultaneously, and use similar movements or gestures.

Body Language Techniques to Create Rapport

1. Mirroring

Doing what the other person is doing so that it appears as though they are looking in a *mirror.*

2. Matching

Doing what the other person is doing but with the *opposite* side of your body (if they move their right hand, you move your right hand). This is less easily detected than mirroring.

What Are Some Of The Things You Can Mirror/Match?	
a) Whole Body	Person's stance or overall position
b) Part Body	Any consistent behavioral shrugs, gestures, head nods, or any other shifts in their behavior
c) Half Body	Upper or lower half of the other person's body
d) Breathing	Match depth and/or speed (this is one of the most powerful forms of non-verbal rapport)
e) Voice	Tonality, volume, tempo, intensity, and intonation patterns

3. Cross-Over Pacing

Using a *different* channel altogether than the one they are using. Crossover pacing is more covert and harder to detect than mirroring and matching.

Channels for crossover pacing:

- Cross arms—cross legs
- Nod in time to the person's speech
- Pace breathing by tapping with your finger or pen
- If they tap their glasses on the desk — tap your pen on your knee

Peak Performance and Rapport

Successful sales people and marketing people, successful therapists, and counselors create rapport and trust extremely quickly, effortlessly, and easily. The influencing process is a model and these people have learned to model behaviors of mirroring, matching, and crossover pacing which helps them to excel at rapport building.

The goal of mirroring and matching and crossover pacing is to make it a habit during situations and to become consciously aware when something changes or when you create disharmony. In other words, you need to recognize the signs for when you have broken rapport or broken trust during the communication loop. If this happens, it is absolutely imperative to reestablish rapport by changing what you are currently doing and going back to what you were doing before the mismatch occurred.

Eye Contact

Mirroring and matching body language and tonality allows you to quickly gain rapport with just about anyone you communicate with. Matching eye contact is something that is extremely important culturally during the communication loop. It is very important to match eye contact in same gender conversations and across the gender conversations. Each sex has its own appropriate eye contact. In business it is extremely important that you notice and tune your sensory acuity to appropriate eye contact, body language, gestures and tonality.

When using mirroring, matching, and crossover pacing it is important to create rapport with sensitivity and with respect. The goal for mirroring and matching and crossover pacing is to build a bridge between you and the other person. When you build this bridge you will enter their model of the world. Remember, matching is not mimicry, which is noticeable, exaggerated and is indiscriminate copying of another person's movement. This is usually considered offensive. It is never appropriate to match large arm movements during conversation. It is not appropriate to mirror them either. What you can do is match them with smaller hand movements. This is an example of crossover pacing.

Rapport Is the Ultimate Tool to Use when Dealing with People

Practice Makes Perfect

Practice mirroring and matching with a partner so that it becomes an automatic part of your influencing skills. As you start to mirror and match others you will find that the process feels unnatural and uncomfortable. This feeling will pass, as you become more fluid with the process through practice. It is just like learning anything new. Do you remember the first time you learned to use a calculator, drive a car, or use a computer? Looking back, you will probably remember feeling better each time you used the device.

The timing of your mirror and match movements is important. When you use this technique, you will feel instinctively that moving at the exact same time as the other person is too difficult and makes you self-conscious. Timing is the key. When your prospect moves their body, wait a second or two until you follow with your movement. If the person crosses their arms or legs, wait for a few seconds before you do the same. To practice try the pattern on your spouse, children, friends, and people sitting in public places, before you attempt it in your professional life.

Using this technique forces you to tune into the other person's world. When you mirror and match another person, you are copying their physiology. When you copy their body language you are also copying their emotional state. If both of you have the same emotional state it will stand to reason you will understand the person's feelings better and really hear what they are trying to say to you.

Calibration/Sensory Acuity

Calibration—is the art of tuning yourself through sensory acuity to the non-verbal signals that indicate a change of state in the person you are attempting to communicate with or influence.

Always Remember:

- External body changes reflect internal state changes.
- The mind and body are completely linked!
- Tune Your Sensory Acuity!
- Practice using pacing and leading until it becomes an automatic response to other people's body language.

50/50 Rule for Rapport

To attain physiological rapport quickly, 50% of your body should be in harmony mirroring and matching or crossover pacing the other person 50% of the time.

This technique takes time and practice to perfect.

Using Mirroring and Matching with Clients

Knowing all of the different channels that you can use to mirror, match, or crossover pace body language, will help you tremendously during an interview. Learn to interchange all of the different channels during your time spent with a client or a peer. Never concentrate on only one channel during the entire time you are with them. Variety will make both of you feel comfortable.

Frequently Asked Question: "Won't the other person realize what you are doing and think that you are doing something funny?"

Answer: I have used this technique for years in many situations and never once has anyone challenged me. I feel I listen better whenever I use these methods of communicating and more important—I know that I make people feel comfortable quickly and easily. My interviews have improved and my income has increased when I sell products or services using the influencing process.

Frequently Asked Question: Often, you are in a room with more than one person. How would you use these techniques to gain rapport?

Answer: Choose the people in the room with whom you would like to gain the highest rapport. Mirror, match, and crossover pace those people with different channels. Perhaps, Mr. Smith has crossed his arms—you mirror him by crossing your arms. Mrs. White is tapping her glasses on the table—you can crossover pace Mrs. White by tapping your finger along with her. By using mirroring on Mr. Smith and crossover pacing on Mrs. White, you can gain physiological rapport with both of them at the same time. Try using this technique at your next meeting.

Remember—mind and body are linked completely!

The way you use your body language will determine the state of your mind and this in turn will control your emotions. Your emotions will always control your behavior and your attitude towards life. The secret to controlling your emotional state is to control your body language. Mirror and match the body language of people you admire. Ask yourself—how does my posture look to people around me? Am I depressed because my head is down or is my head down because I'm depressed? Am I matching the physiology of a depressed individual? What would a motivated, energetic, happy person look like? How **specifically** would I change my body language to mirror and match the behavior that I wish to emulate? Mirror and match successful individuals and success will come your way.

Mastering mirroring and matching techniques will change the way you gain rapport with different types of people. Mastery will enable you to move your prospect towards a specific goal or outcome more effectively, however you must accurately pick up the signals the other person is sending out. You must tune your sensory acuity appropriately and be sensitive and respectful of the other person's views.

Tune your senses into the other person's body language!

Used with permission.

PACING & LEADING

By combining pacing and leading during an interview you will effectively control the level of rapport during the meeting. By controlling the level of rapport, you effectively control the tension level.

Pacing is:

- The art of gaining rapport.
- Establishing the bridge through rapport and respect into another person's model of the world.
- The word we use to combine the technique of mirroring, matching, and crossover pacing.
- Talking about or doing something that is the same as the other person is doing
- Relating something that is verifiably true in a person's ongoing sensory experience.

Leading is:

- Doing something different from the other person in the communication loop.
- Talking about or relating to something that the other person does not believe to be true and/or has not had experience with in their world.
- The goal of leading is to change your behavior so that the other person in the communication loop follows.

Rapport Builds Bridges

Rapport allows you to build a bridge into another person's model of the world, so at some point during the communication loop you will cross over into their world and their point of understanding. With rapport established, you can start to change your behavior so they will follow you into your world. The bridge goes both ways. You can lead them in another direction by entering your world and bringing them across the bridge you have built when trust and rapport are high.

Testing for Rapport

It is important to test to see if you have indeed established high rapport. The simplest method of testing for true rapport is to mirror, match and crossover pace your prospect until you instinctively feel that you can do something different with your body language (lead) without breaking rapport. If the other person follows you with their body language by mirroring or matching, you have established true rapport.

Testing Rapport through Leading

When you lead a person after having gained rapport, you are attempting to influence them according to your outcome or goal. The true test for rapport is to pace someone—use mirroring and matching—then lead—do something different with your body language. If they follow, you have established a high degree of rapport. Rapport has firmly been established when they follow your lead with their body language and **continue to follow**. It is obvious that a high degree of sensory acuity and perception is necessary to understand and gauge precisely how much rapport and trust has been established. Then, when you lead, it is imperative to see the cues that happen when the other person follows your lead. This transition should be smooth and effortless. In order for this to happen, your skill level at pacing and rapport building should be well practiced and at as high a level as possible.

Remember: You can never lead someone or influence him or her effectively unless the bridge has been established between the parties involved in the communication loop.

Perhaps you have been fortunate so far in your career by having success gaining and maintaining rapport with customers, co-workers, and clientele. You may have chosen to keep your behavior the same, expecting others to understand you and your point of view. This may have worked very well for you. Sometimes this approach yields extremely favorable results; but other times it does not. People tend to like and do business with others who act and behave as they do.

Developing the ability to have the conscious choice to influence everyone and to build your rapport bridge into his or her world is a very effective skill set to obtain and explore.

Dan and Larry's Story

I specifically remember the interview that made me realize the personal power I had acquired by learning pacing and leading techniques.

Larry and his partner owned an architectural firm in San Diego. They had decided that their employees were leaving because the company had an insufficient benefits package. The two partners had been best friends since high school. Dan qualified in Civil Engineering at MIT and Larry had graduated from UCLA with a Masters in Business Economics and Marketing. Larry and I had met on several occasions to discuss ideas for the employees. He was outgoing and energetic, with a friendly attitude. I had not had a chance to meet with Dan, his partner, due to his busy schedule.

Today was the day to go over the final proposal and sign the appropriate papers to install the program.

Larry escorted me to the conference room and said that Dan would be in shortly. We chatted about the program and his excitement about finally presenting it to his staff at the company's annual luncheon the next week. He was certain that the program would boost morale and that employee retention would be enhanced.

About fifteen minutes later, Dan entered the room. He was nothing like what my mental picture imagined! Larry was an avid sportsman and had played sports for UCLA; he was a tall, good-looking blond with a healthy tan. Dan was his opposite—He was about 5'4" tall, nearly bald and his pale white skin had not seen the sun for months!

He walked across the room and Larry introduced us. Then, he walked halfway down the conference table and sat down about three seats away from me. He seemed extremely agitated and was drumming his fingers on the table staring at the picture on the opposite wall.

Larry appeared not to notice his partner's behavior and carried on exactly where the conversation with me had ended a few minutes before. I felt very uncomfortable and kept on glancing at Dan. I tried to draw him into our discussion but to no avail. He simply answered my questions with monosyllables and continued to look at the picture.

Larry asked to see the enrollment application. I handed it to him and then he asked, "Where do the company officers sign? Everything looks good to me!" He was really excited about installing the plan immediately! I handed him my pen and he signed all of the documentation immediately.

As he was busy signing I glanced across at Dan again, then I looked at Larry. For the first time since Dan walked in the door I noticed that my body language was nearly an exact mirror of Larry's physiology! Even worse, my physiology was the complete opposite of Dan's! Within the next two minutes, I knew that I had to ask Dan to sign my proposal. Immediately, I started to mirror Dan's folded arms. Thirty seconds later, I crossed my left leg over my right leg and leaned back in my chair. Dan, for the first time since he walked into the room, looked across at Larry and I. Dan then leaned forward and hunched his shoulders. I leaned forward and did the same. Larry crossed his legs and also leaned forward slightly. I was astounded! All three of us were starting to mirror and match Dan's body language. I know that I had been in complete physiological rapport with Larry before Dan walked into the room. We had met before and were very comfortable with each other—the mirroring between Larry and me was completely unconscious and spontaneous. Larry and I were in total rapport with each other.

When I began to change my physiology to match his partner's, Larry automatically changed his physiology to line up with mine! I had the papers that Larry had signed in my hand. I slowly pushed half of them across the table towards Dan and kept the other half in front of me. Along the center of the table was a trough filled with pens and pencils. I knew that Larry had my pen, but I wanted to test to see if I had established rapport with Dan. So, I patted my blazer to find a pen. Out of the corner of my eye I saw him reach into his suit pocket. Then I slowly and deliberately reached out and took a pen from the trough. I pulled my chair closer to the table and began writing on the documents in front of me.

Dan leaned forward, pen in hand, and asked me, "What color ink are you using?" I looked up and he was scowling. I scowled and replied back in exactly his tone of voice, "I always use black." "Good, so do I." As soon as he said that, he pulled his chair closer to the table put his head down and started to sign the papers. I waited until he was finished and I again pushed the papers towards him. He pushed his papers back towards me. I started writing again and he started to sign the final documents. I leaned down to grab a document receipt form because I was going to take original documents out of their office.

Both partners looked down to see what I was trying to do. Dan asked, "What are you looking for?" "I have to give you a receipt document for your records." Dan stood up and went to the telephone. Dan asked his secretary to ask the accountant to bring in the company checkbook. I could barely hide my surprise! Dan came back to the table. Both Larry and I were sitting back comfortably in our chairs. Dan took the chair next to mine and sat back. He looked as relaxed as Larry did.

Larry smiled and almost instantly the hint of a smile touched Dan's mouth. Then he said, "I really feel that you know what we want for our employees. I feel comfortable with the way you handled our program. When I walked into the meeting today, I was really apprehensive about finally getting this program going and I decided to ask Larry to look at other proposals first before going ahead with yours. After meeting you, and seeing how you do business, I feel comfortable with your recommendations."

As I was driving back to Orange County, I thought about the meeting and I suddenly realized the incredible personal power I had mastered through studying behavior and rapport building patterns. I decided to enhance my skills by trying to be consciously aware of mirroring and matching other people and to adapt every negative situation that I come across to become a positive encounter for everyone.

EXERCISE MIRROR, MATCHING & CROSS OVER PACING

Choose a partner and start a conversation. Mirror, match, and crossover pace each other. Remember the 50%-50% rule.

What was your biggest challenge in mirroring, matching and crossover pacing your partner?

Did you find yourself using one technique more often than others – is it acceptable to use just one technique?

Can you establish rapport effectively using only one method (mirroring or matching or crossover pacing)? Why or Why Not?

How did you test your partner to see if rapport had been successfully established?

People Do Business with People They Trust

When people trust you, when you have rapport, this is when communication is most effective. When people are like each other, they feel the other person is trustworthy. When people appear trustworthy they do business together and form personal relationships. These are the basic elements of rapport building using the influencing process.

Be aware that these methods are new to most people who hear them. You will better appreciate mirroring, matching and cross-over pacing, and the strength they bring to rapport building and maintenance, when you experience the power they bring to your conversation and communication loops. To use these techniques it is important to be conscious of what you are doing when you gain rapport and trust naturally. Once you become consciously aware of what you are doing, you can then refine your behavior, use the skill sets that you use naturally, refine the technique and choose when to use mirroring and matching and cross-over pacing.

After you have established rapport you have to understand what it feels like when **rapport is broken.** This usually happens when there is **a mismatch in the mirroring, matching or crossover pacing techniques during rapport building**. Mismatching can be a very useful skill during sales presentations or during marketing presentations. It is important not to offend your clientele. It is equally important for them to know when you disagree with their viewpoint.

If you have gained a high degree of rapport with another person, but you do not want to verbalize your disagreement, you can simply break rapport, or break mirroring, matching and crossover pacing with this person and mismatch them with the appropriate timing during the communication loop. Mismatching is also a very elegant way to end a conversation and to disengage when your outcome is reached. One of the most extreme mismatches that can occur is when someone turns their back on another person during the conversation loop. This is extremely rude and is not advisable.

Think back to a time when you wanted to close a sales presentation and you were locked in harmony and in communication with your client. You knew it was important to get on to the next appointment, but you did not want to be rude or end the trust in a negative way. Often what people do is use a signal to break rapport. The signal to break rapport could be shutting your briefcase or portfolio, putting your pen in your breast pocket, or putting your pen into your purse, picking up a handbag, or it can be as simple as standing up. If you were sitting this is a mismatch and immediately breaks rapport.

Mismatching Rapport to Close the Deal

The tension level during an interview is extremely important. Gaining rapport by using pacing will create an especially high level of rapport. Sometimes you will find that you gain so much rapport that the time you have allowed for your meeting passes without accomplishing much business. If you find that your appointments are too casual or that your clients are friendlier than you want them to be, break rapport slightly by mirroring and matching only one channel of their body language instead of using two or more channels.

Use pacing and leading to move towards your outcome. Do this without becoming so friendly that your client does not take you seriously or they feel that they can brush you off.

When rapport is too high, people feel they can still continue with your friendly relationship without making a decision to do any business with you or your company.

Always remember that too much rapport with a client can be just as bad as too little rapport. Control the tension level during every stage of your meeting.

Betty's Story

One of my favorite clients needed to purchase more life insurance to pay for estate taxes that would be due on her death. She had asked that I meet with her accountant to discuss the death benefit needed to settle the estate. I had already presented the insurance plan and the premium cost to her accountant six months before. I just could not motivate her to sign the papers and give me a check even after four meetings. Whenever I arranged a meeting, we went out to lunch and discussed the insurance. Betty always indicated that she wanted to start the plan.

After lunch, we would drive back to her office and she would manage to brush my proposal off again until next time. I was really becoming frustrated and I knew that I was not being fair to her family by letting her put off the purchase of the insurance needed to pay those pending death taxes.

After I arrived back at my office I picked up the telephone and called the accountant. He asked me if the insurance policy document had arrived yet. I felt just awful telling him that Betty had not even signed the papers yet. I told him that I had scheduled another appointment with Betty next Tuesday at 11:30. I said that I would call him next week and let him know the outcome.

After I finished that conversation, I immediately picked up the telephone to call Betty's secretary. I changed the time and venue of our next meeting to my office at 9:30 in the morning. By changing both the time and the venue I was effectively breaking the strong feeling of coziness that I had allowed to develop during the course of our previous meetings.

I booked the conference room in the building to create the ultimate business environment.

Betty arrived at my office and I led her to the conference room and sat her down. On the table in front of Betty were a copy of the life insurance application, a copy of her will and a copy of her trust agreement.

She looked up at me and said, "Sit down and let's go through the plan."

I moved next to her and went over the details while I was standing. I explained that her accountant had approved the cost and the plan itself, but we had to sign the documents immediately because her next birthday would cause the premium to increase. I casually mentioned that I first met with the accountant over six months ago and had telephoned him last week after our previous luncheon. I also let her know that I promised to let Mark know when he could expect the policy document after today's meeting.

Betty was feeling uncomfortable, so I then sat down and partially mirrored her body language. I placed my hands in my lap exactly as her hands were placed. Unfortunately, she was leaning back. I wanted her to lean forward so I kept my shoulders towards the table. I knew that she wanted to feel comfortable but I also knew that I could not allow her to get so comfortable that she didn't sign the papers again.

The only way for Betty to get on my wavelength was for her to lean forward and come closer to the table. Gradually she started to move forward. As she did I smiled and mirrored her a little more. I could see her start to visibly relax. Her shoulders were definitely less tense than when she first sat down. It was time for me to increase the tension level once again! I pulled my chair further towards the table and crossed my arms as I discussed the consequences again of delaying the paperwork. Her eyes showed that she again knew that I was not happy with delays. She asked me, "If we get the papers signed today, the rate increase won't happen, right?"

I wanted her to know that she was on the right track and thinking along the appropriate lines so I unfolded my arms and matched her upper body completely and smiled again as I pushed the papers towards her. She signed and sat back. I sat back. She looked very comfortable and relaxed and I felt also relaxed. I was thrilled that we had finally managed to sign the papers and get some business completed. She waited for me to clean up the paperwork and we went out to our usual restaurant for lunch.

EXERCISE — MISMATCHING

Make a list of other ways you can mismatch the client and when mismatches would be appropriate. Matching the person's voice and tonality is another way to gain rapport. You can match tonality, speech, volume, and the rhythm of speech. You may also match cultural distinctions or accent patterns. When you voice match or voice mirror, blend in and harmonize with the other person. This is extremely important in gaining rapport during telephone conversations. You can also mismatch, changing the speed and tonality of your voice to end a conversation on a telephone.

Closing a telephone conversation naturally is sometimes very difficult. Learning mismatching of tonality or hurried patterns is extremely important and can reduce the awkwardness that can arise when it is time for a call to end.

Ethics and the influencing process

By now, you realize that these skills can have a profound impact on people. Some of the people that have attended my courses challenge the ethics of consciously using influencing techniques, if the other person does not understand them or know that you are using them. They ask me, "Aren't you telling us to manipulate people?"

My answer is always the same—I have never felt that I manipulate people. I always try to help people with the use of the influencing techniques that I share in this course. When using these skills I feel that I understand other people better. I relate to them on a higher level of awareness. I listen better since I learned how to master the techniques and therefore I communicate more effectively. I use the skills ethically to influence my clients to make the right decisions for their employees, their families and their friends based on my experience of the world.

It is extremely important to use the skills ethically to help people as much as you can. I feel it would be extremely difficult to misuse these influencing techniques for any length of time because congruency is so important. I believe that most people recognize that something is not quite right when dealing with anyone who uses influencing procedures unethically.

Limits to rapport building or rapport maintenance

There are really only two limits in your ability to gain rapport:

1. The degree to which you can accurately perceive the other person's postures, gestures and speech patterns—in other words, your sensory acuity.

2. The skill with which you can match them during rapport building and maintenance.

Your relationship during the communication loop of rapport should be a harmonious mix between your integrity level, what you can do and believe wholeheartedly that you can do, and how far you are willing to go to build a bridge and enter another person's model of the world.

Always remember the 50-50 rule
50% of your body, 50% of the time.

When you first learn to use these skills, you may very well feel uncomfortable mirroring, matching, and crossover pacing another person. As with anything worthwhile, it is very important to practice to perfect your techniques.

Remember, if you are prepared to use rapport-building skills, consciously mirroring, matching and crossover pacing other people will help you gain rapport and trust with just about whomever you choose. You do not have to be like the other person to create rapport. You are simply building a bridge to understand them better.

Recap for Rapport

- Train yourself to be consciously aware of people's body language in every situation. By mastering pacing and leading through mirroring and matching, you will become a master at influencing people.

- Remember: Everyone likes to do business with people who are similar to themselves. You will discover as I have that you can lead people towards your outcome if you first mirror, match, and crossover pace to gain a high degree of rapport.

- Always test for rapport by doing something different. If they do the same action immediately afterwards by following your lead, you have established true rapport and you can continue leading until you obtain your outcome.

- Constantly test for rapport during your interaction. If rapport is broken for any reason—establish it again by mirroring, matching and cross-over pacing until you feel that you can again test it by leading.

- NEVER lead without first gaining rapport! The key to obtaining your outcome with your client is a high level of rapport! Always TEST to see if you have established the degree of rapport that you desire!

- The mind and body are totally linked! External body changes reflect internal state changes. You have complete control over your physiology and therefore you have complete control of your emotions.

Building rapport and creating rapport is a choice that you make during communication. To perfect these skills it is important to use them. Psychologists dealing with autistic children use mirroring, matching, and crossover pacing to enter their world. By entering their world they are then able to lead the individual out and build a bridge to another sphere of reality for the children.

These influencing techniques are extremely powerful if used correctly. When you gain rapport you gain the ability to solicit responses from other people. You also make them feel comfortable so that the communication loop is enhanced. When rapport is built on a high level, people feel confident and comfortable with each other.

Rapport, body language, tonality, and words all form an integral part of the meaning of our communication with others.

Remember: The Mind and Body Are Linked Completely!

Introduction to Language Patterns & Influencing Strategies

Effective communication is vital for many things—great relationships, partnerships, and strategic alliances. Peak performance communication is critical in order to reach goals, to build teams, to work as a team... So how do you become an effective communicator? As soon as you know the keys to unlocking the secret code of communication, you can start learning how to decipher communication messages.

Even more important than being able to decipher messages is the ability to be able to send out effective communication. Your influencing ability is directly related to how effectively you deliver your message and to how well your communication is received. *This book will explain how to decipher and communicate messages effectively.*

Influence & Communication will provide you with your 'Rosetta Stone' to unlock the hidden meaning and intentions that run deep within any communication loop. By learning the communication and language patterns in *Influence & Communication,* you will have the means to break the communication code wide open.

When you understand the communication code, you will arrive at goals more quickly because the better you communicate, the better people can understand exactly what you are attempting to achieve. Since we are more likely to achieve our goals with the help of other people you can see how important clear and concise communication is. If you tell people specifically what your goals are, how you need help and/or whom you need to meet, the odds are they will be better able to assist you in your quest to turn your dreams into reality. If they understand your objective there is a higher probability they will help you.

The bottom-line:
The more effectively you use and analyze language patterns, the more you will achieve throughout your life because your communication will be precise and targeted for peak performance.

Since communication is always relayed in language pattern*s,* pattern recognition is a powerful tool. It can greatly enhance your comprehension and understanding during the communication process. If you can recognize—then decipher—the nuances of the communication code; your personal effectiveness in relationships will be dramatically enhanced.

Competent communicators understand that a person's beliefs are the basis of each individual's communication. Communication patterns based on beliefs—are easily decoded—**if you have the key to unlock the code**. Understanding that all messages are filtered through a person's complex view of the world is of paramount importance.

With all this complexity, is it possible to drop the language of weakness and adopt the language of strength and power?

There is a process to acquire a powerful language base. First, accept that language is complex. Then, learn that there are a variety of practical approaches for you to take. Not all will work in every situation every time. There are many language patterns, convincer strategies, and peak performance skills inherent in powerful language usage. Once you learn the skill sets, you'll be able to grasp the situation more firmly and ascertain which tools will best serve you and lead you towards your goals.

Control is the key to the grammar of success.

As you think about your language choices and learn to control your responses appropriately, you can master many complex situations. There are a variety of possible language patterns that will work effectively in many situations. By unlocking the language pattern code, you will have the ability to determine which ones will work best, depending upon your personal style and the style of the recipient of your message.

Again, common sense is the key to using this material appropriately and effectively. I rarely promise quick fixes or urge you never to say a phrase or word. There are a few occasions when I will try to persuade you to avoid certain words and phrases with certain people or during specific circumstances. Whenever this occurs, please trust me and at least try my suggestion.

Use the lessons in the next sections to help you attain a high level of influence verbally and through your written messages. Incorporate as few or as many and you like. Keep an open mind -- See if they make your communication better. They have worked for thousands of people who have attended our seminars. Only you can judge what will work best for you.

My purpose for this book is to give you a guideline for peak performance communication. When you strive for peak performance, you must be solidly committed to your goals. I have always believed that with other people's assistance, I can reach the highest heights. In order to obtain their help, I need to convince them that my objectives are worthwhile. This is best done by effectively using language. Many people have contributed to this book over the years. It has been a work in progress for peak performance communication.

THE BASIS OF OUR COMMUNICATION—LANGUAGE

People learn to use language primarily by observing and imitating the linguistic behavior of others and secondarily by taking in information through books. Unfortunately, if you want to master influencing techniques there are limitations to informal learning.

In the next section we will be discussing specific influencing methods using advanced language techniques. Our goals are to:

- Increase (and/or refresh) your knowledge about parts of speech and the structure of sentences
- Define language patterns that are used to influence and explain their usage
- Explain the theory of ambiguities—and how to avoid using them
- Establish a method of deduction to give structure to an influencing process
- Define "cause and effect" and explain its significance in changing beliefs

Verbal Agreement Between Parties

Great managers and negotiators gain rapport and trust by truly appreciating what people say and by responding appropriately. Peak performers listen well and assimilate themselves into the other person's mode, or view of the world, extremely quickly. This does not necessarily mean that you must agree with everything the other person says. During effective communication, you should either appreciate their point of view or, at the very least, attempt to understand and empathize with their underlying fears and/or beliefs.

How do we acquire language skills?

As toddlers, we began to learn language by mimicking and imitating people around us. In a short time, we picked up enough words and phrases to make our wants and needs understood to those around us. At first, our parents and those who love us were so terribly delighted to have us speak at all that they willingly excepted anything we said, garbled, clear, or anything in between. Going to bed was "go ni-night", Daddy was "Da-da" and Grandma was addressed as "Mamma". As time went on, however, our infantile contributions to conversations became less cute to those around us.

Societal pressures for us to conform to the common usage of language mounted. These pressures created stress whenever we perceived ourselves to be out of place with our use of language. Whenever we felt we were not communicating well, our self-image suffered. We quickly learned to enhance our communication abilities, bringing them up to the speed and abilities of those we were interacting with to make ourselves feel more at ease. Peer pressure is a strong driving force in communication. We are often remarkably chameleon-like in our ability to 'morph' to the level of communication abilities of those with whom we are currently communicating.

Seeking the respect of those we were communicating with drove our learning process even further as we advanced through life. In adult company, we usually wanted to impress – particularly with adults we respected. For example, our language was normally better with teachers than that which we used with our parents. With our friends and peers, we probably dropped down to a less formal level. This process is based on effective rapport-building techniques. People tend to trust people who act like they do and speak at the same grammatical level they do. Different language is appropriate for different communication loops.

Why is it necessary to communicate effectively?

As we grow and learn, our ability to communicate succinctly and with clarity is paramount to our success. In business terms, many studies have shown that effective communication abilities display a direct correlation to earnings—especially with sales people and management personnel.

Expectations and judgment from others in the business community are very similar to those that we experienced in our childhood. Usually, by the age of four or five, adults ceased thinking that baby talk was adorable. Their expectations began to evolve regarding how they expect children to speak. Adult expectations and peer pressure force most people to conform—especially in business language. It might seem 'cute' for a rookie to mispronounce critical words in an industry, but this behavior will not be tolerated for very long. In business, the learning curve is quick and steep, especially if your goal is to grab the brass ring.

How do we learn how to command our language appropriately for any situation?

At school, as we studied English grammar, the realization that "It is I" and other expressions were correct; and "It is me" and a whole lot more, were not, usually came as a stressful revelation. You say to yourself, "It's me!" sounds okay—so why do I have a big red circle on my paper and a B- instead of an A+? I worked hard, spell-checked, and proofread that paper twenty times! That's when it hit us! English is not just "okay"; it is okay under certain conditions.

We discovered that the way we *just talked naturally* was, in reality, a complex language requiring grammatical rules and syntax - particularly when we wanted to impress others. Our language mastery was of paramount importance when we were being evaluated or graded upon our command of the English language. When we wanted to excel, further introspection uncovered the truth that forethought was necessary whenever we wanted to communicate at a peak performance level.

The Power of Words

Words can contribute to admirable causes or can be manipulated to do great harm. They can inspire, motivate, stimulate, encourage, and spur people toward positive behavior. On the other hand words can be dangerous. People 'shoot from the hip' in anger, wounding those they care about with words. Dagger-like barbs come tumbling out of angry mouths, smiting those at which they are hurled. There is an old saying 'Sticks and stones may break my bones but words will never hurt me.' Words can harm people (psychologically) and yes, vicious words indeed can kill people because they can become so hurt that they choose to harm themselves or others. Wars do not occur because people say nice things to each other! And they continue (or stop) largely based on the impact of politicians' words.

Sticks and stones may break my bones but names can never hurt me.

Since childhood, people have judged you on your use and command of language, and on the breadth and scope of your vocabulary. Work, school, travel, your teachers, co-workers, peers, friends, the media, reading, and conversations have been the feeding ground for your language growth. They have determined the type and number of words you currently possess in your vocabulary. Most people, by the time they reach maturity in their careers, have a fairly good working vocabulary.

Words are the building blocks of communication. By now you have probably experienced the negative impact of choosing the 'wrong' words for a situation. And you probably have at one time or another appreciated the importance of choosing the right words for the occasion.

If names are not correct, language will not be in accordance with the truth of things.
- Confucius (551 – 479 B.C.)

Basically, a word is the name for an idea or for the mental concept that promotes people to form images and thoughts in their mind.

The goal in communication is to choose the correct word to transmit our messages to others appropriately.

Words can name:
Thing (dog, cat, tree, woman, child)
Quality (lighter, darker, faster, slower)
Emotion (sad, happy, excited, angry, motivated)
Action (jumping, moving, speeding, slowing)
Relationships between things or thoughts (and, but, although, in addition)
Person (Bob, Susan, Heather, boy, man, uncle)
Place (St. Paul, Philadelphia, Outer Banks, Left Bank, London, New York)

Be fearless in your choice of words. Use as many words as you need and choose words as big or as small as you think concisely portray your meaning to your audience. Make sure that the words you use are used correctly (grammar and syntax) and be certain that the audience can comprehend them (that the words are in the reader's or listener's realm of knowledge).

> The limits of my language mean the limits of my world.
> - Ludwig Wittgenstein (Tractuatus logico-philosophicus)

Never waste words, and do not waste letters, sounds, nor tax the audience's patience by dragging out a long word when a short word will do the work – providing it is not so short that it lacks accuracy! Brevity is powerful in writing. Concise speaking is powerful for the orator. Winston Churchill's speech during the war years to the assemblage at his old public school is remembered decades after World War II because of the simple and powerful words he spoke: "Never give in -- never, never, never, never, in nothing great or small, large or petty, never give in except to convictions of honour and good sense. Never yield to force; never yield to the apparently overwhelming might of the enemy"

Use New Words Often

Use new words as they come into your world. Sometimes this can be frightening but if you do not use new words, they will fall out of your grasp and you will not keep up with your growing mind and intellect. No one truly knows a word until they use it a few times! Test out words that you have just heard. Look up words in the dictionary that are unfamiliar to you and then pop them into conversations. The first couple of times you can use the new word (or phrase) by simply quoting directly how the word was used. For example: This morning I read an interesting passage in the Wall Street Journal. It said: "The world of corporate governance is being changed by the scandals from the past few months. Company Boards are being forced to look into their ethics codes by shareholders. They also must examine their policies and procedures for handling ethics violations."

Continue to expand your vocabulary throughout your life. Your growing vocabulary will reflect your growing mind -- your character, habits, and the internal workings of your mind -- to your peers, family members, friends, and associates.

Note: If you are using words that may not be familiar to your audience, explain their meaning or make certain the receiver can ascertain their meaning by the context in which you use the unfamiliar word.

> The chief merit of language is clarity, and we know nothing that detracts so much from this as do unfamiliar terms.
> -Galen (On the Natural Faculties)

Correct Word Usage

Just as your life revolves around the customs and protocol of the society you live in, correct word usage (what is appropriate for you) is decided upon by the norms of your society, industry, community, and education. It is not any one person's word usage that determines whether communication is 'right or wrong'; nor does it have to be the majority of the society members, because word usage is 'niched' (e.g. by industry, religion, education, etc.) and is apt to change frequently. The bottom line: Select your words with care.

Always keep in mind that the audience you will be delivering to should predetermine your usage choice. For example, your choice of words should be different when speaking to friends in a casual conversation than when you are addressing your peers in a formal presentation at work.

Throughout the generations word usage has changed considerably. Business and social etiquette change, new industries, services and products are added to common language usage. New words are added and are considered to be 'slang' until they are embraced by the masses. Old words fade out; and so, naturally language has evolved. A word of caution: Until slang words have been adopted, resist being the first in your circle to use slang words during communication. Using slang is dangerous especially when presenting formally, during the influencing process, and also for written communication (the word might go out of fashion 'dating' your written work).

Our range of words is usually reflective of our experience in life, our educational background, and our imagination.

Power over word usage is determined predominantly by two things: First, we must name and express our ideas concisely by choosing the right words to describe our past experiences. Second, we must be able to express ourselves when communicating new experiences and thoughts.

Throughout life we will struggle with both points in our quest to be great communicators as we expand our horizons and continue to grow and educate ourselves. When you stop acquiring new words, and discontinue attempts to fit and refit your old words to how your mind changes ideas and reformulates beliefs, you will have reached the end of your intellectual development.

There are many ways for the mind to expand and grow. As far as getting the words right, it all comes down to finding the appropriate name for what you think, see, feel, taste, hear, smell, and remember. A word is only a word – if it doesn't fit the concept you are trying to portray or accurately describe your emotions or ideas; the words are useless. In fact, they may be worse than useless if they cause you harm because they inaccurately or unintentionally characterize thoughts, ideas, and emotions that you do not have. When this happens they can damage your reputation!

> Every word is a preconceived judgment.
> Friedrich Nietzsche
> (Human All-too- Human)

Danger – Barbarians and Foreigners at the Gate!

Avoid barbarisms, improprieties, archaisms, foreign words, slang, and colloquialisms.

Barbarisms -- An articulation error or misspeaking (slips of the tongue), miswriting (composition error), or substitution of one letter for another. For example: Substituting then for than; compliment for complement; eminent for imminent; council for counsel (legal professional). Also, saying Jamsin for Jazmin (mispronouncing someone's name is the height of rudeness – even if you didn't mean it!) or Chrimsas for Christmas (my daughter's old barbarisms). These aren't so cute when you are an adult. Substituting letters might look (or sound) like this: suspect for expect, excape for escape.

Improprieties – The unacceptable use of a single word or of a phrase. When you use a perfectly good word in the word place, you have committed the language crime of impropriety. The most common mistake is an error in denotation (having a specific meaning). For example, using effect for affect, lay for lie. Note: This example is also a grammatical error!).

Archaisms – Words no longer in common use. Forsoothe is still in the dictionary but you would look silly using 'forsoothe' today instead of the more modern 'indeed' unless you were quoting Shakespearian passages.

> "When I use a word," Humpty Dumpty said, in a rather scornful tone, "it means just what I choose it to mean – neither more nor less."
> "The question is," said Alice, "whether you can make words mean so many different things."
> "The question is," said Humpty Dumpty, "which is to be master – that's all."
> -- Lewis Carroll (Through the Looking-Glass)

Foreign words – There are few times that I might judge the use of a foreign word acceptable. Their use might be satisfactory if the foreign word is so commonly used in the English language so as to have universal understanding or if the word does not have an appropriate translation (then you should take the time to define the meaning of the word for your audience). Words like coup, tête à tête, gesundheit, joie de vivre, and savoire faire have crossed over into our tongue and are defined in most dictionaries.

Colloquialism -- a local or regional dialect expression. Be careful when influencing people from a different region than your own. Word usage can change for selected words (e.g. soda, pop; lift, elevator;)

Slang – the use of new words that have not yet entered the mainstream of standard language usage. Most words enter as a colloquialism or through niche industries and gain a wider audience before they mainstream into our standard language. Slang words may or may not be incorporated into standard usage. For example, some words that have been included in standard usage: groovy, cool, TV, fax, info, the web. Here are others that were not incorporated: phat (for cool), rad for radical, boffo for great.

> Slang is a language that rolls up its sleeves, spits on its hands and goes to work.
> - Carl Sandberg

Generic and Specific Words

We can parallel words to a carpenter's tools. Each type of tool has a special use. Master carpenters are intimately familiar with how to use their tools; and the final product usually reflects their expertise in using the tools in their toolbox effectively. It is the same with master influencers. Their tools are words. If you want to be a master influencer you should know how to use them and how to classify them into categories of usage. The first classification is generic and specific words.

Generic words

Generic words are words that describe non-specific or universal things, groupings, or concepts. If you think of the word 'dog' – dog is a generic word because it does not specify or make a distinction as to what type of dog you are talking about. (*Note:* Never confuse generic words with generalities!)[6]

Specific words

Specific words characterize words that we associate with distinct, specialized, precise, definite, or explicit pictures and ideas in our imagination. For example: Dalmatian is a specific word because it clearly depicts a particular type of dog.

Defining Generic & Specific Words

The waters are often muddied when we try to lock down which words are specific and which words are generic in nature. There are no hard and fast rules – it depends on how you are using the word at that particular moment. For example: If you are discussing animals in general (generic usage) and then you specify the animal to be a dog, you have now transferred the word 'dog' into a specific (through usage) rather than a generic word. Confused yet? No – well, as we go along, you will understand that to be confused is okay. Language and its usage can be confusing and fun! We could debate the finer points of specific and generic usage for hours and still not come to a consensus or conclusion.

Generic	Specific
Dog	Dalmatian
Animal	Dog
Lead	Motivate
Manage	Direct
Flower	Rose
Said	Whisper
Communicate	Email
Contact next week	Telephone next Tuesday
Come over in the morning	Set an appointment for 10:00 AM

[6] Discussed in the Absolutes and Generalities Section later in the manual

CONCRETE & ABSTRACT WORDS

The second method of classifying words is by choosing whether they are concrete or abstract in nature. This type of classification ***depends upon the idea behind the word***. When we name something that can be touched, tasted, felt, seen, or heard, we use a concrete word.

Words that depict the idea of an abstraction or that are conceptual in nature (for example: a quality, state of being, or an action) are said to be abstract words.

Concrete	Abstract
Car	Motion
Fact	Truth
Honest statement	Ethics
White sheet of paper	Whiteness
Books	Educational materials
Horse	Riding
Food	Hunger
House	Home
Flag	Patriotism

The key in language is to find the correct words to transmit your intent and meaning to the audience whether by verbal or written means (listener or reader).

As success in life becomes more important to individuals, so does the desire to communicate better. This desire is preempted by concern about our current command of the English language. We want to feel confident in our choice of words and our pronunciation.

We ordinarily realize that we will have less stress during communication when our command and control of the language is such that we are able to use it readily, effortlessly and presentably in any situation—written or verbal. As we face increasingly complex and demanding situations, our goal of ideal communication becomes more important to us.

What can I do to increase my success?

Confidence and effectiveness in the command of the English language comes from an accurate knowledge regarding the nuances and possibilities that exist. In any situation we need to know how to choose what is most effective for us. Perhaps even more important, we must practice until our command of the language becomes easy and effortless—until peak performance communication becomes an ingrained habit.

Habitual use of competent communication comes with practice. It grows from the process we used as children—from imitating those people whose command of the language we admire.

In business situations, we often have to make choices among words, forms, and constructions within language. Our verbal and written word choices directly contribute to the impressions our clients, peers, and superiors have of us. The bottom-line is this—people make judgment calls about others based on their perception of the other person's command of language.

Within these pages you will find a variety of words, phrases, grammatical rules, influencing strategies and peak performance techniques that will help you enhance your ability to communicate effectively. Throughout our lives we influence others, positively or negatively. This book is designed to decrease the negative thoughts others may have about you and to increase the positive impact you have on those around you.

Description – Painting a Picture of Your World

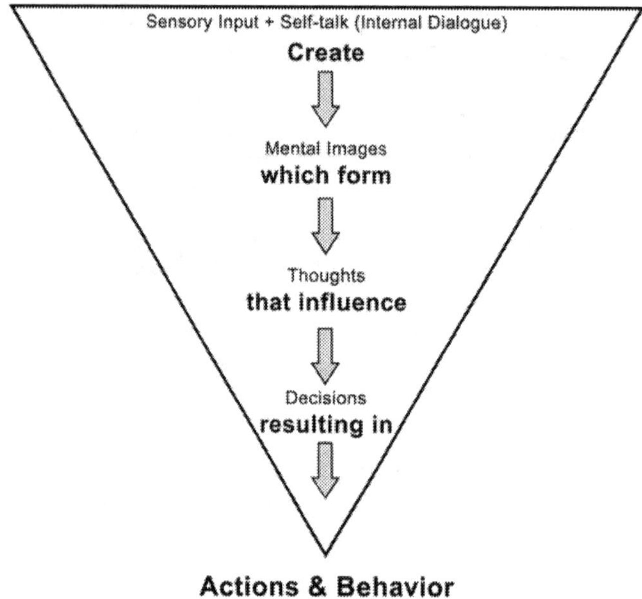

What is the most effective way to describe scenes and beliefs?

Description is one of the most powerful ways the mind creates internal images. Using description as an influencing tool is part art, part science, and process. Descriptions are characterized as words (or phrases) that suggest (or portray) images of persons, places, things, events, emotions, ideas, and/or effects. Properly composed, descriptions should leave a clear and concise impression upon the receiver's mind (listener or reader)[7].

Through description we can let others have a glimpse into our world. Word pictures – descriptions -- can be used to paint impressions from any of our senses. We can describe how something smells, looks, sounds, tastes and feels. Word pictures can also be used to portray emotions, moods, and feelings, as well as concrete things from nature. Word pictures can bring images to life by illustrating motion, behavior, moods, and actions. Word pictures can explain how something looks in addition to how it works. Your ability to influence will be augmented substantially when your descriptions are easy to understand. They should also be interesting so that they come alive in the listener's mind.

[7] Note: During this section of the manual we will assume that the communication is verbal and will therefore refer to the receiver of the message during the communication loop as the listener.

To be most effective, descriptions ideally should be:

1. **Related** to the other person's world -- the words should relate (link) to something the person has experience with. When words can be easily related, the person can readily understand the description we are trying to communicate.

2. **Proportioned** – the words should give us an idea of how the idea can be 'arranged' in the listener's world. Proportion gives the listener a sense of the size and shape of the image being discussed. It attempts to help the person get a sense of how the image correlates to other images in the person's understanding.

3. **Sequenced and have logical order** – put descriptive words down, one after another to form a logical sequence so that the receiver of the information can make a mental map of your description.

EXAMPLE DESCRIPTION

This is an example of how the three elements – relation, proportion, and sequence -- are used effectively in a describing a tall ship as it sails into a harbor.

If the person had never seen a tall ship before, you would try to connect (relate) the description to something that was in their realm of prior knowledge. It was just like the ship in the Disney movie Peter Pan, only it was real! You would then try to provide the listener with a sense of the size and shape (proportion) of the vessel. The ship was 150 feet long – about half the size of a football field. And the highest mast seemed even taller than the entire length of the ship. I stopped counting the sails when I reached thirty in number and there were five substantial masts holding the sails. I have never seen that much rigging on a ship! As the ship sailed into the harbor I first noticed how full the sails were. It seemed odd how they billowed since I had not taken note of the wind until then. As I watched the ship sail toward us as we stood on the quay, I felt the breeze on my face as it gently blew my hair into my eyes. I asked myself, *"How could it be that this slight air current was the force that propelled such a magnificent vessel forward?"(sequence & logical order)*

Edgar Allan Poe's
The Fall of the House of Usher

During the whole of a dull, dark, and soundless day in the Autumn of the year, when the clouds hung oppressively low in the heavens, I had been passing alone, on horseback, through a singularly dreary tract of country; and at length found myself, as the shades of the evening drew on, within view of the melancholy House of Usher. I know not how it was – but, with the first glimpse of the building, a sense of insufferable gloom pervaded my spirit. I say insufferable; for the feeling was unrelieved by any of that half pleasurable, because poetic, sentiment, with which the mind usually receives even the sternest natural images of the desolate or terrible. I looked upon the scene before me – upon the mere house, and the simple landscape features of the domain -- upon the bleak walls – upon the vacant eye-like windows – upon a few rank sedges – and upon a few white trunks of decayed trees – with an utter depression of soul which I can compare to no unearthly sensation more properly than to the after dream of the reveler upon opium – the bitter lapse into everyday life – the hideous dropping off of the veil. There was an iciness, a sickening of the heart -- an unredeemed dreariness of thought that no goading of the imagination could torture into aught of the sublime. What was it – I paused to think – what was it that so unnerved me in the contemplation of the House of Usher?

There is one day when all things are tired, and the very smells, as they drift on the heavy air, are old and used. One cannot explain this, but it feels so. Then there is another day – to the eye nothing whatever has changed – when all the smells are new and delightful, and the whiskers of the Jungle People quiver to their roots and the winter hair comes away from their sides in long, draggled locks. Then, perhaps, a little rain falls, and all the trees and the bushes and the bamboos and the mosses and the juicy-leaved plants wake with a noise of growing that you can almost hear, and under this noise runs, day and night, a deep hum. *That* is the noise of the Spring – a vibrating boom which is neither bees, nor falling water, nor the wind in the treetops, but the purring of the warm, happy world.

-- Kipling's *The Spring Running*

PROCESSING MEMORIES AROUND THE GROUPING PROCESS

Memories are formed around images. We remember images by pulling them up from our memory bank by how we group (or categorize) the memory. It is perfectly natural for us to view objects and to formulate beliefs in groups.

How does Grouping operate in the influencing process?

When you are attempting to influence someone, this is the descriptive process that might occur in the client's mind as the person tries to formulate an image of the product being described. You should help the other person understand the product by working through the details (describing the product) during the sales process.

Step #1 General Overview

Step #2 Inquisitive Interest

Step #3 Context & Perceptual Positioning

Step #4 Filling in the Details

Step #5 Attaching Emotional Involvement

Step #6 Formulating Impressions and Opinions

Step #1 General Overview

The object of every description is to give a single unified impression. Give the listener a brief glance – a general overview – of the concept or idea. The very nature of our eyes and how they operate make certain that we first see only in general and then secondly we take in the details. As we transfer input from our senses, we usually take in general pictures and concepts first, only then does our mind fill in the details.

During the communication loop, the listener tries to identify a General Overview of the idea being discussed or picture being described.

What questions are being asked in the listener's head when they are trying to grasp the general overview?

- What subject is being discussed?
- Do I know anything about the subject?

Step #2 Inquisitive Interest

After our brain has a general understanding of what is going on, and *if there is interest*, the brain starts to become inquisitive. If it does not find the subject interesting, the mind dismisses the ideas and thoughts. Our mind constantly seeks out and moves toward areas that it finds absorbing or attractive. During the influencing process it is critical to keep the other person interested. You can best accomplish this by painting vivid word pictures that impact on the visual, auditory, and kinesthetic levels.

What questions is the brain asking to determine if the listener is interested in the idea or concept?

- How much interest do I have in that?
- Is this the information I've been looking for?
- Are they talking about a (movie, concept, country, town, person, place. etc.) that I want to know more about?

Step #3 Context & Perceptual Positioning

Excellent communicators help their audience understand their vantage point by spelling out their position. They help the listener understand the perceptual position they are speaking from. By doing this, they give the listener a frame of reference for the context of the communication.

To fully understand the intent of the message, the mind will attempt to determine the speaker's stance on the matter. Skilled comprehension begins with concluding which perceptual position the speaker is using. As the speaker, it is best to make this easy for the listener.

Everything people describe is spoken about from a specific vantage point – from one of the perceptual positions – from a definite point of view. Just as a camera can be pointed in different directions to take in differing aspects of a scene, the speaker can position the communication from different points of view depending on how they observe the ideas and thoughts. The speaker's description of the concept can be dramatically altered depending on the specific vantage point (perceptual position) they take.

The brain is inclined to try to quickly figure out from which vantage point (perceptual position) the speaker is talking before it can truly make sense of the communication. In most instances, the listener has to figure this out before they can move forward toward comprehending the message.

Note: Just as a photographer moves their camera to take different shots, the communicator usually shifts their point of view during the communication loop. It is wise to help the listener understand when you have changed vantage points and have shifted from one perceptual position to another. This is called a moving point of view. It can be very confusing to the listener when the communicator shifts perceptual positions (vantage points) too often during the communication loop, Whenever possible, the speaker should clarify their communication stance by explaining from which perceptual position they are speaking. The listener should know when you move from one point of view to another.

Example of effectively shifting perceptual positions: Now that I've finished discussing the product benefits that I have personally experienced, (1st perceptual position), I'll give you some of the financial reasons (3rd perceptual position) why this product has worked so well for other clients.

What statements help the listener determine the speaker's perceptual position?

1st Perceptual Position – the Ego Position -- Individual's description form their personal point of view

From my point of view...
If I had to give you my viewpoint...
Looking at this from my team's standpoint...

2nd Perceptual Position – the Alliance Position -- Another person's point of view laced with their emotional involvement and their values

From my client's point of view...
From Susan's vantage point...
I spoke to Bob and he said, "..."
Through the customer's eyes this looks....

3rd Perceptual Position – The Observer Position – The analysis viewpoint without emotions and devoid of value judgment calls and biases

If we look at this from the financial side...
Our customer's bottom line will be impacted and if we view this purely from their financial point of view...
Looking at this from a clinical standpoint

Step #4 Filling in the Details

Once we have a grasp of the general overview, are interested in the subject, and have discerned the perceptual positioning, we strive to fill in the blanks. We now attempt to add details to the picture our mind is composing. Words create pictures and the more detail we have, the better we are able to compose an image that matches the one the speaker is trying to portray. The details are not only composed from the speaker's words, they are filled in from the listener's internal dialog – their self-talk. If I were describing an angry man, the listener would layer my words with their experience of what they thought an angry person looked like.

From my words and their memory, an image of the person I was describing would be created in their mind. Our imagination works wonders during this process. On the sender's side, imagination helps us paint a picture through our words. On the receiver's side, their imagination helps pull together the pieces of communication that help them build a mental picture. Our imagination will embellish the images we send and receive during the communication loop making them come to life. The images are dynamic and flexible. As the conversation continues we usually add and subtract details.

Step #5 Attaching Emotional Involvement

From the impression we have built so far, we now attach emotions and feelings. Impressions and memories are not just lists of details or inventories of cold, hard facts.

At this stage, emotions and beliefs regarding the impression take shape and we begin to formulate opinions and beliefs.

Step #6 Formulating Impressions & Opinions

As we are creating a detailed view in our mind, we begin to form an impression of the whole.

Using Overall Impressions to Formulate Beliefs

It is our natural tendency to be orderly – to make sense of our world and communication based on how we process information. For many people it is almost impossible to process information unless the information is grouped in a systematic, logically based, orderly fashion. People will attempt to make sense of your beliefs if you have helped their understanding by communicating your beliefs in a logical way.

Grouping

To make sense of the world we live in, people tend to group facts, beliefs, and impressions together. To relate to your ideas, people will group the facts and their impressions of your influencing process together. Groups are formed primarily by two methods:

1. By the general rule
2. By exceptions to the rule.

Grouping -- By the general rule

When we try to view the person as a whole we often bundle their characteristics into groups based on our past experiences and impressions. For example people might group others like this: Italian men like to gesture with their hands when talking. French women dress stylishly. People from the Northeast dislike change and love the status quo. People from the South are hospitable and friendly. Everything is bigger in Texas. This stereotyping clouds our judgment. If the picture we are viewing is of a forest scene, if we are grouping our impression by the general rule, we would glance at the scene and see the forest as a group of trees – you would not look at each individual tree as a separate entity.

Grouping -- By exceptions to the rule

Our eye (and our perception) can be naturally attracted to one striking detail in a picture. Then we use this detail as a basis for decisions, thought processes, and deduction. In other words, we have selectively extracted a few salient details as the central point for formulating and grouping our thoughts. This grouping occurs no matter what senses we use. By examining the forest picture we were viewing in the last example, we suddenly notice that one area contained a bright red maple tree. If we were 'struck' by that image, the image of the one differently colored tree standing out from the rest, our eyes would focus on that detail (the red maple). If the impression has a considerable impact on our mind, we would tend to use that particular detail to structure (or group) our 'overall impression'. If we were asked to describe the scene, we would probably begin by describing the maple tree because it stood out the most in our mind.

Exceptions and Decision Making

The 'exception to the rule' grouping process works as the odd man out in the influencing process. People look for the exception to the rule (or argument) to either believe or refute your message. One point might 'stick' and have much more impact than another. It just depends on how the individual processes the information.

Exceptions to the Rule and Stereotyping

Unfortunately, many people try to make sense of how other people think by looking for the exceptions. They bundle the details of a scene or an idea based on the detail that is different – the one that stands out from the crowd. They classify their perceptions based on the exception rather than the rule. They link the image into their world and to their current beliefs by justifying the behavior on the anomaly rather than by looking for the prevailing wisdom that would govern the similarities. They seek for the answers as to how different they are, rather than automatically see how alike they are.

THE ORIGIN OF AMBIGUITY

What impact does an ambiguity have on the influencing process?

Ambiguous terms or words during communication can lead to heated disagreements based erroneously on misunderstanding facts or statements. They also lead to verbal disputes about specific words and terminology used. Unfortunately, heated arguments can sometimes spiral out of control. When emotions are high, each person thinks their definition is the correct definition. Too much negative energy is spent discerning the different meanings. This negative energy often results in high degrees of frustration and anger, which in turn negatively affects relationships.

Have you ever found that people can say one thing yet mean another, or act one way yet their words contradict their actions? Have you ever found it difficult to decipher another person's intent or meaning? You are not alone! What does the word 'bow' mean to you? If I told you I just bought a bow then images of hunting, a present, or a hair ribbon might come to mind. The image you conjure up in your mind will depend on your experience in life, your relationship with me, the context of our discussion, as well as other factors. When you find it difficult to immediately grasp the meaning of a word because it is ambiguous, misunderstanding and stress are generally by-products. Because words mean different things to different people, miscommunication often occurs - particularly in the arena of verbal communication. People can also become fixated on a word that historically has been associated with negative emotions. If you then happen to use this word in your dialog, you might be surprised by their reaction to what you thought was an innocent word.

How's That Again?
A Wisconsin man in the process of revising his will received the following note from his lawyer:
"Enclosed is a proposed revision of your will. If you have any further comments or corrections, let me know so that we can arrange for your execution."

If ambiguity happens you must acknowledge it. If you don't, people will continue to be confused by it.

Ambiguities and How They Can Skew Perception

There are several ways that ambiguities can muddy the water of clear communication. The bottom line: Make sure that you are communicating clearly and avoiding ambiguities. Especially when you are trying to influence!

Ambiguities occur when the meanings of words or phrases shift or change according to the context they are used in.

Ambiguities can be catastrophic whenever critical decisions are concerned. The consequences of ambiguities can be seen throughout history. A classic example occurred centuries ago when Croesus asked advice from the Oracle of Delphi. Croesus, the King of Lydia, was contemplating war with the kingdom of Persia. Croesus was a prudent man and did not want to fight unless the victory was guaranteed so he went to ask the oracle about his chances of success. Croesus was delighted when the Oracle of Delphi said, "If Croesus went to war with Cyrus, he would destroy a mighty kingdom." Within a short period of time Croesus went to war and was hastily defeated by Cyrus. Fortunately, Croesus' life was spared. He wrote to the Oracle of Delphi, furious that the Oracle gave him the wrong advice. The priests responded that the Oracle had been correct. When Croesus went to war with Cyrus, he had destroyed a mighty kingdom -- his own! Fortunately, ambiguities often do not cause **such** havoc.

Sometimes advertisers purposely use ambiguities to grab the attention of the reader. "Safe driving is no accident!" "Lose some wait!"

Equivocation

In English, as with most languages, many words have more than one literal meaning. For example, the word 'pen' could mean something you write with or an animal enclosure. Through the context of the surrounding words we most often can determine the precise meaning of the word.

> ***There must be lots of jobs available in physical education, because the bulletin announces the team will give a talk to graduating seniors about employment opportunities in the college gymnasium tonight.***

To better understand the concept of equivocation it might be best to state what the opposite of the word equivocal means. **Un**equivocal means that the intent is clear; that there is only one possible meaning or interpretation. When we (accidentally or by design) confuse the different meanings that a single word (or a phrase) may have, by using it in different senses in the same context, we use it equivocally.

Equivocation is the use of unclear statements (and/or ambiguous words or phrases) that can have different meanings, but whose understanding or interpretation is not readily apparent. Often the appropriate interpretation is unclear until the context of how the words are being used becomes apparent. This comprehension of the context often occurs later in the conversation or is spelled out further along in the message. Sometimes, equivocation is only made clear when the other person (the receiver) questions the sender of the communication.

Equivocal words and phrases can mislead and confuse people. The tactic of equivocation is (unfortunately) used by some to hedge, stall, or to delay divulging their position. Fortunately this is the exception rather than the rule when equivocation occurs. Most often the sender does not realize they are speaking equivocally. Questioning the speaker to clear up 'equivocation miscommunication' is the best philosophy.

Unfortunately, this tactic is most often associated with politics. We often hear that politicians equivocate.

Example: *The reporter asked the mayor to state his position on the teachers' strike at the local high school. But the mayor only equivocated, saying "There is no question that this issue needs to be resolved – I have every faith that between the community and the school board that everything will be taken care of". The mayor evaded answering the question by using an ambiguous statement that seemed to share his thoughts on the situation, but really gave no further information on his personal opinion and position.*

To further complicate matters is to look at the context in which the equivocation occurs. When the context happens to be an argument of causation (i.e. for building logic, for using a sequence of cause and effect statements, etc.), we commit the Fallacy of Equivocation.

Fallacies are various types of erroneous reasoning (or interpretation) that cause arguments to be (or be viewed as) unsound, misleading, false, or untruthful. Fallacy of Equivocation occurs because the word/s can have more than one meaning depending on how one interprets them. In the next example, we can better demonstrate the Fallacy of Equivocation by using two different contexts of the word 'end'.

EXAMPLE — FALLACY OF EQUIVOCATION

"The end of the game lies in its perfection; death is the end of life; hence, death is the perfection of life."

The first meaning of 'end' is goal. "The goal of the game lies in its perfection." The second meaning is the last event. "Death is the last event of life." Both of these meanings are correct, however it is the way the statement of logic is formulated with the word "end" that causes the confusion leading to the conclusion that "death is the perfection of life".

EXAMPLE — EQUIVOCATION

Let's look at a humorous equivocation.
Some husbands have red cars.
My husband has a red car.
Therefore my husband is some husband!

EXAMPLE — DOUBLE ENTENDRE

On the lighter side of equivocation are puns, plays on words, and double entendres. Let's look at how words can change their meaning in this funny passage:

On the Job

I've had lots of jobs. My first one was working in an orange juice factory, but I couldn't concentrate, so I got canned.

Then I got work as a tailor, but it was just a sew-sew job, and I wasn't suited for it.

Then I tried to be a chef. Figured it would add a little spice to my life, but I just didn't have the thyme.

Next I worked for a pool maintenance company. It went swimmingly for a while, but eventually it got to be draining.

My last job was in a grocery store, but I didn't put much stock in it, and ended up getting sacked.

By Peter Stone

Relative Context Ambiguities

When dealing with people's perceptions, words that have relative meanings can be ambiguous. When a word is considered to be 'relative' its interpretation is based on the receiver's perception. The word 'large' does not necessarily paint the same picture in the minds of two different people. Many adjectives and adverbs have relative meanings depending on the context. The adjective 'small' is a relative word. A small building and a small person are in very different categories. The context of a building compared to a person sets an entirely different meaning for the perceptual size of 'small'. In addition, imagining a small building in New York City is sure to be different than picturing a small building in a county town. If I just said, "That is small" I have not clearly defined the perceptual parameters of size. As you can imagine, doing this might set you up for miscommunication.

Miscommunication, due to using relative words can have dire consequences in the business world. If, as a customer, I expect you to deliver the product in a timely fashion and my understanding of the word timely is within two to three business days but your understanding of timely is 10 business days -- we have a problem! We have just committed an error of miscommunication through using an adverbial ambiguity because the word 'timely' is an adverb.

Be certain when you use adverbs rather than adjectives, that you are clear and specific about your meaning. Adverbs usually describe action, and actions usually set up people's expectations. You should always check to see if your message has been received as intended. Open up a dialogue to determine, quantify, and clarify the perceptual parameters and expectations – this is vital in avoiding ambiguities.

Accent ambiguities

The meaning of the sentence can change ambiguously depending on which part of the sentence that you stress, denote or accentuate. When you speak, you can accentuate word/s or a phrase within a sentence with vocal inflection or with gestures.

Think about how many meanings you can convey by changing your vocal quality and gestures with this sentence: "Well, I see you're having a great day!"

The most interesting aspect of accent ambiguities is that you can -- consciously or unconsciously -- change the perceptual parameters of a statement into something humorous, menacing or offensive. You can also cast doubt upon a true statement and change it into something that could be perceived as untrue. Newspapers and advertisers have become adapt at skewing perception by using accent ambiguities. Headlines in particular use this technique to influence readers. From a headline in the Philadelphia on Black Friday, "Bearing Any Burden (subtitle) Paying Half Price – in uncertain economy, faithful shoppers."

Purposely Misleading Ambiguities

Never make the mistake of purposely using ambiguities to influence people. Why do we include them in this book? To make sure that you understand the ramifications of using them and because it is important to recognize when they are being used to influence you! What would you have done if you were in the same position as this unfortunate person? A ship's captain and his first mate were at odds from the beginning of a long voyage. Their constant bickering was aggravated by the first mate's tendency to drink a shot of rum at the end of a hard day at sea. The captain was a strict tea-totaler who rarely missed the opportunity to lecture the first mate about the evils of alcohol. After two months the ship docked into port. All the men disembarked for an evening of revelry. The first mate returned to the ship quite under the weather. Unfortunately, he was greeted on deck by the captain. The next morning when the first mate entered his daily observation into the ship's logbook, he saw that the captain had written, "The mate was drunk today." He immediately went to the captain and pleaded that the entry be removed. The captain refused. The mate was beside himself because he realized that the ship's owner would examine the logbook and he would be discharged with a bad reference at the end of the journey. His chances of returning to sea looked grim. He could not change the captain's entry but at the end of his shift he wrote this about the captain, "The captain was sober today." He used a misleading ambiguity to get back at the captain.

Double Negatives and Ambiguous Translations

Double negatives simply confuse and confound the listener. At least if you are reading a double negative you are able to go back over the words and make some sense of their intent! When double negatives are spoken, miscommunication is likely to occur. The communication loop is so rapid and fluid that often there just isn't time to go and ask the speaker to repeat their words. The moment passes and the listener will ignore the words because they can't make sense of them. Another problem with double negatives during communication is that the listener rarely admits they didn't understand. Translation: they are stupid if they ask for clarification of the double negative sentence. Not many people will risk this – especially during the influencing process.

> There is no such thing as knowledge which cannot be carried into practice,
> for such knowledge is really no knowledge at all.
> -- Wang Shou-Jen, Record of Instructions

Historical reference: Ambiguity & Arguments

Some years ago, being with a camping party in the mountains, I returned from a solitary ramble to find everyone engaged in a ferocious metaphysical dispute. The *corpus* of the dispute was a squirrel—a live squirrel supposed to be clinging to one side of a tree-trunk; while over against the tree's opposite side a human being was imagined to stand. This human witness tries to get sight of the squirrel by moving rapidly round the tree, but no matter how fast he goes, the squirrel moves as fast in the opposite direction, and always keeps the tree between himself and the man, so that never a glimpse of him is caught. The resultant metaphysical problem is this: *Does the man go round the squirrel or not?* He goes round the tree, sure enough, and the squirrel is on the tree; but does he go round the squirrel? In the unlimited leisure of the wilderness, discussion had been worn threadbare.

Everyone had taken sides, and was obstinate; and the numbers on both sides were even. Each side, when I appeared, therefore appealed to me to make it a majority. Mindful of the scholastic adage that whenever you meet a contradiction you must make a distinction, I immediately sought and found one, as follows: "Which party is right," I said, "depends on what you *practically mean* by 'going round' the squirrel. If you mean passing from the north of him to the east, then to the south, then to the west, and then to the north of him again, obviously the man does go round him, for he occupies these successive positions. But if on the contrary you mean being first in front of him, then on the right of him, then behind him, then on his left, and finally in front again, it is quite obvious that the man fails to go round him, for by the compensating movements the squirrel makes, he keeps his belly turned towards the man all the time, and his back turned away. Make the distinction, and there is no occasion for any further dispute. You are both right and wrong according as you conceive the verb 'go round' in one practical fashion or the other."

Although one or two of the hotter disputants called my speech a shuffling evasion, saying they wanted no quibbling or scholastic hair-splitting, but meant just plain honest English "round," the majority seemed to think that the distinction had assuaged the dispute.

William James, Pragmatism
New York: Longmans, Green & Company, Inc., 1907

Analyze these historical references of ambiguities

Tzu-king said, "The gentleman is judged wise by a single word he utters; equally, he is judged foolish by a single word he utters. That is why one really must be careful of what one says." -- Confucius, The Analects

Since every third child born in New York City is Catholic, Protestant families living there should have no more than two children.

Oriana Fallaci (1930-), Italian author, journalist, and uncompromising political interviewer, had this scathing remark: "You are a bad journalist because you are a bad woman."

Mr. Browne: I will give no more money to your cause next year.
Solicitor: That's all right, sir, we'll just put you down for the same amount you gave this year.

"Whom did you pass on the road?" the King went on, holding his hand out to the messenger for some hay.
"Nobody," said the messenger.
"Quite right," said the King: "This young lady saw him, too. So, of course, nobody walks slower than you."
- Lewis Carroll, Through the Looking Glass

Robert Augustus Toombs (1810 - 1885) was a prominent lawyer and politician who served in both Houses in Georgia and in the US Senate. Just before the Civil War, after being named Confederate Secretary of State and General for the Army of Northern Virginia, he boasted, "We could lick those Yankees with cornstalks." After the war, when asked what had gone wrong, Toombs said, "It's very simple. Those Damn Yankees refused to fight with cornstalks."

Ambiguities in Composition

What is true of each element within a collection is not necessarily true of the entire collection. Also, what is true of the entire collection is not necessarily true of the individual elements.

Ambiguities in composition -- The Dark Side of Influence

Ambiguities in composition may be best explained by first looking at an example. Which use more gasoline—automobiles or buses? The answer I am looking for is automobiles. I have composed the question ambiguously. It could be answered correctly either way, depending on the context I choose. Collectively, in the entire United States, automobiles do indeed use more gasoline than buses. However, if you look at buses individually, they most certainly use more gasoline per mile than the average car. However, we could take this one step further and truthfully state that my neighbor's car uses more gasoline than the local school bus, which only drives 30 miles per day. My neighbor averages 300 miles per day because he is a traveling Regional Manager. He is on the road significantly more than our neighborhood school bus.

As we can see from the example above, how you pose a question can affect the answer. Politicians have been known to compose surveys ambiguously and then to skew the results for political reasons. Fortunately, as members of society become more adept at recognizing ambiguities in composition, this tactic is less likely to have influence.

Sometimes people use ambiguities in composition to influence others to go along with their ideas and move toward their goals. This motivation need not be for the good of all as you can see in the next example. Many ethical debates occur because of the way words are composed. At the beginning of the 20th century, an excerpt of a transcript of a meeting between more than 20 industrialists revealed this statement. "Each manufacturer is perfectly free to set his own price on the product he produces, so there can be nothing wrong with all manufacturers getting together to fix the prices of the articles made by all of them."

Advertising agencies often use ambiguities in composing advertisements. They often place a small asterisk and/or fine print within the advertisement in case readers think they are being duped and openly doubt the veracity of the ad's claims. They also use footnotes designed to rebuild the trust of readers who might find statements within the advertisement potentially untrue. "Results vary from individual to individual" might appear as a footnote in the advertisement.

Unfortunately, most readers blindly believe everything in print. In fact, many behavioral studies have addressed this phenomenon. Historically, advertising agencies have been able to influence the public using ambiguities in composition. The fine print in the advertisements is there for legal reasons. People rarely read it. Many behavioral studies focus on this issue. And legions of consumers have paid a hefty price for failing to read the fine print. Companies know they must have the fine print to avoid "bait and switch" litigation.

This is not to say that every advertisement with fine print is trying to mislead you. Fine print is also used to clarify intent and to limit offers. For example, a department store might use this fine print to clarify intent (as a special offer for early-bird shoppers): "Limit 15 per store – only available Friday morning from 7:00 AM 'til Noon."

There are many legal reasons that force businesses to explain their offers. Using a normal size font (for the words currently in fine print) would make most advertisements boring and too wording to be eye-catching. For example, when a garden center advertises a sale and says, "50% off everything", they must have an asterisk that explains landscaping and custom floral arrangements are not included. This protects the business, not because consumers believe they are being duped, but because consumers will look for bargains on all merchandise from the retail establishment if the company does not clearly state what the sale applies to in detail.

Ambiguities in composition also happen frequently in corporate communications—intentionally and unintentionally. Flagrant examples occur in sales literature from less than ethical corporations. The FDA has specific guidelines for companies making claims about products under their jurisdiction. The weight loss and cosmetic industries in particular use ambiguities in composition to convince buyers to purchase their products. Just because an individual has lost 10 pounds in one week does not necessarily mean that another person will have the same results. By composing advertising messages ambiguously, the weight loss industry convinces many that these claims are true. If you scrutinize many weight loss advertisements, you will see a footnote that explains that "weight loss varies from individual to individual". This footnote has been mandated by the government to undo some of the perceptual damage caused by the purposeful ambiguity in composition in the ad.

Humorous Ambiguities

Ambiguities in composition sometimes make us laugh. A friend of mine is a professor at Penn State. She told me that once, when handing out grades for a particularly difficult project, one student asked why the students who consistently got A's did so. She replied that she believed they studied harder. The student then joked, "Well, if it's true that all students who get A's study hard, and if you want me to study hard, Professor, the best way to do that is to give me A's on all of my papers."

Miss Smith is a poor woman, and loses whenever she plays bridge. Therefore she is a poor loser.

Let's look at some other examples. Just because the casing that holds a computer is brand new, this should not give manufacturers the right to advertise the entire product as 'completely reengineered'.

In a team situation, just because an individual was the team leader on the last project, should not necessarily set the expectation that they will be the team leader on the next project.

EXAMPLES — AMBIGUITIES IN COMPOSITION

Let's look at a few examples of ambiguities in composition:

Each of these sweaters is on sale at 50% off. Therefore, if I buy two of them, I will be getting 100% off. So I will really be getting one for nothing. (A better point to consider in the argument is that if you only need one sweater you'd be paying twice as much as you actually need if you buy two.)

Societal and cultural perceptions are often based on ambiguities in composition. From the view of people living in Third World nations, America is a wealthy country. Many Third World people assume that because America is a wealthy country that every citizen in the United States must be wealthy.

Stereotyping and Ambiguities in Composition

Stereotyping is often a direct result of people's perception changing due to the thought process inherent in ambiguities in composition. The thought process is very simple, but trying to do damage control after an ambiguity in composition is lodged in somebody's perceptual filter is a complex process. Let's look at the thought process of how stereotypes become ingrained in our perceptual prisms.

Recently, a client from Korea flew to Philadelphia to meet with me. Because his English was not perfect, he asked his nephew (American-born and in his mid-40s) to attend. Over lunch, I complimented my client on his credentials. He was highly educated. He modestly deflected the attention from himself and commented that his nephew had exceeded his own education level. I was very impressed. We chatted further and I discovered that my client's sister was a surgeon in Los Angeles. The man's brother-in-law was an influential banker for the Korean community.

The nephew said that he was proud his uncle had chosen to help so many Koreans establish businesses in the United States. Unfortunately, he also said that he and other Asians constantly had to deal with stereotyping with regard to their grades. He said that most Americans believe that all Asians were awarded with good grades because they were forced to study harder by their parents and their culture. The nephew brought up an interesting point when he said, "Why is it that Americans believe that genetics play such an important role for European descendents with regard to intelligence levels, but with Asians they discount this important information? It is a fact that most immigrants who were able to get into this country at that time were only able to do so because they were highly educated in Korea. Doesn't this play a part in how intelligent their children will be? And therefore, how well they will tend to do in the school system here?"

In Korea, during the time that his parents emigrated, the country lost many of its most brilliant scholars, successful entrepreneurs, and intellectually gifted people. Most of these people were in their twenties and thirties when they immigrated to the United States in the late 1950s and early '60s. When these highly gifted Korean immigrants started families, wasn't it logical that they would in turn produce a high percentage of gifted children?

This stereotype really hurts Asian children in school when they cannot live up to the myths that American society has placed upon them. The incidence of depression in normal range IQ students is inordinately high in the Asian community as a direct result of the stereotype. Normal children sometimes develop self-esteem issues for failing to live up to unrealistic expectations. They can't understand why they are not performing at the levels expected of them. They feel like failures.

I must say even though I try to keep my perceptual judgments as close to reality as possible, I had never thought of this! But, like most people in the United States, I had bought into the stereotype that Asian children were somehow naturally smarter than the rest of the world's children. I actually remember asking my son if an Asian boy in his first grade class was the best reader in the class. When my son said that he wasn't, I asked if he was the best at math. Again my son told me he wasn't. I didn't know this little boy but I had asked about his academic level based on his nationality. Shame on me! I did this without once considering checking the scholastic records from Asia's general population. I had committed the crime of stereotyping based on consistent ambiguities in composition that had entered my perceptual prism about Asians.

The nephew of my Korean client counseled me to pull up the facts about Asian children worldwide. The day after our meeting I did. I discovered that Asia's general population and its children mirror the scholastic ability and IQ of the rest of the world. Here is the question I now face: Now that I have this information, and I'm beginning to grasp how deeply ingrained in my psyche this stereotype is, how do I begin to debunk the Asian child's stereotype that is so ingrained in our culture? Is it something that should be debunked? Is expecting more of children the means to get them to achieve more?

How much different would our stereotype of Asian people be if all we were exposed to were Japanese sumo wrestlers? What would our perception of the male Asian physique be? Might we imagine that all Japanese are very large since most sumo wrestlers are gigantic men weighing well over 300 pounds? How would your perception about Japanese people change if your only exposure to their culture was film footage from World War II?

EXERCISE — AMBIGUITIES IN COMPOSITION

Can you think of some examples of ambiguities in composition?

How do the media use ambiguities to skew our beliefs?

EXERCISE — AMBIGUITIES AT WORK

These words were delivered to a team of managers by an executive vice president last year, "I'm sure that if you'd think it over, you would see that my suggestion has real merit. Remember, it was my idea to launch our European restructuring five years ago, and every division changed for the better. Look at how that has paid off! Now, remember, this is not an order, only a suggestion. As I mentioned in our last meeting, I am thinking about reorganizing the whole business. I still hope, however, that it will not be necessary to curtail the operations of your individual departments."

Interpret how the Executive Vice President is being ambiguous if you were hearing his words from the viewpoint of:

1. A manager in the room from the first perceptual position

____
____
____
____
____
____
____
____
____
____

2. The employees who work for the manager—from the second perceptual position

____
____
____
____
____
____
____
____
____

3. The business standpoint of choosing this executive to lead the initiative.

____
____
____
____
____
____
____

Words that work—words that don't when influencing

During a crisis, you have the choice to escalate stress and negativity or to calm the situation. You have the power to turn negatives into opportunities or to escalate them into disasters.

Realize that peak performance is more likely to occur when people can think clearly with a calm mind. It is difficult to think clearly when you are negatively stressed. The words you use in your head (self-talk) will create negative or positive effects in your mind. When you forget to choose your words carefully when you are under duress, you can exacerbate a negative event. If you choose words and phrases that inflame the situation, the effect of your words will create negative emotions and images in the minds of others. On the other hand, if you choose to be proactive during trying times, you can have a calming effect on others.

Avoid using these crisis-causing words during high-stress times:

Cannot
Crisis
Delay
Due
Fear
Afraid
Bad luck
Blame
Cheated
Expensive
Exhausted
Loss/loser
Impractical
Inadequate
Not negotiable
Obstacle
Overloaded
Stupid
Get back to me
Have to
Impossible
Inadvertently
It's our policy
Never again
No choice
Not my fault
Only once
Think it over
Sacrifice
Spend
Frustrated
Forgot
Insist
Hopeless
Unfair
Unreasonable
Guess
Fail
Impossible
Late
Neglect or neglected
No (or its phonological equivalent know)
Panic
Problem
Slip or slipped
Tired
Unaware
Wasted
Absolutely or absolutely false
Be a fool to pass up
Beyond my control
Bargain
Buy
Can't do it
Cheap/cheapest
Costly
Cut rate—cut to the bone
Don't know
Don't ask

By choosing your words wisely you can be the voice of reason. You will be viewed as a leader – someone who can keep a cool head when others panic. The goal is simple: Avoid crisis-causing words—words that create chaos or negatively impact the situation – at least until the chaotic circumstance is gone.

Words That Create A Positive Mindset or Have A Calming Effect During Trying Times

Rather choose positive, proactive words that imply that the other person has control or at least has choices that lead to a feeling or a sense of control. The words below are positive, proactive words that convey energy, benefits, positive power, and value in working as a team. Some of these words are:

Alter
Aware
Better
Can
Care or careful
Caution
Cost-effective
Effective
Efficient
Emerge
Evaluate
Experience
Expedite
What if... (or If...)
Increased
Improve
Investigate
Manage
Methodical
Modify
Possible
Priorities
Productive
Profitable
Reduced
Re-schedule
Resources
Successful
Valuable
Value
Vigorous
Will

Key Point—the words above effectively shift communication to be focused on bottom-line results, effective collaboration, productivity, profitability, and success. Choose your words wisely for peak performance results!

Highly effective words to use in the Sales Process

Free
Professional
Tested
Limited
Big
Valuable
Unlimited
under priced
Launching
Better
Spotlight
Largest
Unlock
Announcing
Introducing
Wanted
Interesting
Highest
the truth about
Affordable
Attractive
Competitive
Innovative
sure fire
Crammed
Astonishing
high tech
Urgent
Portfolio
Excellent
Surging
Bargain
Pioneering
Genuine
Complete
Quality
Lavishly
Breakthrough
Sampler
Unconditional
Security
Revolutionary
Magic
Weird

sale
guaranteed
improved
simplistic
popular
how to
discount
suddenly
skill
shrewd
useful
colossal
fortune
huge
practical
absolutely
challenge
expert
compare
ultimate
easily
full
it's here
soar
growth
imagination
latest
amazing
revealing
remarkable
revisited
hurry
destiny
informative
last chance
gigantic
reliable
emerging
noted
timely
refundable
personalized
proven
surprise

new
special
immediately
powerful
exclusive
endorsed
fundamentals
perspective
reduced
enormous
survival
now
authentic
gift
focus
lowest
lifetime
advice
colorful
willpower
approved
mammoth
just arrived
beautiful
promising
greatest
important
exciting
sensational
obsession
unique
daring
unsurpassed
mainstream
exploit
love
terrific
profitable
luxury
bonanza
quickly
miracle
reward
delighted

delivered
alert
unusual
instructive
edge
fascinating
bottom line
tremendous
technology
wealth
monumental
last minute
simple
insider
secrets
famous
outstanding
liberal
superior
compromise
zinger
helpful
selected
successful
startling
easy
strange
download
scarce
strong
energy
rare
unparalleled
odd
simplified
special offer
sturdy
opportunities
quick
direct
value
confidential
sizable
wonderful

100+ of the Best Words to Use in Advertising

Absolutely
Amazing
Approved
Attractive
Authentic
Bargain
Beautiful
Better
Best
Big
Colorful
Colossal
Complete
Confidential
Crammed
Delivered
Direct
Discount
Easily
Endorsed
Enormous
Excellent
Exciting
Exclusive
Expert
Famous
Fascinating
Fortune
Full
Genuine
Gift
Gigantic
Greatest
Guaranteed
Helpful
Highest
Huge
Immediately
Improved
Informative
Instructive
Interesting
Large
Largest
Latest
Last
Lavishly
Liberal
Lifetime
Limited
Lowest
Magic
Mammoth
Miracle
Noted
Odd
Outstanding
Personalized
Popular
Powerful
Practical
Professional
Profitable
Profusely
Proven
Quality
Quickly
Rare
Reduced
Refundable
Remarkable
Reliable
Revealing
Revolutionary
Scarce
Secrets
Security
Selected
Sensational
Simplified
Sizable
Special
Startling
Strange
Strong
Sturdy
Successful
Superior
Surprise
Terrific
Tested
Tremendous
Unconditional
Unique
Unlimited
Unparalleled
Unsurpassed
Unusual
Useful
Valuable
Wealth
Weird
Wonderful

ABSOLUTES AND GENERALITIES

GENERALITIES

Broad-based statements that promote:

- Ways of thinking
- Processes
- Practices
- Beliefs

Generalities are statements that are acceptable or applicable in most situations.

Most of the time, morning meetings have higher attendance than afternoon meetings. People who like to leave 'wiggle room' in their statements use generalities. When people communicate using generalities it is more difficult to refute their statements. Generalities do not have to be true in every instance. If you look hard enough at any generality, there is almost always a situation where the general rule does not work or is inappropriate. Note: Never confuse generalities with generic words.

The Negative and Positive Aspects of Generalities

As you can imagine, speaking in generalities can create confusion. Depending on your goal, confusion can be seen as a negative or positive factor during communication.

Negative Uses of Generalities

If you give feedback with generalities, people might think, "Are you talking in general terms or are you talking about this specific instance?" The person might need clarification before letting you continue your dialog. When delivering feedback with generalities, misunderstandings can occur. The best feedback is clear, concise and specific. This goal is rarely achieved when you use generalities.

Specific Feedback is delivered best without generalities

Using generalities might be a negative if people need specific feedback and coaching about a particular issue. It is unwise to use generalities like the one below when you expect specific outcomes as a result of feedback.

EXAMPLE GENERALITIES

Incorrect method of delivering specific requirements (using generalities):
"Sarah, most situations require that you be on time for our monthly staff meetings."
Sarah might think that she can be late or not attend as occasions arise because of the word 'most'.

Correct method of delivering specific requirements (using absolutes):
"Sarah, our monthly staff meetings begin promptly at 8:30 AM. Your punctuality is required."
Sarah clearly understands that her on time attendance is mandatory.

Positive Uses of Generalities

However, if your goal in delivering feedback is to foster debate about a behavior, thinking, practice, or belief, then the use of generalities may be very appropriate. For example, if you want to check information and deliver feedback immediately, but also want to give yourself wiggle room in case the information was incorrect you might use generalities like this:

"One of the team members has complained that you come late to a lot of Monday morning staff meetings. Are they correct?"

By using generalities in this manner, you give the person an opportunity to refute the charge and/or to explain their behavior. Another reason to use generalities is to help the other person define their actions. Is this their normal behavior? Do they understand your expectations? Or do the specifics of this particular situation warrant the exception?

EXAMPLE — POSITIVE ASPECTS OF GENERALITIES

Two team members have had multiple conflicts over a period of several months but one team member, Steve, has constantly refrained from commenting. One day, the situation boiled over and the normally passive team member, Steve, lashed out verbally at the aggressive team member, Tom. Tom has made a complaint to Steve's solid line manager. The solid line manager has chosen to use generalities to give feedback about this situation to Steve.

"Steve, normally you hold your temper and you usually choose your words carefully with most employees. What happened with you and Tom the other day is not something I would expect from you. Even so, you will have to make a plan to reconcile your differences with Tom and move forward. Before speaking with Tom, you might consider how you plan to avoid this type of behavior in the future. If I can assist you in any way, please let me know. "

This is a great way to use generalities to uncover the reasons for the out-of-character behavior.

Generalities

When you spend the money you yourself have worked to earn, you are likely to exercise some care in how you spend it; you know that it will take lots of work to replace what you spend.

- John Hospers, Free Enterprise As the Embodiment of Justice

Underline the word/s that makes the sentence a general statement.

We tend to get what we expect ***~NORMAN VINCENT PEALE***

When people who are tolerably fortunate in their outward lot do not find in life sufficient enjoyment to make it valuable to them, the cause generally is, caring for nobody but themselves. ~ ***JOHN STUART MILL, Utilitarianism***

*Love is something eternal. ~****VINCENT VAN GOGH***

*Few people have any next steps, they live from hand to mouth. They fail to plan, and so they are always at the end of their line. ~****RALPH WALDO EMERSON***

Look around for a place to sow a few seeds... ~**HENRY VAN DYKE**

A young man is not a proper hearer of lectures on political science; for he is inexperienced in the actions that occur in life, but its discussions start from these and are about these; and, further, since he tends to follow his passions, his study will be in vain and unprofitable, because the end aimed at is not knowledge but action.
~ ***ARISTOTLE, Nichomachean Ethics***

Check Your Perception by Using Generalities

Another way to use generalities is to check your perception about the situation.

EXAMPLE - CHECK YOUR PERCEPTION BY USING GENERALITIES

Situation:
The IS Department's response time to the Accounting Department in the afternoon is typically more than one hour as opposed to a response time of fifteen minutes or less in the morning.

Perceived Behavior:
The IS Manager is slacking in the afternoon and IS not working a full day.

Actual Behavior:
IS Manager arrives at 5a.m. to do systems back-ups and his day is supposed to end at 3:00. He typically stays, without compensation, until 4:00 before leaving.

The Account Manager wants to verify his perception, so he uses a generality: "Most of our system crashes in the afternoon take more than an hour to fix, as opposed to the morning when it tends to take 15 minutes. I can't help but notice that most of the time you aren't even on the premises after 4:00pm. How can we remedy this situation?"

The Account Manager realizes that if he communicates with the IS Manager using absolutes, HE would create potential conflict with his word choices. For example: "You're never on the premises when we need you each afternoon. Because you're not here, your afternoon response time is quadrupled compared to the mornings. How can we remedy this situation?"

Generalities and Personal Power

Communicating in generalities can also take away your personal power and make you look less authoritative and/or assertive. **Using generalities can be perceived as a weakness.** Let's look at an example. If a team leader wants a team member to submit status reports on time, the team leader can communicate in terms of generalities or absolutes.

Weak generality

Getting your report on time usually makes my job easier.

Strong absolute

Receiving your status report late (after close of business on Friday) makes it impossible for me to fulfill my job responsibility of delivering budgets on Monday afternoon.

Consensus and Generalities

Consensus of opinion is difficult to obtain when dealing with generalities because there are always exceptions to the generality. And people view most generalities as relative words. 'Most' means different things to different people. If you are trying to influence people, and you need 'wiggle room', you should try to use generalities when you communicate. Avoid generalities when providing feedback. It is important to be as factual and specific as possible.

> You always have the choice during the communication to use generalities or absolutes. Strive to make your choices reflect your intent.

ABSOLUTES

Absolutes are defined as statements (or words) that cannot be refuted. Absolutes are statements of fact that are true for every situation. Absolutes are rarely effective during the influencing process when trying to build rapport because they are not open to much interpretation and are rigid. During the influencing process, the flexibility of generalities is preferred when building relationships and keeping an open dialogue with others.

> Almost every rule has exceptions. Absolutes are the opposite of generalities.

ABSOLUTES EXERCISE

Underline the word/s that makes the sentence an absolute statement.

It is always your next move.
NAPOLEON HILL

Knowing that you have complete control of your thinking, you will recognize the power…
MIKHAIL STRABO

I've never been poor, only broke. Being poor is a state of mind. Being broke is only a temporary situation.
MIKE TODD

If we do what is necessary; all the odds are in our favor.
No one can make you feel inferior without your consent.
ELEANOR ROOSEVELT

All things are difficult before they are easy.
THOMAS FULLER

EXAMPLES ABSOLUTES, GENERALITIES & PERSONAL POWER

1. Generality: "You are late to work **just about** every day and this **probably** shouldn't continue."

Absolute: "You are late to work **every** day and this cannot continue."

2. Generality: "A few people have mentioned that you **sometimes** don't give them full credit for their ideas."

Absolute: "**Six** people from your department have come to me and said that you have not given them credit for **any** of their ideas that you used in your presentation last week."

3. Generality: "I felt your report was **a little** on the **ambiguous** side and **most people** will be confused about our sales figures, it probably needs **some** adjustments."

Absolute: "The **third** and **fourth** sections of your report need to be clarified and expanded in order for this audience to fully understand our sales figures."

EXERCISE — ABSOLUTES & GENERALITIES

ABSOLUTES	GENERALITIES

1. Fill in the chart above with words that are either absolutes or generalities[8].

2. Write 3 more sentences that utilize generalities and then write a second version of them to use absolutes.

1. G: ______________________________

   A: ______________________________

2. G: ______________________________

   A: ______________________________

3. G: ______________________________

   A: ______________________________

3. Explain the pros and cons of delivering the message in either style.

____

[8] Answers at back of book

PARTS OF SPEECH IN ENGLISH

Summary of Characteristics

Formal characteristics	Typical position in sentences	Traditional definition	Example
Nouns	Before and after the verb: after a/an, the, our, this, some, etc.	The name of a person, place, relationship, thing, etc.	Woman, room, toothbrush, friendship
Pronoun	Before and after verb; after preposition	A word used in place of a noun	He, she, it, they, one, you, I, we
Verb or predicate	Follows the subject in statements; often first in commands and questions	A word indicating action, state-of being-s, -ing, -ed	Act, acts, acting, acted, is, am, was, being, were, have
Adjective	Comparison, (that comes between a/an, about, etc. and a noun); after linking verb	A word comparing, qualifying, making more exact, the meaning of a noun -able, -ible, -al, -ant, -ary, -ic, -sh, -ous	Warm, warmer, warmest, big, bigger, biggest, more, better, best, formidable, edible, final, sugared, sure-footed, soulful, darkish, fearless, callous
Adverb	Variable; after verb plus object	A word modifying a verb, adjective, or another adverb -ly, -wise	Loudly, quietly, really, fortunately
Preposition	Before noun or noun and its modifiers; often at the end of construction	A word relating a noun to another word; joining a phrase to a word or sentence	As, by, since, behind, below, with, between, of, through, until, via
Conjunction	At the beginning of a clause or sentence	A word joining two words, phrases, clauses, or sentences	And, but, for, however, therefore, because, since, when, consequently
Interjections or Exclamations	May be regarded as a subtype of adverbs	Used to attract attention	Oh! Ouch!

POWERFUL VERBS

Assertive language begins with the use of powerful verbs. By making use of words that have a powerful impact on the mind, you will successfully influence people with whom you are communicating. The spice of communication is the versatility of powerful word usage. Below is a list of powerful words to pepper your vocabulary.

absorb
achieve
act
add
administer
advise
analyze
apply
appraise
approve
arrange
assemble
assist
attend

balance
bought
budget
build

carry
centralize
change
check
clarify
clean
coach
collate
collaborate
compare
compile
complete
compose
compute
conceive
condense
control
convert
convey
coordinate
correct
correspond

counsel
create
cut back on
cut cost/s

deal with
decide
define
deliver
demonstrate
design
determine
diagnose
direct
discover
divert
distribute
drive
duplicate

edit
encourage
enlist
establish
equip
ensure
evaluate
exact
examine
expand
expedite
experiment
extract

facilitate
feed
finalize
finance
fire
fold
foster
find

found
furnish

generate
govern
guarantee
guide

handle
head
help
hire
hypothesize

identify
illustrate
implement
improve
improvise
increase
influence
inform
initiate
innovate
inspect
install
institute
instruct
integrate
interpret
interview
introduce
invent
invest
investigate

judge

launch
learn
lecture
lead

liquidate
list
locate
log
lower

maintain
manage
measure
merge
minimize
modernize
modify
motivate

negotiate
notify
number

observe
obtain
open
operate
organize
overhaul
oversee
outline

pack
patrol
persuade
photocopy
pick out
plan
post
prepare
prescribe
process
produce
program
publish
purchase

qualify
question

raise
read
realize
receive
record
recruit
reduce
refine
relate
reorganize
report
represent
research
respond
restore
restructure
retrieve
revamp
review
revise

select
serve
service
set up
ship
show
simplify
sell
sold
solve
sort
staff
standardize
start
strengthen
study
supply

support
supervise
systematize

tabulate
tailor
tape-record
teach
taught
tend
tell
told
total
track
train
transact
transfer
translate
transport
treat
type

uncover
undertake
undertook
unify
update
upgrade
use
utilize

verbalize
verify

weight
withstand
withstood
work
write
wrote

People are judged—positively or negatively on their command of verbal and written language.

SUBJECT, VERB, OBJECT

Remember—Powerful communication uses the strongest language pattern --

Subject, Verb, Object.

Appeals are riskless for the defendant: penalties cannot be increased nor partial acquittals overturned. The prosecution cannot appeal. This makes it safer for judges to help produce acquittals if they so desire. At any rate, they become defense minded: if the judge bears against the defendant, and it is often likely that he may be overruled. If he bears against the prosecution, the judge is safe. No appeal is impossible. Hence, when in doubt, it is in the judge's interest to rule for the defense. -- Ernest Van Den Haag, Punishing Criminals

EXERCISE — SUBJECT, VERB, OBJECT

Identify the subject, verb and object in each sentence.

A man is free who is not master of himself.
EPICTETUS

What is freedom? Freedom is the right to choose. The right to create for one alternatives of choice.
ARCHIBALD MacLEISH

Write the five subject, verb, and object sentences for an influencing process that would fit into your business.

1. ______________________________
2. ______________________________
3. ______________________________
4. ______________________________
5. ______________________________

INEFFECTIVE "I"

Always Avoid the Ineffective "I". Ineffective "I" sentences are based on **your personal perception**. Your perception can be easily dismissed as **just your opinion.**

- I think...
- I feel...
- I have a problem with...
- I like...
- I noticed...
- I believe...
- I heard...
- I don't have...

A test of maturity is the process of realizing that the universe does not revolve around the self.

When your communication starts with the word 'I' you consciously (or subconsciously) send the message that your primary focus during the communication loop is centered on you instead of on the issue at hand.

Often, when you begin sentences with "I", the other person in the communication loop becomes *confused about the intent* of your message. This can be best illustrated by examining the following sentences:

Ineffective 'I' Adds To The Confusion During Communication

The pilot is flying the airplane. In this sentence, 'the pilot' is the subject; 'is flying' is the verb; and 'the airplane' is the object.

I heard that the pilot is flying the airplane. In this sentence, there is confusion about the intent of the message. *Note* - Is your communication intended to relay the fact that you overheard someone talking about the pilot or that the pilot is flying the aircraft?

In the first sentence, your audience understands the message you are trying to send clearly, concisely, and specifically. In the second sentence, the listener may wonder if they have missed the true intent of your communication and will flip flop between either intent, wondering which is best for this particular situation.

Let's examine another set of sentences.

- ***You have invested heavily in blue-chip stocks.***

'You' is the subject; 'have invested' is the verb; 'heavily' is the adverb describing the verb; and 'blue-chip stocks' is the object of the sentence. The statement made with this sentence is clear and concise.

Now, let's change the sentence into the **Ineffective "I" format.**

- ***I noticed that you have invested heavily in blue-chip stocks.***

From this sentence, you can easily see that the listener may have to analyze the intent of the communicator within the context of the intended message. The listener may think that the communicator is simply stating that they took note of the fact that blue chip stocks were in the investment portfolio or they may think that the communicator is making a judgment call on the investment because the sentence began with "I".

Weak phrases that often accompany the Ineffective "I"

Like (or do not like)
I really like the way you...

Want (or don't want)
I want to make sure...

Feel
I feel that we need to...

Need
I need to convey...

All these sentences convey the emotion rather than action! Ask yourself: Do You Need Action or Emotional Involvement? If the answer is action: Then use the power of Subject, Verb, and Object statements during the influencing process for the appropriate impact.

Leadership -- The Exception to the General Rule

As with most language patterns, there are exceptions to the general rule of how and when to use (or not use) the pattern. If you are in a leadership position or are known as the expert in your field, your opinion holds weight in the listener's mind (e.g. the CEO of a company, VP of a sales and marketing division, etc.), you can soften your words by using the Ineffective "I". You would do this in the influencing process so that your words do not appear as a decree or give the impression that people should take note of your words or else ('your way or the highway' syndrome).

EXAMPLE — WHAT THE LISTENER IS THINKING -

- ***I want you to start thinking about how you are going to protect your family if something should happen to you. I think the best way to look after them is to buy permanent life insurance, but I also think that you might want to supplement it with some ten-year term because I feel the kids will need it until they go to college.***

What can I say! Just for fun let's go inside the listener's head:

- ***I want*** (who's really cares what you want – it's my money you're spending***!) you to start thinking about how you are going to protect your family if something should happen to you. I think*** (well, that's just your opinion and I read in the Wall Street Journal that...) ***the best way to look after them is to buy permanent life insurance but I also think*** (well, how many other of your opinions are going to cost me a bundle!) ***that you might want to supplement it with some ten-year term because I feel*** (You haven't even met them so how can you have feelings about them? I'll be lucky if my son gets through Middle School with his grades – they'll be living with me forever. So much for your feelings!) ***the kids will need it until they go to college.***

What a mess! These were the actual words (We taped them!) from a financial professional's typical closing statement. Luckily, he has learned to take out the Ineffective "I" and stay on track with the issues.

EXAMPLE — INEFFECTIVE "I" IN MANAGEMENT

The "Ineffective I" is particularly common in management situations. It should be avoided because of the confusion it creates.

Our team must complete the report, put it into binders, and deliver it before the Monday morning sales meeting.
The team is clearly the subject, there are three clear action verbs and the subject is the report. There is no confusion regarding the tasks or due date.

I think our team must complete the report, put it into binders, and deliver it before the Monday morning sales meeting.

If the manager (or team leader) delivers this sentence rather than the first, the team members may feel that the tasks are just the person's view of the best way to handle the meeting. It may not come across as a directive – it may be perceived as just their opinion and therefore open to non-compliance.

HEDGES – TRIM THEM OR CUT THEM ALTOGETHER

Hedges are words that add doubt to your statement. Hedges make you look indecisive. They give the perception that you doubt your ability to think decisively or autonomously. Hedges make you appear submissive. Notice how many hedges start with the Ineffective 'I'.

In The Elements of Style, William Strunk and E. B. White write, "If your sentence admits a doubt, your writing will lack authority." What is true for the written word is true for the spoken word.

Simple hedges

- You shouldn't...
- ... really.
- Well...
- Sort of...
- I'd like to...
- I'd like to see...
- In my opinion...
- Basically,...
- The way I see it...
- I know that it...
- It may sound silly but I think...
- Clearly,...
- The point is...
- I'd like to add...

Self-Deprecating hedges

I'm not sure...
I'm not sure I know all the answers but...
I'm really not happy with the way things turned out but...
I'm not sure I'd go to war on this but...
I guess I'm trying to say...

I guess I mean...
I'm pretty sure...
I guess...
I'm not an expert, but...
I may not be right, but...
I'm not a specialist but...

Self-deprecating (within the context of the group)

We really shouldn't—-, should we?
We usually...
We almost always...

AGAIN—Use powerful language in the format – Subject, verb, and object – to avoid using hedges!

Stop Playing Tag!

A tag is a short expression attached (tagged on to) the end of the sentence or statement. Tags do damage during the influencing process because:

1. *They can appear to be coercive. People might think they would appear rude if they disagreed with your point of view. You take their option of debating with you away. This is not a good thing to do during a communication loop.*
2. *They can also be perceived as arrogant or pushy. They can give the listener the sense that the speaker is just a bit too sure of himself.*
3. *Tags can also give the impression that you are not sure of your service, idea or product. It might seem like you are looking to others to validate your decision, right?*

Some other examples of 'tag' expressions:

- ..., isn't it?
- ..., don't you think?
- ..., right?
- ..., okay?
- ..., won't you?
- ..., are you?
- ..., doesn't she/he?
- ..., don't they?
- ..., see what I'm saying?
- ..., you know what I mean?
- ..., you know?

There are situations where using tags is appropriate when influencing. Remember, the examples below should be viewed as exceptions to using tags. ***The general rule is to avoid using them.*** *If you choose to use them, do so sparingly with an awareness of the risks.*

- *If you seek compliance from people who are not as powerful as you, a tag can give the appearance that you are willing to receive input or that you are soliciting input.*

- *They are also useful as a power play. If you must have compliance from an individual who is resisting you and you have power over the person, you can use a tag to drive home your expectations. This report will be on my desk on Monday morning before 11:00 AM, correct?*

'BUT' & HOWEVER IN INFLUENCING

An excellent way to let others realize you appreciate their point of view (or can see where they are coming from in the communication loop) is to eliminate the word 'but' from your vocabulary during any communication loop. Only use "but" when you have chosen your words carefully and have planned for the psychological impact of the word "but".

Recently, I had lunch with Pat Croce, part owner of the Philadelphia 76ers. Pat Croce is one of the most positive, upbeat individuals you will ever meet. Over our meal, we spent some time discussing the negative impact of the word 'but'. He told me that he always thinks of 'but' as **B**ig **U**gly **T**rouble!

> **Key Point: Think of BUT as**
>
> **B**ig
>
> **U**gly
>
> **T**rouble!

By eliminating the word "but", and replacing but with 'and', you will give people the sense that you truly appreciate their viewpoint. It also is indicative of the fact that you trust their judgment regarding the issue at hand. This simple communication technique will positively enhance your communication.

'But' can be (and often is) an extremely destructive word during the communication loop. It implies that you have heard what the other person said, BUT have some objections that discount their point of view. When you use 'but' in conversation, people think you cannot see where they are coming from during the communication loop. 'But' is a confrontational word if used improperly.

> **Can I use however instead of but?**
>
> *'However' is 'but' in a tuxedo!* Whenever *you used the word however, you may be viewed as arrogant or patronizing! Be careful!*

The Structure of a 'But' Sentence

Imagine a 'but' sentence being structured as two separate statements with 'but' as the joining word.

THE BUT RULE		
First statement	**but**	*Second statement.*

First statement
Psychologically, when you use 'but', the first half of the 'but' sentence (the first statement) is made more negative because of the word but. But casts doubt on all concepts and words that immediately precede it. 'But' leaves confusion regarding your true feelings and/or intentions regarding the situation.

But
As soon as 'but' is said, people wait for you to 'zing' them. People mentally cringe and wait for the words that follow 'but'. For example: That's a great shirt but I wouldn't wear it tonight. The shirt owner understands that a negative judgment about his choice of attire has been made. The long-term risk is that the person will avoid wearing the shirt in the future, because of the negative memories of your 'but'.

Physiological react to 'but'

Whenever people hear you say but – they tense up – waiting for you to 'zing' them with the words that follow.

Second statement
But also gives more weight and apparent value to the second half of the sentence—all the words that follow 'but'. This weight can be either more negative or more positive.

EXAMPLE — BUT WITH NEGATIVE & POSITIVE WEIGHT

Negative: That report was well written **but** you should have run it through spell-check before you gave it to Sue.

Positive: Our department lost the contract **but** in the long run I think that we would have lost money on the service aspect.

EXAMPLE — USING "BUT"

You are doing a great job but...
I hear what you are saying but...
I am trying to be patient but...
You have a great point but...

The 'But' Kills the Compliment!
I've always wanted to dress with more style. You know, a little out of the corporate-norm like you do. That's a great shirt **but** the tie isn't one I would have chosen for myself.

Even if my true intent was to give a heart-felt compliment—the "but" killed it! The fact that I thought the shirt was great is probably not what the other person remembered or even heard. Now, let's swap the two halves of the sentence and see what the difference is from a psychological viewpoint.

I've always wanted to dress with more style. You know, a little out of the corporate-norm like you do. Your tie isn't one I would have chosen for myself **but** that's a great shirt.
What is the message I left you with after I swapped the last sentence around?

EXAMPLE — BUT & JOINED STATEMENTS

Management

I understand that you are growing impatient with Kelly. *But,* you have to remember that she is learning a new task that usually takes people three months to master. Her performance on Kathy's team was always outstanding. I am certain, after she is up to speed, she will be a great asset to your team, too.

Sales

I understand that you want time to mull over this decision but, you have to remember that you said the same thing at our last review and we are still talking about the same problem! Shouldn't we put a deadline on this and put it to bed?

> **Bottom-line with But & However**
> When you want to deliver good news then bad news –
> **never** use the word "but" or "however" if the two statements are going to be joined.

Key point—Understand that if two statements are not technically one sentence (because they are separated by a period) *but* are joined by implication of thought-flow (e.g. 'But,); the "but & however rules" hold true.

For example: That's an interesting point that Bob just made. But, it would be prudent to research the facts before we commit.

Use 'But' Effectively

Never use but or however when you move from a positive to a negative statement.

Use but or however when you want to lessen the impact of a negative statement.

Negative BUT Positive

Which statement would you prefer to hear?
That's a great outfit you have on (positive statement) BUT, that color really isn't your best (negative statement).
OR
That color really isn't your best (negative statement) BUT, that is a great outfit that you have on (positive statement).

THE EFFECTIVE USE OF BUT AND HOWEVER

Sometimes we have to communicate bad news. Like Mary Poppins said, "A spoonful of sugar makes the medicine go down." Always try to plan for bad news to be delivered as pleasantly as possible, with the least amount of negative impact.

An effective way to relay bad news is to plan to use “but” or “however” appropriately. We know that ‘but’ and ‘however’ negate and cast doubt upon the first half of a sentence and they give more weight to the second half of the sentence. Why not take this information and use it to benefit communication during troubled times?

EXAMPLE — POSITIVE BUT

We missed our quarterly sales objective by 11 percent **but** with what we have in the hopper, and if we keep up the momentum we created in the last six months, our next quarter will far exceed the numbers we have currently projected.

There is nothing either good or bad, but thinking makes it so.
WILLIAM SHAKESPEARE

You cannot always control circumstances. But you can control your own thoughts.
CHARLES E. POPPLESTONE

It is not ease, but effort, not facility, but difficulty, makes men. There is, perhaps no station in life in which difficulties have not had to be encountered and overcome before any decided measure of success can be achieved.
SAMUEL SMILES

Success is not measured by what a man accomplishes, but by the opposition he has encountered, and the courage with which he has maintained the struggle against overwhelming odds...
ORISON SWETT MARDEN

The most important thing in life is not the triumph but the struggle. The essential thing is not to have conquered but to have fought well.
BARON PIERRE DE COUBERTIN

A little philosophy inclines a man's mind to atheism; but depth in philosophy bringeth a man's mind about to religion.
FRANCIS BACON, Essays

Men scan with scrupulous care the character and pedigree of his horses, cattle, and dogs before he matches them; but when it comes to his own marriage he rarely, or never, takes such care.
CHARLES DARWIN, The Descent of Man

EXAMPLE — POSITIVE HOWEVER

I realize you are disappointed in my team's performance. However, let me go over our numbers on this project and compare it to our overall progress. You mentioned that Susan said she expected the program to be completed by April 8th but she didn't realize that the customer changed the specs mid-course. In fact, our customer is more than satisfied with our timetable and with the service we have delivered so far. They have actually recommended that we deal with their divisions in Florida and Texas for similar projects. Even though our schedule slipped, our willingness to be flexible and change our timeline actually brought in two new sites as customers for the company.

EXERCISE — EFFECTIVE USE OF BUT

Write five examples you can use that make an effective use of but:

EXERCISE — EFFECTIVE USE OF HOWEVER

Write five examples effectively using 'however':

However in the Professional Arena

EXAMPLE — EFFECTIVE USE OF HOWEVER IN THE LEGAL PROFESSION

"However" is frequently used by attorneys to discount the other side's causation arguments and to influence the judge or jury members.

The prosecution says that my client was willfully negligent by manufacturing this product. **However**, the facts clearly show that this product helps alleviate the suffering of tens of thousands of people across the globe. They say the evidence they will put before you will prove this negligence. **However**, if the evidence they will present was readily available at the time, my client would not have manufactured and sold the product. My client has a long, solid history of delivering outstanding innovative products to the medical field and of pulling products from the shelf at the slightest hint of a problem.

EXAMPLE — EFFECTIVE USE OF HOWEVER IN ACADEMIA

"However" is frequently used in academic circles. When used effectively, it can make you seem more knowledgeable or learned than others.

My colleague has an excellent point, **however** there are several research papers that deal with a contrary point of view. Let me give you several examples...

Key point #1
Use "however" whenever you need to be viewed within the context of an expert.

Key point #2
Never use "however" or "but" to self-deprecate.
Example: I'm not sure about this **but...**
I'm not in expert in the field **but...**
I'm not completely convinced of the facts **however...**

Key point #3
Use 'however' sparingly – using this word frequently might mark you as arrogant.
However is also viewed as a power play between peers when too frequently used during meetings. Also avoid using words that imply but and however:
Nevertheless
Although
Regardless
Et cetera
What should you use instead?
Pause or Use "And"

AND IS INNOCENT

'And' is an innocent word. 'And' simply adds to and expands what has already been said.

But is a difficult word that is too often associated with negative thoughts and actions. Unfortunately, but is often used as a conjunction instead of 'and'. By consistently using the word 'but' you add tension and aggression to the communication loop. When you eliminate 'but' you will find that communication will be immediately enhanced. You will optimally gain and maintain more rapport, more quickly, than in the past.

By being consciously aware of when you use 'but', 'however' and 'and', you will become more effective in reducing stress and conflict during times of change. Trust and morale within your organization will also be enhanced.

EXAMPLE INEFFECTIVE USE OF "BUT"

An unhappy alternative is before you, Elizabeth. From this day you must be a stranger to one of your parents. Your mother will never see you again if you do not marry Mr. Collins, but I will never see you again if you do."
JANE AUSTEN, Pride and Prejudice

Avoid "Yes, but..."

Nothing drives people crazy like a "Yes, but...". You can often see this phrase forming on their lips before you have even finished speaking! What is a "Yes, but..."? These are words that the other person says right after someone speaks. If a but in a but statement has the power to negate the first half of the sentence, a "Yes, but..." has the psychological power to entirely nix what the other person just said. "Yes, but's" are rude and give the other person in the communication loop the perception that you really don't care about their opinion or their words.

> Most of our so-called reasoning consists in finding arguments for going on believing as we already do.
>
> - James Harvey Robinson (1715-1747)

You're not listening with an open mind!

If you are just about to "Yes, but..." to the speaker, it means that you haven't really been listening to what the speaker has said. You cut off your listening by formulating your "Yes, but..." response. What you are doing is really waiting for the other person to inhale or pause just long enough for you to refute their words, concepts, goals, or ideas.

The bottom line on "Yes, but's" - Never use them!

> Listening, not imitation, may be the sincerest form of flattery.
>
> Dr. Joyce Brothers

Common Views & Common Language

Fortunately, most people you interact with will be in the same culture and have similar beliefs and viewpoints. These people—and you—will tend to share common values and have a common view of the world. They may also share common interests, friends, work, hobbies, likes, dislikes, and political and religious persuasions. Any of these similar 'degrees of commonality' might result in some degree of rapport.

Human beings tend to get along with others who share similar values and belief patterns, and/or with people who have a degree of commonality with them. You might like the same sports team, or play the same sport—golf, tennis, or swimming. You might share similar interests in reading materials, books, magazines, or other types of literature.

To communicate effectively and efficiently, rapport, trust and respect for other people's models of the world must be established. Try to establish a degree of commonality with all your clients and prospects. When you achieve this, you assume a positive intention for the basis of all communication. This is a powerful way of moving toward agreement or a shared outcome. In order to gain the trust of the other people in the communication loop efficiently and successfully, you should pay attention to the other person. What do they enjoy? Who do they interact with? What do you know of their likes and dislikes? What values do they hold dear? It is imperative that you have enough versatility to enable you to be flexible in your own behavior to respond to their cues.

LANGUAGE PATTERNS

We now understand the method for gaining verbal and non-verbal rapport, but what do we say to move toward our influencing goals and affect our subjects on the sub-conscious level? By mastering psychological language patterns and assertive word usage, you will be able to command and recognize sentence structures that form the basis for formulating beliefs as well as decision-making and value judgment processes. Mastery allows you to create an incredibly powerful impact on the mind of others within the communication loop.

One of our goals is to learn to analyze other people's pre-taught responses – their communication habits and patterns. If you are trying to influence others, you must make a plan to try to link your goals and theirs. If you are selling, you should be able to make a plan to link your products and services with their communication patterns. Your desire is to achieve those pre-taught responses whenever you want them to happen during the communication loop. For example, if you want your sales prospects to say, "YES". The most desirable way to get to 'yes', is to key into those pre-taught responses that your clients have been programmed to deliver by society. For instance, Madison Avenue firms – the capital of the advertising world -- have conducted several studies that prove that several key words and visual stimuli elicit interest and programmed responses in the average population (free, sale, buy one get one, red stickers, end caps at supermarkets, etc.).

The bottom line on this information -- Learn what habit patterns are appropriate for your business and/or industry and work them into your presentations for maximum impact.

If you become a master of reading and using people's pre-taught responses, most of your influencing can be done on the subconscious level. If this is done effectively the others will not perceive you as aggressive or 'pushy' whenever you attempt to influence them.

Power of Silent Communication

During the influencing process, give the other person enough time to process information. Only by processing cause and effect relationships can their beliefs change. This is critical to the influencing process.

The mind needs time to process information. How do you know that the other person is processing information? Simply use your sensory acuity and look at their eyes. Internal dialog looks similar to a vacant stare. When the other person's mind is processing (and storing information, using self-talk, or making a decision their eyes will help you see how (and when) their processing 'hardware and software' is working. The following chart will show you how to recognize what mode the other person is in while they are processing the messages you are sending.

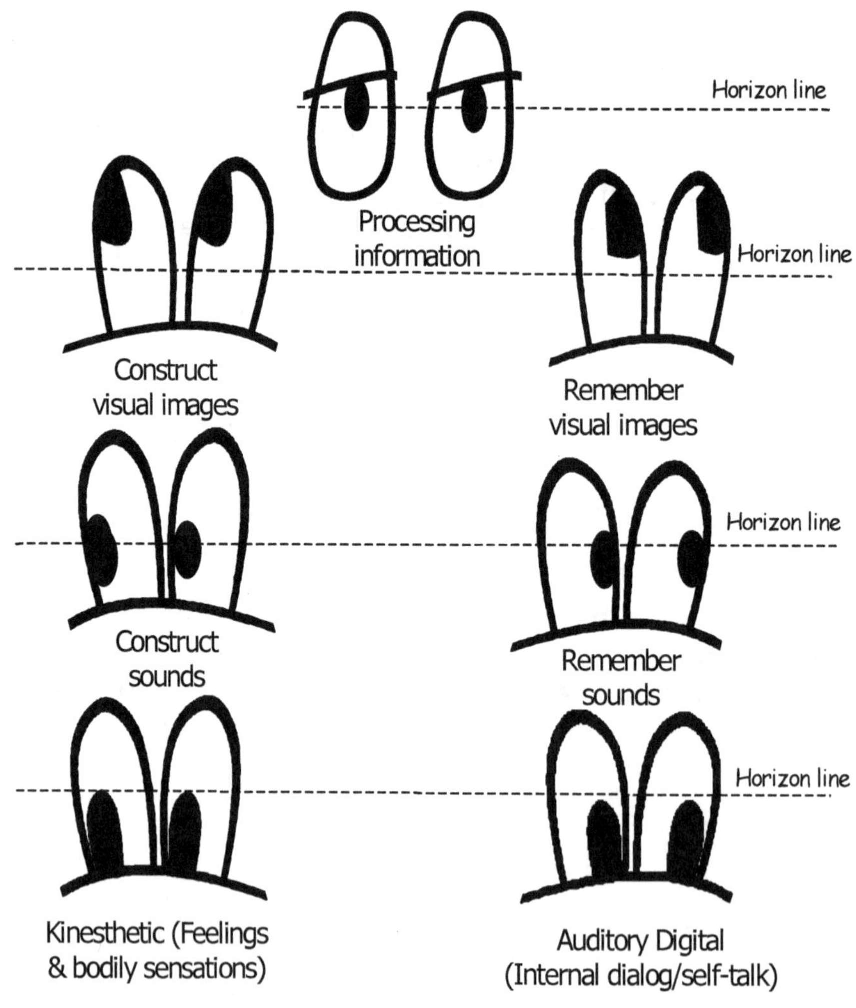

The chart above is depicted as if we are looking at the other person. The horizon line is the reference that will assist you in determining which mode the person is in. The horizon line will shift depending on the angle of the head. If the person is accessing information and their eyes are scanning across the horizon line (from ear to ear), the person is most likely accessing auditory information. When eyes are above the horizon line, the person is in a visual mode and when eyes are below the horizon line, the person is in the kinesthetic mode or is talking to himself.

When we are remembering information, processing information, or simply engaged in self-talk, our eyes provide clues as to how our mind is working. When accessing feelings, a person's eyes will tend to move down and to the left. In a situation where an individual actually saw something prior to being asked a question about the incident; and they are first asked to remember it, their eyes will typically go up and towards the right. If they never witnessed the event or saw the image, their eyes will try to create an image and will move upwards to the left. When the eyes are staring straight ahead and appear 'slightly unfocused' or as if they are looking into the distance, the person is probably storing, trying to grasp a situation, thinking about the future and is in the visualization mode (Note: Not the visual mode!), making decisions, or processing information. This is not a good time to talk to them about information that is vital to your influencing process -- they rarely hear what you are saying when they are in this mode. Give them a chance to come back to you (refocus) before you continue or just converse about things that are easy for the other person to talk about without much thought (weather, sports, etc.).

LANGUAGE PATTERNS FOR INFLUENCE

Language is a wonderful thing. It can be used to express thoughts, to conceal thoughts, but more often, to replace thinking.
- Kelly Fordyce

LANGUAGE PATTERN #1—EMBEDDED COMMANDS

What Is A Command?

Before we can address the first language pattern we need to establish a working definition of the word command. When you command someone to do a task, you give a ***direct order stating what you would like to be done***. Commands are always given in the ***present tense***.

An embedded command therefore is "a direct order stating what you would like to be done" that is HIDDEN within your message. **Embedded commands fit into the normal structure of a sentence without drawing attention to their existence.** Embedded commands relay a command in a manner that sounds less demanding and more suggestive. They are an effective way to subtly get messages across to the people you are attempting to influence.

"How do I know if the words I am using form the true structure of embedded commands?"

Test for commands

Use this simple test to keep you on the right track:

1. Make certain that the verb you are testing is in the **present perfect tense**. It helps to add the words 'right now' or 'now' to test if the command works in the present moment (and therefore is in the present tense).

2. Say any person's name.

3. Use the words that make up the command combined with any person's name in front of the command to ensure that the command is a full sentence.

4. If the sentence that you have just created is a **complete sentence that can be used on its own**, then and only then, have you used an embedded command.

Test Example #1:

1. Test the words "feel confident".
2. The verb "feel" is in the present perfect tense. I test this by saying "I feel confident right now".
3. Then I test that the command is a full sentence by saying a person's name directly before the command. "Rob," and use the words of the command, "Feel confident".
4. "Rob, feel confident."
5. Then I ask myself, could that sentence be used by itself and make good sense to Rob?
6. The answer to both (in this case) is yes.

Test Example #2:

1. Test the words "call me tomorrow".
2. Test for the present tense by removing 'tomorrow' and inserting 'now'. 'Call me now' works so the verb "call" is in the present tense. Let's put it together—
3. "Mary, call me tomorrow".
4. The sentence again can stand on its own and make sense to Mary.
5. "Feel confident" and "call me tomorrow" are both commands that I can work into sentences to create the structure of an embedded command.

Test Example #3:

1. Test "signing a check".
2. The verb is "signing". Is the verb in the present tense? No, it is <u>not</u> in the present tense. "Signing" is the present participle of the verb "to sign".
3. By using the verb test, we realize that the words "signing a check" cannot form an embedded command

Note: Present participles end with the suffix '-ing' and are NOT the present perfect tense of the verb in question. Commands are powerful – but they become 'wishy-washy when they use verbs that end in –ing. Only use the present participle (-ing conjugation) for verbs that are unimportant in moving you further toward your influencing goals.

*Note: Always remember that any present tense verb ending in – 'ing' will **not** form an embedded command.*

EXAMPLE MULTIPLE COMMANDS

Now, let's look at an example that has more than one command in it:

- Bob, sit down at the head of the table. Sally, you sit next to him. Holly, please bring the butter and set it next to me.

In the example above, the commands can be highlighted by using voice inflection. Could you recognize the commands easily?
Did you count four commands? Now that you can recognize commands, you can learn how to effectively use them to obtain your outcome.

Embedded commands form the backbone of effective verbal influencing techniques.

Practice learning to recognize them in your everyday life and learn to use them effectively to influence people below the conscious level. In order to do this, you should understand a little of the psychology of commands and how they have been used to train us since childhood.

We have been commanded throughout our lives to do various tasks. By doing instructed tasks, we gain knowledge from our peers, associates, teachers, parents, and friends. Peer and societal pressure usually force us to comply with orders and commands. It stands to reason, therefore, that society as a whole does not easily condone or accept people who "go against the grain" when they constantly fail to perform tasks they are instructed to do. To gain acceptance in any social circle, we have been "programmed" since birth to act on other people's verbal commands. By using this knowledge in a sales or management capacity, we can greatly enhance the impact we have on the people that we want or need to influence.

By understanding the background of commands, you can immediately **recognize the power** of being able to use commands that affect your clients on the subconscious level.

Phonological Marking

To deliver any command so that it has maximum impact we have to make use of our voice. By changing our tonality before the command and also changing tonality after the command, we are able to deliver the message effectively, and at the same time are able to hide the intention within the sentence that we use. This technique is called **phonological marking**. By hiding the command, we get the message across to the other person; without being perceived as pushy, bossy or aggressive. Practice delivering effective embedded commands so that they have a powerful impact during any presentation.

Congruency and embedded commands.

IT IS IMPORTANT TO BE CONGRUENT WHEN YOU USE EMBEDDED COMMANDS!!!

Have you ever heard or seen something that just did not seem quite right? Most often, anything that jars your mind on either the conscious or subconscious mode lacks congruency. Congruency is lacking or nonexistent when verbal communication does not agree with body language. (For example, A person saying "yes" while shaking their head from side to side.) Or when actions do not correspond to accepted behavioral norms. (For example, someone telling the interviewer how exciting their last project was while sitting in their chair and looking bored or uninterested.) In both examples the interviewer will subconsciously feel that something about the person just does not quite 'gel'. Most often, people do not understand exactly what it was that made them uncomfortable during the interview. They will not be able to put their finger on the cause for their uneasy feeling about the person. It is imperative that you are congruent in your speech and body language, as well as the non-verbal and verbal messages you convey.

Congruency is expressed and heightened by consciously sending out the message you want your listener to hear. If you want your client to get excited—first, get excited yourself! If you want your team to be motivated—first act motivated yourself. If you want the interviewer to get enthused about the prospect of hiring you or having you on their team—first, get enthused yourself! If you want your prospect to be interested, look interested and act interested in what you are presenting. Then be interested when they are presenting their ideas.

To deliver maximum impact commands:

- Test the command.
- Your body language directly affects the impact you have on others.
- Make sure that you are congruent with your verbal and nonverbal actions.

EXERCISE — EMBEDDED COMMANDS

Let's evaluate the next four sentences.

As you read through them—THINK CAREFULLY—How could these sentences have more impact? Rewrite the sentences using embedded commands. Underline the embedded commands in the sentences you write.

1. Julie, I'm sure that you are going to find this proposal interesting.

____

____

____

____

2. Joe, it's so exciting to see that you're using this material in your business life and profiting from it!

____

____

____

____

3. Richard, after our meeting on Wednesday, I mailed you a copy of my resume. You said you were interested in putting my name forward as a candidate for the computer programmer position in Baltimore, Maryland.

____

____

____

____

4. Jackie, during our last networking meeting we had discussed Biotech, Inc. You said they were interested in employing a sales representative for their Center City office. I have enclosed my resume and references from three previous managers that I have worked for. We talked about getting together again next week. When are you free? I'm sure that you'll find my resume interesting.

____

____

____

____

EXAMPLES	EMBEDDED COMMANDS
Answer my past letter	Believe me
Be interested	Be open
Be receptive	Buy into the idea
Buy it	Buy now
By now	Call me to make an appointment
Check my references	Check/review on my qualifications
Consider me as a candidate	Consider my application
Contact me with any questions	Convince yourself that it's right
Consider my abilities (as a team player in your new department/for the position)	Discuss openly
Do it now	Expect a call from me on Friday
Expect my call on Tuesday	Feel content
Feel confident	Feel relieved
Feel happy	Feel good inside
Figure out how we can do business together	
File my resume for perusal (in January when you hire personnel for your Washington, D.C. office)	Forward my name and resume to your department head
Forward my resume to the appropriate person	Forward my fax to the appropriate person
Get excited	Get it
Get sold on the idea	Get together to go over my qualifications
Get together to discuss the position	Get together soon
Invest now	Look over my resume
Make a decision	Make an appointment
Move quickly	Purchase it
Put in a good word for me	Remember me
Read my resume	Read the enclosed resume/materials
Read the last section of my resume	Refer me to your human resources department
Refer to my recent letter	Reply to my request
Schedule an appointment	See that this is an excellent match for your requirements/position
Set a date for a future meeting	Set an appointment
Set up a telephone appointment	Sign up now
Sit down together	Start investing
Start saving now	Take my word
Trust me	

When using embedded commands during the influencing process, the use of the person's name strengthens the command. You can use the name before or after the command and still get the exact same results. Embedded commands using a person's name work most effectively if they are short and to the point. More power is added to the command if you pause slightly just before giving the command and pause slightly after the command. This is called analogical marking. **ANALOGICAL MARKING** means drawing attention to an embedded command either verbally or physically, making sure that it has an extremely powerful impact on the subconscious mind.

EXERCISE RECOGNIZING EMBEDDED COMMANDS

Let's evaluate the next five sentences and count the embedded commands. As you read the commands, try to mimic the technique.

1. Let's sit down together and discuss the options available to you.

2. Can we get together soon so that you will feel comfortable with the program?

3. Because today's financial environment is constantly changing, you need to be open to new ideas and concepts.

4. I will call you next week to make an appointment for you and your partner to meet me for lunch to go over the details.

5. By now, you can probably see the benefits of dealing with our company. Believe me, we have specialized in handling hundreds of accounts that are very similar to yours.

Practice delivering embedded commands until you have mastered the technique!

Phonological Ambiguities

Notice the command—**by now**—this is a **phonological ambiguity**. When you hear the word spoken, the mind tries to translate the words into all the meanings it has stored in memory. It could mean 'by now' as in time, 'buy now' as in purchase, or 'Bye now' as in goodbye. If there is no context surrounding the word or the vocal qualities do not provide a clue as to the meaning of the words, your mind must search for the meaning. It searches for the meanings of the words separately and looks at the possible meanings for those words with regard to the whole idea within the sentence [context]. The mind then acts by choosing the correct meaning for the word and disregards the inappropriate definitions; completing the thought process.

Think about the impact the word "know"[1] has during your presentations. It makes sense to eliminate "know" from your sales presentations, doesn't it? Substitute 'understand' for 'know'.

WRITE NOW is also a phonological ambiguity. When heard in conversation, 'write now' could be translated in two ways - 'Write now' as in to sign a document or 'right now'—meaning at this moment.

Exercise — Phonological Meanings

Can you think of any other phonological ambiguities? What about "check with me"? This phonological ambiguity works well when it is necessary to command your client to get out his checkbook to give you a check.

____

____

____

Another fun phonological ambiguity is the word "yesterday". By drawing out the syllables you can make the word sound like "yes today!" Wouldn't it be wonderful if all of our prospects said, "Yes today"?

____

____

____

____

Language Pattern #2—Embedded Quotes

We hear about constitutional rights, free speech and the Free Press. Every time I hear these words I say to myself, "That man is a red, that man is a Communist. People in America should talk like an American talks. "You never heard a real American talk in that manner.

Frank Hague: speech before the Jersey City Chamber of Commerce, July 12th, 1938

Embedded quotes are yet another way of directing someone's action or belief through a command hidden within the structure (in this case specifically within a quotation) of a sentence. Instead of telling the person directly what they should do, an embedded quotation suggests the action that should be taken based upon what another person in a similar scenario said or did. Quotes, traditionally, are what another person says. **You can easily bring a 'third party endorsement' into your conversations for more impact and believability** by using embedded quotes. This technique can be one of the most powerful influencing and selling tools at your disposal. Embedded quotes work best if you use logical flow and sequence. This will keep people on track with the story line.

I heard (person) say to (tell) (person), "(exact quotation)"

Recant the details of a discussion—He/she said, "(exact quote)". Then I said, "(exact quote)"

As you practice this technique, you will quickly realize that you can subconsciously command prospects to move toward your influencing goals with greater ease, and it will be perfectly acceptable to them. They don't think you are commanding them when you hide the commands in this language pattern. Embedded quotations are much less detectable than always using embedded commands.

Quotes provide the perfect format for using embedded commands because they fit so naturally into normal conversations.

For example, if I wanted a water filter for our house, I would tell my husband that John, our next-door neighbor, told me he just bought a water filter and now his water tastes better than bottled water.

The way I would weave the command into a direct quote from John might look like this: Honey, I was talking to John this morning and he said to me "Hellen, the best thing I did this year was to buy a water filter. The water tastes so different! My kids drink less soda and enjoy pure, clear water now. On top of that benefit, Judy can save so much money every year because we're not buying bottled water at all now!"

The underlying message of my communication is BUY a water filter. Through embedding the commands that get me to my goal through recanting the gist of John's words (buy) in a quotation, I am asking my husband to buy us a water filter so that we can have great tasting water too! Notice how many commands we were able to successfully weave into the quotation!

Embedded quotations can be used in several ways. The most powerful is in building metaphors. **Embedded quotes take on the format of 'mini-metaphors'**. A metaphor is an analogy or story that relates a concept that is known to the other person to another concept that is (or might be) unfamiliar to them. For example: When trying to explain how a computer works, people often use metaphors that describe the brain, guts and memory of the machine. By likening the workings of a computer to the workings of the human brain and body, people can better grasp how a computer functions. We use metaphors to link the two concepts so that the other person can better grasp the meaning of our communication. We use metaphors in recanting details because storytelling is one of the oldest forms of belief-based learning in history.

People remember information best when they can relate facts to a story. The process of metaphor building is imperative for great communicators. Embedded quotes form the basis of rich, believable analogies and metaphors. The mind creates pictures and images best from strong analogies and stories rich with details and emotions.

> In a motion picture featuring the famous French comedian Sacha Guitry some thieves are arguing over division of seven pearls worth a King's ransom. One of them hands two pearls to the man on his right, then two pearls to the man on his left. "I Think I will keep three and save them for later," he said. The man on his right says, "How come you keep three?" "Because I am the leader." "Oh. But how come you are the leader?" "Because I keep more pearls now and later."

Personal

Something odd happened in the meeting the other day. **I listened to Frank tell Susan**, "I know you don't like the new system. We all have to adjust to changes. Go with the flow and soon you'll see the benefits of this computerized process." Susan was feeling a bit out of sorts and frustrated but after Frank's comments, she seemed to become at least more open to the new implementation.

Learning

Just the other day I had a similar discussion with Janet. **She said**, "I am so excited about the course I'm taking! I'm really happy about the information. I feel that I can easily implement the techniques into my life and make them part of my presentations."

Management

I now ask myself, "Did I do everything possible?" Then I ask, "Is it time to escalate this issue to upper management?"

Sales

I sometimes ask myself, "Why don't you just get on the phone and make appointments, immediately?"

Telecommunications

While discussing the status of our new service development with Mark, he asked me, "Why don't you focus on the doable and ensure market readiness?"

Financial

Just last week, another client, we'll call him, Mr. Jones, said to me, "I like this product. It will fit my current needs for security and long-term growth." And naturally, I agreed with him. It's perfect for his situation. I thought about him right now because your needs and his are very similar. It looks like you appreciate your client's confidentially when you use "we'll call him or her" when telling a story. If you use a client's name, it appears that you are gossiping and you are not trustworthy.

Insurance

I was discussing your portfolio with my partner last week and he said to me, "Hellen, this family has a major problem if Frank gets seriously ill." I told him that at our last meeting we had briefly discussed life and disability insurance. Then he said, "Mr. Holt should get covered for at least basic expenses. He should buy disability insurance immediately!"

Health & Well-being

My doctor has always said, "Exercise regularly—just take a walk instead of driving to the corner store—take the stairs instead of the elevator. Do these things plus eat a balanced diet and you will live a long, happy, healthy life." Sounded like a good idea to me, so I'm following his advice. My wife and I walk the dog every day. We walk about two miles. It gives us a time to catch up on the day and spend some pleasant time together. Guess what, in the last year, I lost ten pounds without trying!

EXERCISE — EMBEDDED QUOTATIONS

To perfect your delivery of embedded quotations—write three examples directly pertaining to your profession or personal life. Say them aloud and practice them for perfect delivery.

1. ____

2. ____

3. ____

LANGUAGE PATTERN #3–EMBEDDED QUESTIONS

Just like with embedded quotations, embedded questions are used to hide a statement or a request. Embedded questions are an especially effective way of softening commands because they allow the receiver of the message to take responsibility for applying the command to him/herself – without requiring the speaker (or sender of the message) to do it. The receiver plays an active role in the application of and answer to the question (command). The indirect nature of the command frees the speaker of the awkwardness that can arise sometimes when asking someone to take action (especially on your behalf). By appealing to the receiver in a style in which they appear to be the decision maker and the one with the control, then you empower them to actively participate in helping YOU to meet your goal!

> The way a question is asked limits and disposes the ways in which any answer to it – right or wrong – may be given.
>
> Susanne K. Langer

Memorize these preludes to embedded questions—

- I (sometimes) ask myself if....
- I'm wondering whether....
- I'm curious as to....
- Someone (person's name) asked me...
- I heard (person) ask (person)..." (embed exact question)"
- I just wanted to inquire (whether)
- Joe mentioned that...
- I think we should ask ourselves this question...
- Susan said that she would be interested in finding out if...

> What is the use of political liberty to those who have no means to bake bread? It (political liberty) is only a value to ambitious theorists and politicians. And these people do not need to bake bread—they have plenty to eat. Perhaps, we should bake bread and ask these questions first?
>
> ***JEAN PAUL MARAT***

Personal

I used to suffer from a lack of confidence when meeting new people, too, especially in a business situation. Normally, I can talk to anyone, but I'd find myself faltering in some situations. **I would often ask myself** if reading a book about how to control internal dialog—how to make self-talk positive would help? I searched and found a wonderful book at the local bookstore. **I was wondering whether** you should you buy it and study it for some tips? I noticed that you face the same types of situations in our staff meetings.

Learning

I'm curious as to how I can incorporate these techniques even more quickly into my business and personal life. I guess I should take one at a time and master each individually. Is that the best way? Is there another method to make the process dovetail into current skills more quickly?

Management

I now ask myself, "Did I do everything possible?" Then I ask, "Is it time to escalate this issue to upper management?"

I'm wondering whether it's possible for you to file your expense vouchers on time?

Sales

I sometimes ask myself, "Why don't you just get on the phone and make appointments, immediately?" By just asking those questions, I somehow propel myself into an action state. Maybe that will work for you, too.

Telecommunications

While discussing the status of our new service development with Mark, **he asked me**, "Why don't you focus on the doable and ensure market readiness?"

Financial

I sometimes ask myself, "Hellen, can I trust this instinct and put money into this investment?" Then, I say, "Of course I can! The company has a great track record and I feel comfortable with the decision to go ahead immediately!"

Insurance

I'm wondering whether you will be interested in the program or simply see the value of my proposal?

Health & Well-being

I am wondering whether you will enroll in the program and do the exercises regularly?

EXERCISE — EMBEDDED QUESTIONS

Write three examples of embedded questions by rewriting your embedded quotation exercise:

1. ____

2. ____

3. ____

CAUSE & EFFECT LANGUAGE PATTERNS 4 & 5 – DIRECT & IMPLIED

Recognizing and using cause and effect language patterns will enable you to:

- **Use a naturally occurring language pattern to install suggestions.**
- **Speak in the way beliefs are organized in your prospect's mind, making you more believable.**

Powerfully strengthen your understanding of pacing and leading techniques and their impact.

During communication, especially in the language patterns called "*cause and effect*", we take advantage of the way the mind works. Since childhood, we have been programmed to think that our actions, whatever they may be, have a direct relationship on the way the rest of the people in the world react to us. Based on other people's reactions, we are given feedback and stimuli to further respond and react. This interdependence on others in the communication loop and the reactions of people in the loop forms the basis of the study of cause and effect during communication.

Cause and effect language patterns have been used in our realm of interaction with other people since birth. Is vital to understand that our beliefs take the format of cause and effect.

Cause	Effect
Being afraid of sharks	Not swimming in the ocean
Thinking that life insurance is not necessary	Family inadequately covered if you die prematurely
Unwilling to provide timely feedback to staff	People do not develop professionally as quickly as they could
Inadequate communication throughout the corporation	Attrition is higher when compared to other companies in your industry
Failing to ask for referrals	High stress, not enough people to call, insufficient level of activity to achieve financial goals, production suffers, financial objectives slip

People form beliefs based on their interpretation of cause and effect relationships. If I think that a cause will result in an effect, my mind paints a picture for me to remember. If I think that bungee jumping will result in me having a heart attack, I will believe that bungee jumping is dangerous and I will avoid the activity altogether. However, if I think that bungee jumping will be exhilarating and fun, I will believe that I would enjoy participating.

The bottom line: Whichever picture my mind conjures up (i.e. the result of the cause and effect relationship) will be transformed into beliefs, which in turn will form the basis from which I make decisions and act.

People and Cause and Effect

When we looked at the first, second and third person perceptual positions, we discovered that most of the time, most people remain in the first person perceptual position – the position of EGO. Human beings have a quirk that makes them think that the universe revolves around 'ME' and secondary—my relationship to others. We naturally assume that interdependence (based on how we view the situation) is logical and so we usually follow cause and effect statements without question. People often become frustrated, angry and reactive when their view of how cause and effect should occur is questioned, put in jeopardy or whenever an unexpected result happens. The tension level dramatically increases at times when people who do not like change experience situations that evolve differently from what they planned on occurring.

Building a Case During the Influencing Process

Our judicial system revolves around proving cause and effect relationships. Attorneys for the prosecution must prove causation. Defending members of the profession seek to refute the cause and effect statements of the prosecution lawyers. To accomplish this, the attorneys must use the psychological theory of replacement. This theory states that in order to change a belief, you must replace it with another, more effective or more logical belief. Since all beliefs take the form of cause and effect, the new belief must be put forth in cause and effect language to take hold and be effective.

Science and Cause and Effect

In 1905, Albert Einstein published two important papers on the Theory of Relativity. These papers started a debate that continues to this day. We can use the basis of his theory to better understand the dynamics of communication and the interaction of events that surround specific messages.

The fundamental hypothesis of the theory was grounded on the idea that the state of absolute rest did not exist in the universe. In other words, nothing ever stopped. Events moved on; as did time and our position in space. A brief synopsis of Albert Einstein's Theory of Relativity states that every action in the universe causes some form of reaction in the universe. In plain English, there is an interdependence of bodies on one another. This interdependence can only be accurately measured, analyzed and studied when the relative positions of <u>all</u> entities are studied. The study should be based on where each entity was and now is with regard to their individual positions and specific characteristics within the specific circumstances of the event.

Language Pattern #4 Direct Cause & Effect

X Causes Y

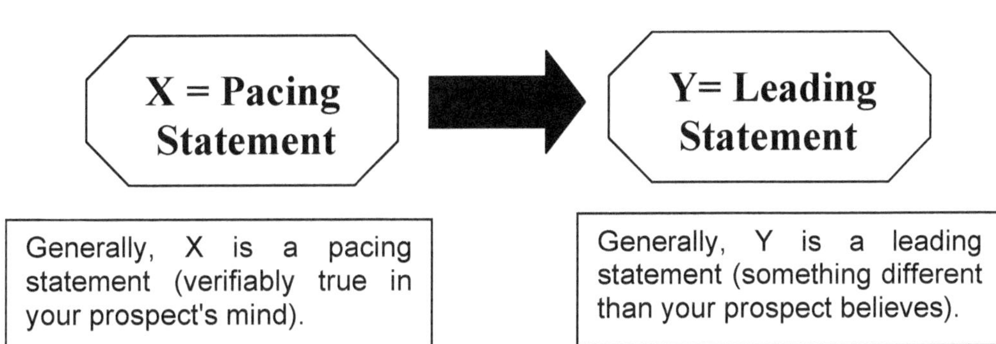

The cause does not necessarily come before the effect during communication. You must learn to discriminate within the sentence to determine which is the cause and which is the effect statement. You can have more than one effect for a cause.

Examples of Cause & Effect from History

It is the way we react to circumstances (cause) that determines our feeling (effect).
DALE CARNEGIE

He who would accomplish little (effect) must sacrifice little (cause); he who would achieve much (effect) must sacrifice much (cause)…
JAMES ALLEN

The world is so constructed; that if you wish to enjoy life's pleasures (effect), you must endure its pains (cause). Whether you like it or not, you cannot have one without the other.
SWAMI BRAHMANANDA

Among other evils which being unarmed (cause) brings you, it causes you to be despised (effect).
NICOLO MACHIAVELLI, The Prince

The only thing necessary for the triumph of evil (effect) is for good men to do nothing (cause).
EDMUND BURKE, letter to William Smith

The government in its wisdom considers ice a "food product." (cause) This means that Antarctica is one of the world's foremost food producers (effect).
GEORGE F. WILL, Government, Economy Linked

The greatest discovery of my generation is that human beings can alter their lives (effect) by altering their attitudes of mind (cause).
WILLIAM JAMES

Words that *Suggest* a Cause and Effect Relationship

How can you recognize a cause & effect statement when the word 'because' is not apparent?

The words in the table below will assist you in quickly determining when cause & effect is in play during the influencing process.

as	**and**	**while**	**causes**
since	**during**	**forces**	**makes**
invokes	**settles**	**stimulates**	
becomes	**verifies**	**determines**	
brings to pass	**kindles**	**creates**	

Memorize These!

EXAMPLE — CAUSE AND EFFECT

Personal

Sitting in your chair listening to my voice *(cause)* causes you to completely <u>absorb this material</u> *(effect)* and <u>accept it</u> (*effect*) into the deepest levels of your subconscious mind.

Accepting this material *(cause)* deep in your mind causes you to **<u>use it ethically</u>** *(effect)* whenever you are influencing people.

Learning

Thinking your next thought *(cause)* causes you to be consciously aware that you have to **<u>practice this language pattern</u>** *(effect)* to completely master the technique.

Management

Meeting with a diverse team *(cause)* of experienced company personnel forces (causes) you to <u>be aware</u> *(effect)* of the full range of implications and possibilities for the new product.

Listening to customers *(cause)* causes you to <u>evaluate your course of action</u> *(effect)* and <u>consider better matches</u> *(effect)* with their buying criteria.

Telecommunications

The passing of legislation *(cause)* causes a change *(effect)* in the construct and capabilities of our competition.

Financial

A change in the valuation of our stock *(cause)* causes fluctuations *(effect)* in investment levels.

Insurance

Introducing new products *(cause)* causes industry analysts to look more closely *(effect)* at how they perceive our company.

Health & Well-being

Since starting my exercise program and new weight loss program *(cause)*, I feel so motivated *(effect)* and I'm sleeping better *(effect)*, too.

Exercise — Cause & Effect

Write five cause and effect statements pertaining to your industry. Write them with the cause before the effect, then swap the order and deliver the effect first.

1. ____

2. ____

3. ____

4. ____

5. ____

How can you make a Cause & Effect Statements even more powerful?

Cause and effect --because optional

Numerous studies have proved that people comply with requests more easily (and quicker) when they are told why you are asking them to do something. When you explain the importance of the request and also explain how much you appreciate their assistance, others will help you attain your influencing goals. This is an exceptionally powerful technique to use when you are attempting to change beliefs (through cause and effect language patterns).

EXAMPLE — CAUSE & EFFECT AND BECAUSE...

I know that many of you believe that it would be best to outsource this project because we are overloaded with work *(cause = too much work for too few people; implied effect = we'll never be able to do this and we'll never get free time!)*. But, our team must complete this phase of the project internally because the information is too sensitive for outside consultants to see (cause = external people will see – effect – they might potentially leak sensitive information).

> Cause and effect... because optional
>
> Just as some penalty (effect) deters a prospective offender by making the prospect of crime less attractive (effect), so does the more severe (cause) penalty make crime still less attractive (effect), and so less likely to occur (effect). Because death penalty (cause) is perceived by most potential lawbreakers as the maximum feasible penalty, it is probably the effective deterrent force (effect).
>
> -- Frank G. Harrington, Neither Cruel nor Unusual

LANGUAGE PATTERN #5 IMPLIED CAUSE & EFFECT

(As X, Y)

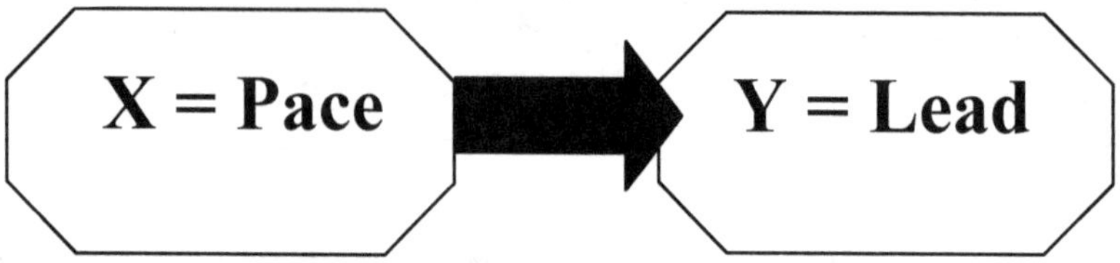

X = Pace → Y = Lead

Implied cause and effect forms the pattern—as PACE happens, LEAD naturally follows.

The same rules apply to indirect cause and effect with regard to pacing and leading.

This pattern is basically the same as direct cause and effect. The difference is that **instead of directly indicating a link, we imply the link.**

You don't need to complete the Y statement for this to be effective. My mother used to tell me "You might want to walk on the sidewalk when you get closer to the mall." The implication is that if you don't, you could be hit by a passing car. Make sure that the other person's reaction matches your expectation of their understanding of the effect before you continue. If it doesn't, you should be prepared to use a DIRECT cause & effect statement. You have to be certain that they have enough knowledge to draw the conclusion you want them to draw. You need to know how they will think through the cause and effect relationship if the effect statement is not stated.

> Note: **Implied cause and effect patterns are** less detectable **in conversation than direct cause and effect patterns,** but have exactly the same effect on your prospect's mind during the influencing process. **If you are on the same wavelength as the person you are communicating with, then you have a greater chance of ensuring that they will draw the conclusion (regarding the effect) that you imply.**

EXAMPLE — IMPLIED CAUSE & EFFECT

What conclusions would people come to regarding these statements?

You always do what you want to do. This is true with every act. You may say you had to do something, or that you were forced to, but actually whatever you do, you do by choice. Only you have the power to choose for yourself.
W. CLEMENT STONE

These, then, are my last words to you: Be not afraid of life. Believe that life is worth living and your belief will help create the fact.
WILLIAM JAMES

Things turn out best for the people who make the best of the way things turn out.
John WOODEN

What happens to a man is less significant than what happens within him.
LOUIS L. MANN

Your living is determined not so much by what life brings to you as by the attitude you bring to life; not so much by what happens to you as by the way your mind adjusts to what happens.
JOHN HOMER MILLER

A man bears beliefs, as a tree bears apples.
RALPH WALDO EMERSON

As I grow older, I pay less attention to what men say; I just watch what they do.
ANDREW CARNEGIE

Invariably it is true—as is the inner so always and inevitably will be the outer.
RALPH WALDO TRINE

Exercise — Implied Cause & Effect

As you begin to master *(cause)* this language pattern, you will definitely have a deep sense of accomplishment *(effect)*.

Write three sentences that use the implied cause and effect pattern as follows. Use at least one embedded command in each pattern.

1. As a statement

___

___

2. One with quotes

___

___

3. One with an embedded question

___

___

LANGUAGE PATTERN # 6 IF... THEN... (SPELLING OUT CONSEQUENCES)

The mind translates 'if... then...' in this manner.

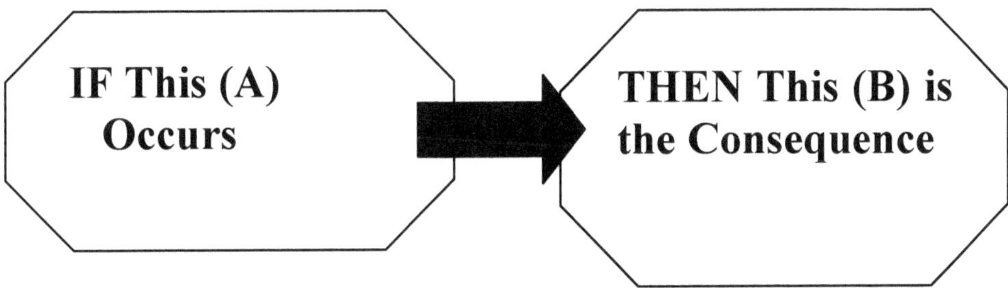

IF (in the event that A occurs)
THEN
the consequence would be (or probably be) B.

The if...then segment should be something that is familiar to the listener (a pacing statement) so that the compliance level is as high as possible. The second portion of the if...then (the segment after 'then') can be new information to the audience (a leading statement) OR it could simply reiterate facts they already knew (another pacing statement).

Note: It is important to understand that a statement must be verifiably true in the perception of the audience to be considered a pacing statement. If they do not yet believe it to be true because they are still in denial, act as if the statement is a lead. If the person is still in the denial or resistance phases of the Transitional Time Line[9] the statement that you might think is a pacing statement is actually a leading statement because the person does not believe it to be true.

If statements can be used to propel people to take action, make decisions, or to guide decisions in a different direction. They can be used subtly or not (depending on your intent, level of authority and motivation). They are also considered to be cause and effect statements.

[9] Discussed later in the book and discussed in depth in the Moving Forward with Change Manual.

If you see yourself as prosperous, you will be. If you see yourself as continually hard up, that is exactly what you will be. ***ROBERT COLLIER***

A set definite objective must be established if we are to accomplish anything. [10] ***JOHN McDONALD***

If a man knows not what harbor he seeks, any wind is the right wind. ***SENECA***

If you believe you can do a thing, you can do it. ***CLAUDE M. BRISTOL***

[10] As with cause and effect, the 'if' does not have to come first in the statement.

'NESTED IF' STATEMENTS

Influencing with
If… then…

Logical flow and sequence is important when 'nesting' if's. The term 'nesting if's' originated in the computer industry. An 'if' statement is a line of code that tells the computer how to process based on input. For example, if the customer lives in New Jersey, charge them 7% sales tax. Under this scenario, the computer will not charge sales tax to anyone else in the database besides people who live in New Jersey.

When the data does not comply with the 'if' statement, the computer goes sequentially to the next statement. This is the same principle that the brain uses to process information.

Unfortunately, life is seldom reduced to 'this or that' choices in series. There are often nuances that allow for exceptions. In the tax example from New Jersey, what if tax did not have to be levied on people of certain professions even if they lived in New Jersey? To correctly assess taxes, programmers formulate 'nested if's' based on various circumstances. The goal in programming is to skip unnecessary if statements to preserve processing time. 'Nested if's' are structured to skip over – ignore – the if's that are not relevant.

'Nested if' statements can be formulated to give people the illusion of choice during the influencing process.

They can be used to shorten the time it takes for people to make decisions and take action.

EXAMPLE 'NESTED IF'S'

If the person lives in NJ then test to see (If they live elsewhere; skip all the if's that are inside this 'nested if' statement)

If they are in certain professions then…

EXERCISE 'NESTED IF' STATEMENTS

Write a series of 'nested if' statements that will help you move a team from exploration to making a decision.

Establishing Criteria, Understanding Features and Benefits, & Uncovering Expectations

Step 1 Features & Benefits

It is true that the general features and benefits of your product or service are important during the influencing process, but even more important are the **specific** features and benefits that are perceived as being important by your client/customer. Your client is going to be more inclined to listen to you and take interest in learning more about your product if you explain what they will receive (how they will benefit) in terms of what **they perceive to be of value**. Ask them the "What's important..." questions in all pertinent perceptual positions to find out what they value.

The easiest way to explain the difference between a feature and a benefit is to describe the difference as it exists in a sales environment. Once we firmly grasp the concept as it applies to selling, we can easily translate the features and benefit process to motivating, leading, and managing people.

If you are selling a service or product you have probably heard the expression "Sell the sizzle, not the steak!" This expression is a metaphor for highlighting (selling) the benefits (the sizzle that the customer values), rather than concentrating solely on the features (the steak).

People are usually interested in the some of the facts about the product or service – the features – BUT what they really want to know about is what the product can do for them – the benefits.

Benefits

BENEFITS EXPLAIN what it DOES (ACCOMPLISHES) for the buyer. Benefits focus on HOW the product SOLVES A PROBLEM for the person or addresses a NEED. Benefits are often centered around emotional involvement and tempt the individual by solving a problem. Benefits are highly personal and are focused on what the product or service will do for that particular person and their personal situation based on what they perceive to be valuable.

Features

If the person wants to know about the features, they usually ask specifics about what the product IS rather than what it DOES. Features are usually facts and data about the service or product. They tend to be impersonal and unemotional. Features usually are what they are, and are often not open to interpretation.

EXAMPLE: FEATURES AND BENEFITS

Product: Microwave Oven

Features: 80 watts, revolving tray, convection capabilities, auto-defrost, etc.

Benefits: Saves time – cooks food 5 times faster than on the stovetop, avoids waste because you can easily freeze leftovers and reheat them within minutes,

EXERCISE FEATURES AND BENEFITS

Select a product or service within your company and fill in the chart below with its features and benefits.

Features	Benefits

STEP 2–FINDING HOT BUTTONS (CRITERIA)

The information you receive from your prospect is the information that they use to decide if a communication message, product or service is appropriate for their individual needs. It is what drives a prospect to act on a proposal or to avoid it. Personal criteria are what individuals need to satisfy if they are going to become a team player within an organization.

> Criteria - What a prospect must have (or believe they have to have) before they will take action, make a decision, or buy something.

The more closely your message, product or service matches your prospects buy-in criteria, the more impact you will have on them and the better your chances of success.

When managing people, the person's buy-in criteria for motivation and decision making must be established for peak performance to exhibit its full potential. When you know what the person values, you can motivate them and assist them in reaching their professional goals.

Finding a person's criteria for buying is the most important goal in any sales interview. "Hot buttons" are a person's buying and decision-making criteria. The most effective way to influence your client to purchase your products or services is to first establish his criteria for purchasing and then link the criteria emotionally to obtain your desired outcome.

Often, the criterion for buying evolves from the buyer's perspective of What's In It for Me? They are in the first perceptual position at this point in time. If you can find out what they want and link your ideas (and dialog) to their personal wants and needs, you have a better chance of persuading them to be open to input and suggestions. If you remember to clearly communicate on their personal WIIfm, you increase the odds of having them come around to your way of thinking. By communicating the WIIfm message, they will tend to have an open mind regarding your message. They will also be more inclined to discuss your products and services. If you are managing people it is important to deliver your message on their WIIfm airwave. If you don't, you are in for a rough ride as the leader of your department.

> **The most effective way to make certain that you are communicating on the person's station 'WIIfm' is to talk about features and benefits as they relate directly to the person.**

Format for Finding Criteria (Hot Buttons)

You must establish both personal and business hot buttons to link your message, product, or service for maximum impact in any business negotiations.

Once you have uncovered your customer's personal needs/criteria, you need to uncover any other decision makers' criteria that will be critical to your influencing process. You do this by looking at all three perceptual positions, then you link all criteria (if possible) to the features and benefits of your service or product. You should integrate internal and external hot buttons for maximum communication impact. Asking a series of questions does this:

1st Person Perceptual Position Criteria

What's important about (context) to you (personally)?

Or

What's important to you (personally) about (context)?

2nd and 3rd Person Perceptual Position Criteria [11]

What's important about (context) to your company (manager, decision-maker, profitability, etc.)?

Or

What's important to your company (manager, decision maker, profitability, etc.) about (context)?

Note: Try not to ask these questions one right after the other when gathering criteria. Make sure both are asked at the appropriate time during the fact-finding and criteria-gathering interview.

Never prompt your prospect by assisting them to verbalize their criteria; even if their reasons seem trivial, unimportant or frivolous. Remember, their criteria are what they will base their decision on to do business with you, be motivated by you, or tell others about your plans. The most effective way to link their criteria to your message, product or service is to listen to the exact words they use when describing their criteria. Maximum impact is attained when those exact words are repeated to the person during the linking criteria or closing phases of the communication loop or sales process. This will drive anyone's effective communication, closing ratio and client retention rate higher because all parties in the process will be working towards clearly understood outcomes/goals.

[11] Make certain you ask about the criteria of all involved in the buying/decision-making process. It is especially important to establish the criteria for anyone who has 'veto power' over your products and services.

Learning

What's important to your company with regard to you mastering the right skill set for your new position?

Management

To a transferring executive:
What's important about a new home to you and your family? AND
What's important about the neighborhood's proximity to your office?

To the Vice President of Sales and Marketing:
What's important about having your people become more effective in the marketplace to you personally?

AND

What's important to the company about increasing revenue through having a highly effective sales and marketing force dealing with your client base?

Telecommunications

Q: What is important to you about streamlining your communications supplies from vendors?
A: It will enable me to spend more time with my customers so that I can achieve greater understanding of their priority needs. (This is a towards statement.)
A: The streamlining will help me achieve my goal of focusing the department's limited resources on the most important projects. (This is a towards statement.)

Q: What is important to the company about developing a strategic relationship with a leading communications organization?

A: It will mean that we can avoid surprises and avert superficial solutions. (This is an away-from statement.)

Telecommunications

To the Information Systems Specialist—decision concerning updating telecommunications hardware:

What's important about purchasing new equipment to you?

AND

What's important to the corporation about this acquisition?

Financial

To the benefits director—deciding on a new investment company for the corporate pension plans:

What is important about 401k investments to you personally?

AND

What's important to your corporation with regard to the investment mix for all employees?

Insurance

To a newly married husband and wife:

What's important to both of you individually about making sure your spouse is adequately covered if you are no longer with us?

AND

What's important to you as a married couple (replaces corporation) about having the right coverage in case anything happens?

To a Human Resource manager when discussing a new life insurance benefit for employees:

What's important to you personally about making sure your employees and their families are adequately covered if one of them dies?

AND

What's important to the corporation about having the right amount of coverage for employees and their families in case anything happens?

Health & Well-being

What's important to you personally about being active well into your seventies?

What's important to your family (replace corporation) about you being active well into your seventies?

Linking Criteria to Your Prospect's Outcomes

For influencing purposes, the more you refer to the other person's criteria and link it to your product/service the more impact your presentation will have.

In traditional sales courses, participants are asked to match benefits to client needs. Often the clients' needs are based on what the selling company **thought** the client might need. Without uncovering the client's true criteria for buying you can set the salespeople up for a difficult sale.

Important – Without solid influencing skills, it usually takes longer to change a prospect's criterion to match your product/service/management goals than it does to find people whose criteria match your product/service/management goals. You have to know when to cut the process off if you cannot establish a match between their criteria and what you are offering If you fail to do this, your client might have buyer's remorse or your new hire might be a poor fit for the team.

What are some of the benefits of properly matching people's criteria?

In today's intensely competitive global marketplace, a higher than average closing ratio traditionally has the following benefits:

- The sales force earns more money.
- The corporation receives more revenue, which drives growth.
- The company gains a reputation for innovative products/services. Clients, prospects and the competitor's sales force hear this throughout the marketplace.
- Enhanced reputation becomes a vehicle to recruit and retain a highly qualified sales team.
- As the sales force's level of expertise increases, the level of motivation to close sales increases. Success breeds success!

As the drive continues for higher closing ratios, sales, marketing and customer service people will be forced to hone their communication skills. Listening to the client or prospect is not enough, **you must uncover what their expectations are and deliver accordingly**.

Uncovering Expectations -The Function Of Linking Criteria

During the influencing process, others will weigh the option of adopting your goal. They will imagine themselves complying with your plan of action. Then they will picture alternatives. They will decide which direction they will choose according to their criteria and how their criteria links with their expectations.

Your influencing goal will meet their criteria expectations or not. The options are that the goal will:

1. **Meet expectations** – The influencing process should be accomplished to the satisfaction of both parties.

2. **Exceed expectations** – They will be delighted because they believe you will deliver more than they expected. Make sure you do!

3. **Fail to meet expectations** – In this scenario, you must evaluate whether the person's expectations are too high. Are there valid reasons why their expectations are high? Is the person's perception reality-based? Or have they based their opinion on erroneous or false information? Are your products/services priced higher than your competitors'? You have several options during the influencing process to counter objections. All of them should be based on the individual's criteria linked to their expectations. If you fail to meet the other person's expectations you run the risk that they will comply now, but change their mind later.

Towards (pleasure) & Away From (pain)

All criteria serves to make you want to move **towards** (attain—usually associated ***with pleasure*** or positive emotional impact) or move **away from** (avoid—usually associated ***with pain*** or negative emotional impact) something. These terms do not refer to whether they are moving toward or away from the decision to purchase your product/services or to help you accomplish your influencing goal or not. Moving "towards or away from" is how the product (if they had it) would help them move toward pleasure rather than help them avoid a painful situation.

For example, let's imagine you were purchasing a life insurance policy for your family. You could purchase with the criteria of helping you attain peace of mind knowing that your family will have enough money to continue with their current standard of living and that you have left funds to help your local elementary school build a new playground. These reasons make you happy – you are moving toward pleasure with your criteria for purchasing a life insurance policy. On the other hand you might decide to purchase the policy out of fear (avoiding pain). Your reason for the policy purchase is to move away from something that would negatively impact your happiness - that your children will not be able to go to college if you were to die prematurely and that your spouse would have to sell the family home. These thoughts cause you psychological angst (pain) if you did not make the decision to cover the risk with life insurance. The decision (to still purchase the insurance) is not different but the motivation for doing so is completely different depending on your thought process.

The key is to link the thought processes involved in the prospect's decision-making process to an appropriate strategy in your influencing process.

Note: Listen carefully when people communicate their criteria - the "What's important to you" answers. Write the information down verbatim to use in your presentations and communication during the influencing process.

To Determine Whether the Person is Moving Towards (Pleasure) Or Away From (Pain) Ask:

Direct Method:

What will having (exact criteria) mean to you (or do for you)?

Indirect Method:

Just imagine that you had (the criteria delivered – the 'what's important to you?' answers). What would you expect from that product, service, corporation, representative, etc? Note: To soften your request for expectations, you can use a language pattern (suggestion pattern #4[12] – Just imagine - as the examples does) to solicit the person's expectations.

TOWARDS

Words you will hear when a person wants to move towards their criteria:

attain
complete
Get
take over
fulfill
procure
gain
include
enable
accomplish
consummate
acquire
reach
achieve
appropriate
secure
accomplish
carry out
realize (the goal of)
obtain
finish
arrive at
earn
goals
solutions

AWAY FROM

Words you will hear when a prospect moves away from their criteria:

avoid
Get away from
shun
lose
Escape
rule out
Relinquish
withdraw (from)
back off from
Sidestep
forfeit
elude
count out
Defeat
Avert
evade
Fail
Dodge
Exclude
Ban
Surrender

---

[12] Discussed in the language pattern section of the manual.

EXERCISE EXPECTATIONS & 'TOWARDS' OR 'AWAY FROM'

People move 'towards' or 'away from' because they have expectations about what will happen if they take a course of action.

You must uncover their expectations to determine if the person's expectations are in line with what your product, service, and or influencing goal will deliver.

Make a list of phrases[13] the person might say that will help you determine whether having your product or service will be linked moving toward or away from:

Toward (Pleasure and Goal attainment)	Away (Pain and Avoidance)

[13] Answers at back of book

Examples — Towards

Q: What will having passive income do for you?
A: It will enable me to buy more things that I want.

Q: What will having this new equipment do for you and your department?
A: This new equipment will really lighten our workload by transferring the customer service calls for our ABC Product to another department.

Examples — Away From

Q: What will having passive income do for you?
A: It will ensure that I don't have to work when I get older.

Q: What will having life insurance mean to you?
A: It will make sure that my wife and kids won't have to sell the home that we live in to pay estate taxes.

Q: What will having this new equipment do for you and your department?
A: Half of my team's unproductive workload will disappear when we get rid of the old system.

Examples — Multiple Links and Towards & Away From

The person might have a combination of towards and away from if they buy your products or services OR go along with your goal.

Q: What will having life insurance mean to you?
A: It will mean that my estate taxes will be paid *(towards)* and I don't have to worry *(away from)* about that problem for my kids.

Q: What does being able to communicate better as a leader mean for you and your team?
A: It will mean that we won't waste a lot of unnecessary time *(away from)* spinning our wheels always trying to second guess one another. It will also dramatically improve our levels of trust and morale *(towards)*.

EXERCISE TOWARDS & AWAY FROM - LINKING CRITERIA

Underline the "towards" and "away from" linking words in the above examples and write two examples pertinent to your industry.

1. ____

____

____

____

____

2. ____

____

____

____

____

Language Patterns that Bind – Convincer Strategies

Use **Convincer Strategies to Influence Opinions, Beliefs, and Decision Making Processes**

Convincer Strategy #1 Single Binds

The more you X, the more you Y.

All through our lives we have heard this language pattern. The *more* you think about the pattern, the *more* you will realize just how often you do hear it. A single bind is simply two statements that express a single cause and effect relationship. Single binds always reflect only one – a single – comparison (with no alternatives) of what will occur (the positive and negative consequences inherent in the cause and effect) for the two statements.

This language pattern falls into the cause and effect language pattern category. In cause and effect, and in single binds, embedded commands powerfully increase the impact of single binds.

To leave the best impression on the receiver's mind, single binds should be structured so that they move the other person toward a state of abundance (more efficiency, save more money, lose less money, solve a problem, attain status they currently do not possess, etc.) and move you closer to your influencing process goal.

Note: Even by using single binds that contain the word 'less' and words that appear to reduce what the listener currently has, the person might perceive this as attaining a goal. This is especially true when you link the person's criteria in an 'away from' manner[14]. For example, a weight loss industry advertisement promises: The more visits you have to (the weight loss center), the less your dress size will be. In marketing insurance products, a brochure reads: We make certain the worst thing that can occur is covered (picture of house on fire with family standing outside watching firemen), so that you'll worry less about what will happen to your most valuable possessions.

The bottom line: This gives you a subtle way to let people know that by going along with your ideas and your influencing process, things will be better for them.

[14] See Linking criteria – towards and away

Patterns for Single Binds

The best way to learn single binds is to **recognize the patterns** and **practice them**. These are ranked in the order where they have the most psychological weight for the receiver and the most impact during the influencing process.

The more you X, the more you Y **MX = MY**

The more you X, the less you Y **MX = LY**

The less you X, the more you Y **LX = MY**

The less you X, the less you Y **LX = LY**

The more you X, the more you Y, and the more you Z **MX = MY & MZ**

The less you X, the more you Y, and the more you Z **LX = MY & MZ**

You can further enhance the impact by stringing together several phrases that link a couple of consequences (effects). Again, for the maximum impact, try to create more abundance.

EXAMPLES USING LESS TO SPELL OUT CONSEQUENCES

Note: Single binds can be highly effective as a means to create anxiety and fear. This pattern can be used to help people look clearly at the consequences of negative behavior.

Management: (direct cause and effect, MX = MY & ML, combined with an effective 'but' statement, suggestion pattern #4, and embedded commands)

Goal: To get the manager in the Information System department to work cooperatively with the sales department to implement a new product for a customer.

Example:
I realize that it has been stressful working with Susan and Jim on this project because your department has had to do 90% of the work and you only have 10% control over the client specifications. I know that you think that we should be talking directly to the customer and that we need to take more control of this project. But Susan and Jim and their sales people have been working on this deal for over 15 months. They believe that they know the client's needs intimately. The **more** you think about the consequences of going around them, you'll (**more**) quickly realize that and they'll feel that we would be stepping on their turf (rightly so!), and our company might look **less** efficient. Just imagine, for instance, if someone from our department asked the client questions that were already answered by Jim or Susan last year. It would make us all look bad. I think we should avoid this at all costs. It's simply not worth the risks. Let's just go with the flow here and work together cooperatively as best as we can under the parameters set out.

Financial Sales: (MX = MY & ML, combined with an effective 'but' statement, direct cause and effect, suggestion pattern #2, double bind, and embedded commands)

Goal: Get the client to put their paperwork together so that you can finalize their financial plan.

Example: I understand that you are busy and that it takes time to find these documents. But, the **more** you resist the thought of completing this financial plan within the next few days, the **more** you'll realize that you'll have even **less** time to prepare for your tax burden because your business is growing so rapidly. Ignoring the problem doesn't make it go away, doing it will make it go away. When you think about it, the problem is just getting bigger! You said it would only take an hour to find the documents. Do you think it would be fair to come back and collect them on Monday or would it be better to pick them up Tuesday morning?

The more deeply the path is etched, the more it is used, and the more it is used, the more deeply it is etched.
JO COUDERT

The greater the obstacle, the more glory overcoming it.
JEAN BAPTISTE MOLIERE

The harder the conflict, the more glorious the triumph.
THOMAS PAINE

Personal

The more you help others, the more you realize what a good feeling it gives you and the better your opportunity for self-actualization.

Learning

The more you use this language pattern, the easier it will become for you to incorporate it into your sales presentations.

The more you become aware of the uses of single binds, the more you will realize when they are being used on your mind and the better you will be able to make the choice to be influenced by them or not.

Management

The more your team understands the process, the less confusion will exist.

We should leverage the entire World Telecom team to help make sales happen. The more team members we get involved the better our chance to increase revenues and improve customer interaction.

Telecommunications

The more your company thinks about using ISDN, the more you'll see the benefit in the speed capabilities and cost savings.

Financial

The more you invest in __________, the more you'll feel confident as you see your account grow. If you're wondering if ____________ is for you, you'll immediately feel sure as I show you their past performance.

Insurance

The more life insurance you purchase, the more secure you'll feel. And if you're wondering about life insurance as a product in your family's portfolio, you'll realize that without it your family doesn't have a future if you're gone, right?

As we discussed last week, Joe, the *longer* you wait to buy life insurance, the *more* it will cost you, and the *more* it costs you the *less happy* you'll be about paying the premiums. None of my clients like paying for insurance, but the *quicker* we get started the *faster* your cash values will build up. The *longer* we wait to start this policy, the *older* you'll be when you buy life insurance. For all of these reasons I feel that the best thing I could possibly do is to advise you to *start now* and *pay less* over the long run.

Health & Well-being

The more you exercise the better your body functions. If you even have the slightest doubt about the truth of that, just try to remember how well you slept after your last long walk. It made you sleep wonderfully, didn't it?

EXAMPLE USING MULTIPLE LANGUAGE PATTERNS

Here are some examples from the health insurance industry that combine:

- **Cause & effect -- X causes Y**
- **But/However**
- **Single Binds -- The more you do X, then the more you do Y**

Can you spot the different language patterns that are used?

1. Medical trend has increased therefore your PPO rates are going up; however if you considered modifying your benefits to our Direct Access Plan you could greatly reduce your rate increase.

2. USA Health Care has lowered their commissions, which has caused your income to go down; but if you bring more business to ABC Corporation you will make a higher commission and you will be eligible for our broker bonus program, which really could up your income as you bring us more cases.

3. You could go to XYZ Health for a lower premium; however, your 10 employees in CA would be forced into an indemnity plan and this could cause dissatisfaction for those employees, a higher premium cost for them, and possibly increased administrative costs for you.

4. Your prescription costs will exceed the 150 prescription limit. However, you will continue to get the ABC MediPlan Discounts so you will always be saving money.

5. You could be turned down for Plan I due to your health. However, Plans A, C and F are guaranteed issue and offer a prescription discount which will help lower your prescription costs.

6. You could get a balance bill, if you choose to go to a doctor who is not associated with that particular group. However, we have the largest network providers in the state so the majority of our clients rarely have balance bills to pay out of their pocket so that lowers your actual costs.

EXERCISE — SINGLE BINDS

Write five sentences using single binds with embedded commands that follow different language pattern formulas. These examples can be statements, questions or quotations. Try to use a variety of your new influencing skills as we showed you in the health care industry examples.

1.

2.

3.

4.

5.

CONVINCER STRATEGY #2 DOUBLE BINDS & HIDDEN DOUBLE BINDS

Formula For Double Binds

B (choice) OR C (choice)

Where either choice is basically the same (and leads to your outcome), but is worded differently. The specific goal when using a double bind is to get the other person in the communication loop to think about making decisions that align with your outcome. To produce an effective double bind you use two commands that would have basically the same outcome (moving the influencing process forward) in a suggestion sentence.

By using double binds and hidden double binds you:

- Create the illusion of choice
- Utilize that illusion to install suggestion
- Hide your suggestion so that it is unrecognizable
- Learn a means of controlled confusion to install suggestions

The Illusion of Choice

A double bind is a sentence structure that subtly influences the receiver of the message by giving them the illusion of choice. Two commands are used within a sentence that is formatted in such a manner as to allow the person being influenced to make a decision on which option to choose. Both decisions will yield in the favor of the sender's goals and will propel the influencing process forward. The differences in the two options might simply be: the time frame in which the influencer's goal will be met, the specifics of how the process of meeting the goal will come about, how the details of deal will be structured, which day you will meet, the time of day that is best, etc.

The bottom line: You get someone to do what you want them to do by giving them two options - and you don't really care which one they choose! You get closer to your goal - they feel that they are in control.

Note: You are not necessarily required to hear a verbal response when dealing with double binds and multiple pattern double binds. You can assume that the person will consent to either option. Don't wait for a response, simply assume compliance and continue communicating.

Use sensory acuity to gauge whether a person is moving forward or not.

Rules for the Effective Use of Double Binds

- Gain rapport!

- Progress from mental to physical. Always try to bind a person's thoughts first, then work progressively towards binding physical movement. You can, however, bind them to sign a contract right from the start if you bind making the decision and **not** the physical act of signing.

- You must deliver the double bind effectively and meaningfully, as if the meaning of the words make good sense and are logical.

Embedded Command Combinations For Double Binds	
Establish a position to support this process	Recommend that the department continue with this initiative
Be open	Be receptive
Be interested	Get excited
Trust me	Believe me
Make it a habit	Use it daily
Work it into this quarter's budget	Set it up for next month's billing cycle
Get enthusiastic in a few minutes	Invest in it
Buy it	Lease it
Consider the cost savings	Let it positively impact your bottom line
Agree to new price increases	Approve new business plan
Withdraw money from savings plan	Simply borrow against it
Recognize accomplishments	Look at personal initiatives
Make a referral	Tell me about a few friends who might be interested
Apply it	Use it
Consider alternatives	Choose an option
Make an appointment in your office	Sit down over lunch/coffee
Accept it as fact	Take it as truth
Give me a referral	Let me know of a few contacts you think might be interested
Use this knowledge daily	Integrate it into your daily life
Invest right away	Buy the product after I explain a few more details
Get excited immediately	Think about how happy this will make you

EXERCISE DOUBLE BINDS

Underline all of the double binds that you can find in each statement.

A man sooner or later discovers that he is the master-gardener of his soul, then his life.
JAMES ALLEN

We must all hang together or assuredly we shall all hang separately.
BENJAMIN FRANKLIN, to the other signers of the Declaration of Independence

I will not accept if nominated and will not serve if selected.
WILLIAM TECUMSEH SHERMAN, message to the Republican National Convention

I have tried—as we all must try—sedulously not to laugh at the acts of man, nor to limit them, nor to detect them, but to understand them.
BARUCH SPINOZA, Tractatus Theologico-Politicus

Personal

I've been thinking about losing weight and starting an exercise program for months. I just have to decide how and when to start. The choice isn't completely clear yet—count calories and walk a couple times a week or just reduce food portions and climb the stairs at work instead of using the elevator?

Learning

So far, you have been learning different ways to speak to people to make it easier for them to do what you want them to do. As you continue to learn to use these patterns, do you think that you will find them useful in your professional life or simply be able to integrate them into your behavior to enable you to be a more efficient businessperson?

Management

Just suppose you were to give me a raise right now. Would that impact this year's budget or could you slide the costs into next year's?

You can justify this proposal on cost savings or consider its merits based on customer services.

Ed, if you want to meet our 1997 revenue objectives, you can agree to price increases on these services or approve this business case.

When you review my performance you can either recognize my accomplishments against my performance agreement or consider the innovative achievements that were not planned but were implemented on my initiative.

Telecommunications

Now that we've explained the benefits of SMDS Service, would you like to begin conservatively with the first service we discussed or go ahead and install the second option and avoid expensive equipment upgrades next year?

World Telecom places tremendous importance on our customer's level of satisfaction. As you evaluate us for this proposal, do you think the dedicated Corporate Account Manager or the technical strength of our Systems Engineers will be the deciding factor in giving us the (your) business?

Financial

You can either buy now or lease it, short or long term.

Diane, if you want your children to go to college you can withdraw money from your savings plan or borrow against it now.

Insurance

After considering the options I've presented in your financial profile, I'm wondering whether you think the term insurance or permanent coverage is your best option?

Health and Well-being

Mike, you can either count calories or give up your cookies and ice cream every night, you make the decision. Either way will help you reach your weight loss goal.

EXERCISE — DOUBLE BINDS

Write five double bind embedded command combinations pertinent to your industry or field.

1. ______

2. ______

3. ______

4. ______

5. ______

Write down five outcomes you would like to achieve either in your business or personal life.

1. ______

2. ______

3. ______

4. ______

5. ______

Compose five sentences that use embedded commands within a double bind to accomplish your five different outcomes.

1. ______

2. ______

3. ______

4. ______

5. ______

Convincer Strategy #3 Multiple Pattern Double Binds

Multiple pattern double binds are a series of double binds and hidden double binds (with or without a verbal response from the other person in the communication loop) preplanned to achieve a desired outcome. Multiple pattern double binds are used just the same as multiple nested "ifs" are used in computer programming. The other person in the communication loop is taken through a series of planned double bind combinations leading to a specific outcome.

This process has evolved from traditional fact finding.

Traditional Fact Finding—*Traditional fact-finding consists of a series of close-ended questions (Yes or No responses).*

Q: Has your company considered options for your long distance carrier?
A: No

Q: World Telecom has just introduced a package that I think would suit your company's needs. Are you available on Wednesday morning? I will be in your area.
A: No, that doesn't work for me.

Q: What about Friday?
A: No, I have a weekly staff meeting.

Q: I will be back in your area next Thursday. Can we meet in the afternoon?
A: That won't work either. Why don't we touch base in January (At this time the client is tiring of the questions and is frustrated with the process...).

Open Ended Fact Finding

> The specific goal of open-ended fact-finding is to keep the conversation flowing and never allow a simple yes or no response.

Q: What's the process your company uses for considering various options regarding your long distance carrier?
A: Usually we do a budget analysis of our usage on a quarterly basis. Then we receive quotes from various vendors.

Q: World Telecom has just introduced a package that I think would suit your company's needs. When are you available in the next few weeks in order for me to gather your information? I'm in your area every Tuesday and Thursday.
A: The next couple weeks I'm booked. How about three weeks out?

Q: Tuesday or Thursday— the week of the 20th is fine. Which suits you best?
A: Tuesday the 21st at 2:00 is fine.
Response: Great, I'll be in your offices Tuesday the 21st at 2:00.

Q: Most companies consider various options regarding their long distance carriers on a regular basis. We have found that companies similar to yours usually do a semi-annual __ or quarterly analysis of their usage for budget requirements. We provide prospective clients with an analysis quarterly.

A: We usually do quarterly analysis.

Q: I've noticed that we've never had the opportunity to offer you a competitive analysis. World Telecom has just introduced a package that I think would suit your company's needs. I'm in your area every Tuesday and Thursday. When are you available in the morning or afternoon in order for me to gather your criteria?

A: The next couple weeks I'm booked. How about three weeks out? Tuesday at 2:00pm on the 21st would work for me.

Response: Great, I'll be in your offices Tuesday the 21st at 2:00.

Hiding a Double Bind

Hiding a double bind is an exceptionally powerful influencing strategy. This is a controlled confusion tactic. By hiding a double bind you intentionally try to create confusion in your prospect's mind. Armed with the knowledge that the mind, when put in confusion, will accept the first logical suggestion that it is given as a means of pulling itself out of a confused state, we can perfect the technique of controlled confusion in a sales interview.

Structure for Hidden Double Binds

B (choice) OR C (choice).... QUESTION?

The structure for a hidden double bind is the same as the structure for a double bind. Instead of completing the thought you continue talking and then ask a question. The double bind is sandwiched between the structure of the sentence and the question at the end.[15]

The double bind creates the confusion and the question provides the anchor needed to bring the person out of confusion and back to reality.

The effect is that when the person answers the question at the end of the hidden double bind, they come out of their confusion and the subconscious mind immediately accepts the validity of the double bind.

The bottom line: When you hide a double bind, the mind usually first forces itself to make a decision about which option it prefers – choice A or choice B – because it seeks closure before it can move on to answer the question at the end of the sentence.

[15] The question at the end of the sentence does not have to lead on from the double bind's question. They can be unrelated.

Personal

I've been thinking losing weight and starting an exercise program for months. I just have to decide how and when to start. The choice isn't completely clear yet—count calories and walk a couple times a week or just reduce food portions and climb the stairs at work instead of using the elevator? Maybe I'll do a combination. The only thing I know for sure is that I'm starting Monday. I set up a weight loss tracking session with a counselor. Doesn't that sound like a great idea?

Learning

So far, you have been learning different ways to speak to people to make it easier for them to do what you want them to do. As you continue to learn to use these patterns, do you think that you will find them *useful in your professional life* or simply *be able to integrate them* into your behavior to enable you to be a more efficient businessperson. I have found that speaking indirectly can be more tactful in a sensitive negotiation. Did you know that the Japanese communicate this way?

Management

Just suppose you were to give me a raise right now. Would that impact this year's budget or could you slide the costs into next year's? I've been planning a trip to Europe with my mother for my 40th birthday in the spring. Have you ever been to London or Paris?

Telecommunications

Now that we've explained the benefits of ABC Service, would you like to begin conservatively with the first service we discussed or go ahead and install the second option and avoid expensive equipment upgrades next year? I have found that most customers like you send electronic messages through these networks. What type of e-mail system are you using today?

World Telecom places tremendous importance on our customers' level of satisfaction. As you evaluate us for this proposal, do you think the dedicated Corporate Account Manager or the technical strength of our Systems Engineers will be the deciding factor in giving us the (your) business? Back to customer satisfaction, have you ever noticed that more problems seem to happen when solid decisions concerning the best company for customer service aren't made right up front? I think some research studies have even been conducted on that topic and proved its validity.

Financial

In business I find that my clients can *be interested* or *be intrigued* by the concept of financial planning. I don't know whether you'll *get excited* or simply *see the value* of the service my company has to offer your business. Most of our clients like the retirement and tax planning service we have to offer. Does that sound like something you would like to hear more about, so that you can make sure you have the best plan for your future?

Insurance

After considering the options I've presented in your financial profile, I'm wondering whether you think the term insurance or permanent coverage is your best option? Most of my clients choose permanent coverage. They think they are going to live a long time and the term will become very costly or run out. How long do you think you are going to live?

Health and Well-being

Mike, you can either count calories or give up your cookies and ice cream every night, you make the decision. Either way will help you reach your weight loss goal. I found that cutting back on snacks worked for me. It's not such a sacrifice, is it?

Exercise — Hidden Double Binds

Take the sentences you wrote for the double binds and write them in the hidden double bind format.

1. ____

2. ____

3. ____

4. ____

5. ____

CONVINCER STRATEGY #4 INSTALLING SUGGESTIONS AND IDEAS WITH 'JUST' AND 'YET'

When trying to influence anyone, it is imperative to install new ideas and positive suggestions in their mind that will move you (and them) towards your objectives. You first have to open someone's mind up to prime them for a new idea. This can be accomplished by using the simple words 'just' and 'yet' (language patterns that occur naturally in normal conversations). Language patterns give form to the process whereby new beliefs, thoughts, and ideas are formed.

Here are some opening phrases to use. The goal is for the people in the communication loop to think along the same lines in a soft non-aggressive manner.

- **Can you just imagine...?**
- **Have you ever thought about just...?**
- **Have you ever just considered...?**
- **Have you thought about...yet?**
- **Have you had time to think about... yet?**
- **Did you imagine the consequences of ... yet?**

Note: Even if they have not previously thought about the subject in question—**they will now** because you have successfully installed the idea.

EXERCISE — INSTALLING IDEAS

What phrases do you use to open the conversation to your ideas?

____

____

____

____

____

____

____

____

____

____

____

Suggestion Patterns

Military recruiters are extremely successful at convincing individuals to join the armed forces—even though there is nothing romantic, exciting, or enticing about basic training and working your way up through the ranks.

Top military recruiters possibly have one of the most difficult influencing jobs in the world. Precisely for this reason, the language patterns they use are particularly persuasive.

After studying recruiting techniques used by the military, I have found that there are several patterns that fit effectively and easily into the communication influencing loop and/or a sales interview. All suggestion patterns are very flexible and become even more effective when used in conjunction with a high degree of rapport.

The outcome you want to achieve by using these patterns is to:

1. Inject doubt (confusion) about the issue
2. Start the confusion process (in order to open up the person's mind to be influenced) and then
3. Control the confusion (doubt) in your prospect's mind.
4. Change the person's beliefs.
5. Move them toward your influencing goal

Note: They will begin to doubt the validity of their particular beliefs about the subject (or product or service) being discussed if you deliver the pattern efficiently.

After you have established confusion and doubt regarding your prospect's preconceived beliefs, you can then, by using influencing techniques, alter their thoughts and beliefs with respect to your products or services.

SUGGESTION PATTERN # 1A

Have you found (outcome)?

The first suggestion pattern asks the prospect the above question, with the intention of helping them to see if their current beliefs are aligned with the outcomes of those beliefs. Using this pattern forces them to think through their beliefs with regard to the subject. Is what they are getting truly what they want? If they are getting what they want, then use this suggestion pattern to find what other information they need to move towards your way of thinking. By answering and then dialoguing about their answer to this question, you can uncover the information that you need to discover how they think **historically** about the product, goal, service, or idea. Note: This acts like a trial balloon, tentative proposal, or an exploratory discussion. You are responsible for supplying the facts and the cause and effect statements to effectively influence their thinking.

SUGGESTION PATTERN # 1B

Have you EVER found (outcome)?

How do attorneys make certain people on the witness stand think through their answers and tell the truth? They add the word 'ever' to suggestion pattern #1. "Have you found..." is simply asking a general question whereas "Have you EVER found..." insists that you go deep into your memories to find the truthful answer to the question. The person usually pauses before answering and is more serious about pondering the question when you add EVER to this language pattern.

Responses to Suggestion Pattern #1A & 1B

There are only two ways for your prospect to answer this suggestion pattern. Fortunately, both methods of answering are beneficial to your outcome.

The first answer is the affirmative. The obvious benefit is the knowledge that your client agrees with the statement that was designed to help you achieve your influencing outcome with the prospect. Another positive aspect of the affirmative answer is the acknowledgment during the meeting of a high degree of rapport between yourself and your prospective client.

If your prospect gives you a negative answer, your response should **always** be: **Not yet?**

Not yet? What information would you need to verify the truth of that comment?
or
Not yet? What facts can I let you have to convince you?
or
Not yet? What data do you need for me to give you to convince you of that?

The reply given will be the information your prospect feels he needs to have to ensure that he feels comfortable with making the decision to go further towards your outcome. In other words, your prospect has given you the method to dispose of his main objection to buying your service or product, or of going along with your ideas and goals.

Personal

Have you found the more you strive positively toward your goals, the easier they seem to be achieved?

Learning

Have you found the more hands-on the training, the better the retention and the better the material is incorporated into solid business practices?

Management

Have you found that the more appointments you make, the more people you see and the more sales you make from increased activity?

Telecommunications

Have you found that flexible pricing options enables companies to use new and better communication systems?

Have you found that the more you look at World Telecom, the more you understand that our data strategy is superior to all our competitors, or do you simply find that our data services meet your needs today? (combined with double bind.)

Have you found that switched data networks offer more flexibility than dedicated networks? Or have you found that you can reconfigure them more easily than point-to-point circuits? Our customers often feel that using a modern switching technology gives them a "high tech" look. That is very impressive in the annual report.

Financial

Have you found that most successful investors put their money in well-known mutual funds?

Have you found that the more you invest in retirement savings, the more likely you'll be able to retire without having to work part-time?

Have you found that the more you remain open to new ideas, the more you dramatically increase your chances of making more money?

Insurance

Have you found that most people with a net worth of over $ 1.5 million have invested wisely in permanent life insurance to alleviate their death tax burden from their families?

Health and Well-being

Have you found that the less you think of your own self-image, the more your self-confidence grows?

Have you found that:

- the more you exercise the better your mind works?
- when you walk regularly that you feel better?
- the more you walk, the more you want to?
- making it a habit to walk makes it easier to do it daily?

SUGGESTION PATTERN #2

Would it be fair to say (outcome)?

Suggestion Pattern #2 "Would it be fair to say?" encourages the prospect to either agree or disagree with your question according to their beliefs and their understanding of the information you provided. This pattern is used to provide reiteration of the positive aspects of your presentation. The goal is to establish a relationship between the prospect and how your product/idea/service/goal can serve and best benefit them.

Responses to the Pattern

Affirmative

The response to this question is almost always affirmative because since childhood we have been taught to be fair and polite to everyone. Affirmation drawn from this pattern is a positive reinforcement of your rapport with your subject.

Negative

If your prospect replies negatively, you should re-establish rapport immediately. You should try to find out why the person is uncomfortable and become more aware of your prospect's body language. In my opinion, if the client responses negatively to this pattern, you have not established a high degree of rapport and your sensory acuity during the sales process has been lacking.

Rarely will a person be rude enough to say that anything is unfair unless they are trying to directly antagonize you. If this happens during a closing interview, my suggestion would be to back off and re-evaluate your strategy. Again, I must emphasize the extreme importance of regaining rapport with your prospective client.

> This pattern should not be used until rapport has been established and confirmed.

In the studies we have done, this pattern works best when the receiver is a male. It is most effective when the sender is female and the receiver is a gentleman. This pattern is usually less effective when used woman-to-woman.

Personal

Would it be fair to say that helping other people makes you feel great and moves you closer to self-actualization?

Learning

Would it be fair to say you realize the value of the information we have gone over so far?

Would it be fair to say that when you consider all the alternatives that the best option is often to choose the one sitting right in front of you?

Would it be fair to say that when you consider all the alternatives and haven't yet made a decision, that simply choosing an option is easier and less stressful than not doing so?

Would it be fair to say that when you consider all the alternatives, it will make life easier in the long run?

Management

Would it be fair to say that you feel this proposal addresses your needs?

Telecommunications

Would it be fair to say that World Telecom can offer you more choices for data solutions than any other competitor in your area? Would it also be fair to say that our service contracts offer more choices than anyone else's?

Would it be fair to say that you recognize World Telecom's expertise in communications?

Financial

Would it be fair to say that you prefer the long-term lease option?

Would it be fair to say that you recognize the opportunity for you to increase your profits by making this move now?

Would it be fair to say that you are happy with the figures I have presented to you so far?

Insurance

Would it be fair to say that you feel that permanent life insurance is better than you thought it was?

Would it be fair to say that you realize the importance of disability income for your employees after looking at the statistics I have just shown you?

Health and Well-being

Would it be fair to say that losing weight and exercising regularly will prolong your life?

Suggestion Pattern # 3

What would happen if ____________,
Because... (leverage values) ?

This pattern is especially useful when your prospect expresses necessity (can't, have to, must not, shouldn't, etc.). When you ask your prospect this question you are helping them to explore the possibilities of what can happen from a different viewpoint. You are asking them to prepare themselves for a different outcome (a better outcome perhaps) if they are willing to do/try something new.

In this pattern, BECAUSE links the information together. For maximum effect, use cause and effect, single or double binds, or embedded commands in the second part of the pattern (after because) to move the client closer to your outcome.

People in general never like to think of missing out on any opportunity. Human nature certainly works to your advantage when you effectively use the third suggestion pattern. Try to create a sense of urgency when you employ this powerful pattern to help you during your sales process.

Personal

What would happen if you wrote thank you notes to the people who impact you the most?

Learning

What would happen if you made the commitment to read one new motivational book a month? Do you think it would have a positive impact on you, your business, and your family?

Management

What would happen if you managed your time better now? The sooner you start, the more free time you will have to spend on yourself.

What would happen if you make it a habit to manage your time efficiently and use it better everyday? You know you have so many things you want to achieve and this would help you accomplish all your goals.

Telecommunications

What would happen if your company decided to make the decision to expand services today because of a competitive threat? Would you see the benefit of deploying our services because they can migrate to higher speeds so easily or would the flat rate pricing be more important to your company's bottom line?

What would happen if you waited to implement this network because your organization isn't convinced that our services will make your operational costs lower? Would it positively impact your budget during this calendar year or wouldn't your company see the benefits until next year? Industry analysts look at the corporate bottom line very closely these days. Have you found that your management team worries if the stock price drops?

Financial

What would happen if you start to invest now in __________, because the sooner you get started the younger you'll be when you're financially independent?

Insurance

What would happen if you decided not to buy disability insurance today because you felt like thinking it over and tomorrow while you were waiting to make your decision, something happened and you weren't able to get the insurance now? We have a ten-day free look with a full refund if you don't like the policy benefits.

Health and Well-being

What would happen if you took a long walk with your children everyday? Think of the benefits—better health, time away from the TV, time to talk and relax, and the best thing is that you will be establishing great healthy habits for a lifetime.

SUGGESTION PATTERN # 4

Just Suppose...
+ (optional—because)

Just Imagine...
+ (optional—because)

Note: This pattern is designed to put the person into a visual mode. When your influencing goal centers on visual images, this pattern is great to use for soliciting expectations.

This suggestion pattern is another way to encourage the prospect to entertain an idea that they may not have considered before. You can help them to create a mental picture that suggests that taking a (different) course of action could lead to an outcome they might not have considered until now. You help prepare them for future positive and negative possibilities by looking at them now.

"Just suppose" is much more subtle than "just imagine". The implication is that you are not locking down decisions, you are 'just supposing' and having an open dialog about options. By carefully structuring the suggestion pattern, you start to build an image in your prospect's mind that moves toward your influencing process goal, without blatantly leading him towards your outcome.

EXAMPLES SUGGESTION PATTERN #4

Personal

Just suppose you decided to change your attitude about rush hour traffic? Instead of getting stressed, enjoy the quiet time and reflect; or listen to something motivational.

Learning

Just suppose you concentrated on changing one aspect of your habit patterns by incorporating a newly learned technique into your behavior? Just imagine the positive changes that will happen in one short year!

Management

Just suppose you use some of our services. Which ones do you think would benefit you and your company most?

Telecommunications

Our pricing really makes it easy for you to figure out your network costs. **Just suppose** your vice president asked you to expand service into the next state. Would he expect you to give the team a budgetary answer immediately or would he give you a couple days to put the prices together quickly? With our pricing strategy, you can figure out the costs fast, on the back of a napkin during lunch. That would ease your workload and stress level during a budget crisis.

Financial

Just suppose you were to make the decision to implement this investment strategy today. The more you think about the consequences of delaying your decision, the more you realize that you need to make your decision now to appreciate the positive impact on your bottom line.

Just suppose you did make the decision to transfer your IRA from your CD to an equity-based mutual fund to ensure you take advantage of the long-term growth options the stock market traditionally offers.

Just suppose you invest $200 per month for ten years? Imagine the peace of mind that action will bring to you and your loved ones.

Insurance

Just suppose you chose term insurance now instead of permanent? What would happen if you became ill after your policy runs out in ten years? Just suppose you selected permanent coverage? In ten years the premium might be paid by dividends and paid-up additions.

Health and Well-being

Just suppose you stopped smoking today? Imagine how proud your family would be.

EXERCISE JUST SUPPOSE...

Practice using all four suggestion patterns by composing three examples of each.

The first in each pattern should use cause and effect, the second—single binds, and the last either double binds or hidden double binds.

1. Have you found...

a. Cause and effect________________________________

b. Single bind________________________________

c. Double/hidden bind________________________________

2. Would it be fair to say...

a. Cause and effect________________________________

b. Single bind________________________________

c. Double/hidden bind________________________________

3. What would happen if...

a. Cause and effect________________________________

b. Single bind________________________________

c. Double/hidden bind________________________________

4. Just suppose.....

a. Cause and effect________________________________

b. Single bind________________________________

c. Double/hidden bind________________________________

CONTROLLED CONFUSION

The theory of controlled confusion states: give people enough time and the correct stimuli and they will confuse themselves about their steadfast ways or change their own beliefs (based on new suggested ideas). The goal is just to put a little doubt in their mind about what they currently believe. Remember the psychological rule of replacement.

Harry Truman once said, "If you can't convince them, confuse them." This tactic is used by politicians in smear campaigns. I find the practice unethical when used by people who know precisely what they are doing. However, I think that it is often used unintentionally and without malice.

The theory of controlled confusion is simple: when confusion sets in, so does doubt about current beliefs. When this happens, a window of opportunity presents itself for current beliefs to be replaced.

The key is to recognize the practice and also to know what controlled confusion feels like. Consequently, when your mind experiences it you can avoid getting your mind and emotions sucked into the controlled confusion vortex. When you know what the tactic feels like, you can arm yourself against the practice.

The story below will attempt to put you into a state of controlled confusion. Have you ever felt like this before? It takes a while for the mind to figure out what the purpose of the story is. This is the moment when the window of influence opens. Be warned – people open your window of influence with this tactic. It happens more than you think!

Once upon a time there were two neighbors. One guy owned an elephant. It was becoming a nuisance and very expensive to maintain so he said to his neighbor, "Listen, I'm going to sell my elephant. It's only $500. Want to buy it?"

"Not a chance!" responded the other friend. "Besides, what am I going to do with an elephant? My wife will complain, I have two small kids to support. Susan, the cat, doesn't like elephants. We thought about getting an elephant years ago, but we lived in a small apartment. The weather has been really interesting lately. It reminds me about how good the crops will be this year. Elephants sure do eat a lot of food. We can barely pay our bills right now. Besides, $500 is too much...I'll give you $100, all right?"

Can you think of a time when controlled confusion played a part in your decision making process? Discuss this!

ACTIVE LISTENING

VERBAL BACKTRACKING OR PARAPHRASING

Verbal backtracking is one of the most *successful* methods to make sure that you are asking the correct questions in an interview. With this technique we **ensure** that the prospects **true objections** can be dealt with **before** any closing attempts are made. Another great benefit of this technique is that it makes your prospect **think through his objections**; perhaps, they might even start to question the **validity** of some. With the power to select certain words to backtrack, you can selectively reinforce the ideas that will help you influence and ultimately close your prospect. Backtracking and paraphrasing *make certain* that you are able to gain rapport in a person's verbal model of the world.

How Do You Do Verbal Backtracking?

You have to listen to the exact words, ascertain their context, and then simply choose some of the pertinent words that your prospect has just spoken and **repeat the same words** in the form of a question. Make sure you inflect your voice so that the other person understands that you are posing a question to establish better understanding of their point of view. Make certain that your body language reflects curiosity and open-mindedness

The goals for verbal backtracking are:

1. For the other person to think through their position.
2. For that person to explain their standpoint to you while you listen – without interrupting or prejudging!
3. For you to have complete understanding and clarity regarding their feelings and beliefs regarding the subject being discussed.
4. To uncover objections so that you can work through the objections to solve the problem, attain your influencing process goals and their fulfillment objectives, and/or to come to resolution regarding an issue.

> I never learned anything while I was talking.
>
> Larry King

EXAMPLE — VERBAL BACKTRACKING

Prospect: I have never believed in buying life insurance.

Backtrack: *So, you've never believed in buying life insurance?*

Prospect: Yes, my accountant has always told me that it's a total waste of money.

Backtrack: *Your accountant told you that it was a total waste of money?*

Prospect: He says that I really don't need insurance right now.

Backtrack: *He says you don't need any now?*

Prospect: Yes, I'll only need it when I reach retirement and sell the business or my kids take it over to pay for any taxes due on my estate.

Backtrack: *That's interesting – when you discussed paying taxes on your estate when you reach retirement, did the unpleasant option of not reaching retirement come up? I know it's a nasty thought, but my job is to help make sure we look at all the options and protect your assets no matter what.*

Prospect: Funny, but we didn't really talk about premature death and estate taxes. My parents both lived to be older than 80 and I just figured I'd do the same. But, my wife's dad passed away at 58. His pension plan has barely covered his wife's mortgage and real estate taxes – luckily we've been able to help. My wife told me that he didn't have any life insurance except enough to cover his funeral expenses. I guess I should see what would happen to my family if that ever happened to me. I don't even know what our taxes would be. My kids are too young to take over the business and my wife doesn't want to run it.

As you can see verbal backtracking helps the person look at options and helps you ascertain their thought processes in respect to the issue at hand. The more you backtrack, the more they clarify their thinking so that you can understand their position better.

Note: Too much backtracking can make you look incompetent! If you use this process too much you might seem unable to appropriately grasp the issue. If the prospect thinks you have taken to much time to 'ramp up to speed' or understand him, he might look elsewhere for the expertise to help him solve his problem. The bottom line: Use your common sense to appropriately use verbal backtracking.

Why use Verbal Backtracking?

The traditional method used to respond to prospects' objections can lead you to a dead end.

> Using the Traditional Method
>
> Does not help you to get closer to your goal!

Prospect: I have never believed in buying life insurance.

Response: *Why is that, Mr. Prospect?*

Prospect: I just never have.

If you have the nerve to go on with direct questions to find out why your prospect never believed in life insurance, you will probably be perceived as a pushy, aggressive salesperson. **Certainly not the image that you would like to get across to a new prospect!**

Furthermore, if you do NOT find out your client's reason for his attitude about your product or service, your effectiveness during the close will be severely diminished. How can you possibly attain an effective close when you really do not know your prospect's **true** objections about your product?

Do you wait until you bump your head against them when you are presenting your sales ideas?

> **Use Verbal Backtracking to Uncover Objections During the Influencing Process!**

70 Phrases That Stimulate Action for Written Materials

1. Start with your goal – What do you want them to think, do, and feel?

   Do you want to the prospect to:
   - ✓ Attend a seminar
   - ✓ Write for information
   - ✓ Give you their email address
   - ✓ Book an appointment
   - ✓ Schedule an annual review
   - ✓ Schedule an examination
   - ✓ Call to order
   - ✓ Telephone for information, etc.

2. Write your closing line (or phrase) first. The goal is to close your ad, brochure, marketing piece, or letter with an **action-getting** phrase – this is a leading (not a pacing statement).

3. Compose a series of commands that lead the person logically toward the goal. For example, if the goal of your email or letter was to schedule an appointment (goal) the logical flow of the commands you would choose to use might be: expect my call Monday, let your assistant know I'll call you, look at your schedule, pick a couple of options on Tuesday morning, work out time on Thursday instead, lock it down in our calendars by email, confirm the appointment the day before with your assistant. If you were promoting a seminar through a newspaper advertisement and wanted to gauge the effectiveness of the ad, the commands might be: Get excited, come see five of the top motivational speakers in the country, set the whole day aside in your calendar to start learning power secrets of the country's best salespeople, rip out this ad, call before Dec. 15th for a super discounted early bird special rate, have your payment information ready, mention this ad for further savings. Note: Weave the sentences within your text into language patterns for maximum impact (e.g. Formulate the text by using a variety of influencing techniques and language patterns -- embedded commands, embedded questions and quotes, etc.).

4. Promote action. Give the reader something to write or do. The scratch off discount cards used in stores have been found to be highly effective in getting people to act. In the influencing process, if you can start the ball rolling and get your prospect to act – (even if it just a small action) – your chances of getting them to comply on more significant actions (writing a check, giving you the order, setting up an appointment, etc.) dramatically increase. Studies have proven that this tactic works well in just about every industry. In the insurance industry, if you can get them to come to a free seminar or complete a fact-finding process, the likelihood of the prospect continuing through to the completion of the sale increases each time they take action in the influencing process.

Here are 70 suggestions for words to weave into your influencing process that stimulate action.

Study these phrases. They will help you prepare your copy so that it revolves around (and is in harmony with) your influencing process.

- ✓ Act now!
- ✓ Amazing literature .
- ✓ Ask for free (samples, folder, information, etc.)
- ✓ Be the first to qualify.
- ✓ Call now
- ✓ Description sent free
- ✓ Details free!
- ✓ Everything supplied!
- ✓ Everything included!
- ✓ Fax your information and receive free
- ✓ Free plans tell how
- ✓ Free selling kit.
- ✓ Free with approvals
- ✓ Full particulars free
- ✓ Get facts that help
- ✓ Get started today!
- ✓ Interesting details free
- ✓ Investigate today
- ✓ It's Free!
- ✓ Act Now!
- ✓ Literature free
- ✓ Mail material to:
- ✓ Money making facts free
- ✓ No obligation!
- ✓ Don't Delay!
- ✓ Request free literature
- ✓ Rush name for details
- ✓ Sales kit furnished.
- ✓ Send for free details
- ✓ Send for it today.
- ✓ Simply call now
- ✓ Unique sample offer
- ✓ Valuable details free
- ✓ Write us first!
- ✓ Yours for the asking

Influencing Audiences – Formal Presentations

The key to effectively influencing an audience (or prospect) with a presentation is to know your audience **and to send the appropriate message with the appropriate words**. If your audience learns something and then finds that they can use the information you delivered to their benefit, you have successfully influenced their thinking and they will appreciate your message more in the long run. In this section, we will examine word usage and how to use phrases for maximum impact during a presentation -- specifically, focusing on how you choose words that send the appropriate message during your presentation.

Choosing the **correct words** starts with thinking about exactly **what** you want to accomplish, then tying your presentation goals to the **expectations** of the other person. The bottom line is this: **To give a successful presentation, you have to get the words right.**

The message that you want to send must be written with great thought as to the most influential and appropriate words. Care and time must be given to stimulate the intended images in the minds of individuals in a diverse audience.

A politician was asked to give a speech to a woman's group. His theme revolved around government spending and personal responsibility. Previously, he had delivered the same speech to audiences and received good reviews. Unfortunately, because he'd delivered his message so many times, he became bored with some of the words. Despite the fact that the words had been delivered before and were effective, he decided to change them a bit.

In previous presentations the politician used these exact words, "Our government is taking care of people from womb to tomb". These clever words received smiles and a number of people in the audience applauded the line. However, at this particular women's group luncheon, he chose these words instead, "I am sick and tired of our government taking care of people from sperm to full-term." He paused -- with a smile on his face, waiting for the impact of the words. As you can well imagine, the women in the audience were shocked. You could cut the silence with a knife.

Great word choices will be remembered by your audience, poor choices will not -- it's that simple.

Your word choice is critical to the communication of your ideas. Your word choice must be appropriate -- and convey solid, well-defined images. Here is another example.
Do you remember John F. Kennedy's words, "Ask not what your country can do for you, ask what you can do for your country." These powerful words, delivered during his inaugural address, will be forever associated with President Kennedy. What many people do not realize is that the idea behind these powerful words had been delivered **many** times prior to that memorable speech.

Only a few months earlier, during a campaign appearance in 1960, candidate Kennedy tried to deliver the same message using very different words. -- "The new frontier is not what I promise I'm going to do for you, the new frontier is what I'm going to ask you to do for your country." As you can clearly see, **word choice** and the **arrangement** of the chosen words made a critical difference in how the audience responded to Kennedy's message.
Another great example would be to imagine if the immortal first line of the Gettysburg Address, " Four score and seven years ago..." began instead with the words, "87 years ago..." -- I seriously doubt if school children would be compelled to recite that!

By now, you're probably thinking – I'm just in sales! Or I'm just in management! Or I'm just in customer service! I really don't have to deliver memorable speeches! Well, you do if you want to be #1 in a competitive arena. Just think about this for a moment -- If your competition can deliver a more memorable message - one that sticks in the client's mind better than yours - **I'll guarantee you that they will get the business – not you and your company!**

Delivering Your Message

Okay – so where do you begin? How do you deliver a consistently powerful message? How can you influence people positively with your words? Which words should you use? The process is actually simple, but does require forethought and planning.

1. **Start with your influencing goal**. What do you want them to think, do or feel when you are finished?

2. **Start with the image you see in your own mind**. Then, use simple words to describe that image in an outline format.

3. Next, **flesh out the details** of your image. Think of yourself as an artist painting a beautiful mental picture.

4. **Use simple power words** to embellish your image. Instead of saying implement – say the simpler – and more powerful word -- ACT. Restrain yourself from embellishing the image with words that are either too flowery or too bland. You can easily kill your message by using too many words. Just think of Nike's successful slogan "Just DO It" Suppress yourself by constantly asking – "Are these words redundant? Will they mean the same thing to the people or person I am speaking to?"

5. **Deliver the words aloud**. After you have the basis of your message complete -- and you like the words you have chosen – say them aloud. Are there better phrases - or words - you could have chosen? Jot them down next to the words that first came to mind. Next -- examine your words according to the guidelines that we are giving you.

6. **Write great opening and closing lines!**

Power Words for Impact

Powerful verbs, nouns and adjectives can generate emotional reactions and create a scenario where everyone is "on the same page". To deliver a great presentation, it is vital that each person in your audience be in the same place at the same time. People's interpretation of words depends on many factors -- our experiences in life, our emotional state at that particular moment in time, our culture, gender, age, and value system. Each person in your audience may interpret your words differently. It is up to you to make sure that your word choices establish the exact intent you desire. Avoid ambiguities in context and content.

Words like urgent, really, compelling, and critical often mean the same things to different people. If I say, "This is really urgent", I will convey a sense of urgency to most people. In English, there are many powerful simple words that convey universal meaning -- free, hot, exciting, new, improved -- to name a few.

It is imperative that you use adjectives that give meaning to your images. Descriptive words set the tone so that the context for your words comes shining through. As a presenter, you need to produce the exact image **you want to create** in everyone's mind at the same moment. If you want to **grab and keep** your audience's attention throughout your entire presentation -- make sure you feed them a steady diet of powerful words.

Let's look at an example -- If I want to describe a rose, I have to first decide the emotions I wish to evoke in my audience. Do I want people to think about gardening, love, or business? Make your rose come alive – if the rose is red, make it **blood-red, if it reminds you of glowing embers make it fiery-orange or if your rose is the first rose of spring make it spring-like – perhaps pale pastel yellow**. During your presentation, your audience's emotional involvement will be dependent on the words you choose and the images you create with your descriptive words.

Try to avoid words your audience doesn't know. If you just can't avoid words that they are unfamiliar with, make sure you give the meaning of the word. For example, the word 'paradigm' has often been used in corporations to describe a way of thinking, but the original definition is 'to show something side-by-side' - in other words – to compare something to something else. From this translation came the current meaning – that a paradigm is an example or a pattern. In the last few years this unfortunate word has been over-used, mis-used and should now be 'Not-used'.

The same 'explaining the meaning' rule applies to acronyms that your audience might not know. An acronym is a word that is created through the combination of the first letter of each word in a series of related words. For example, USA for the United States of America. Many people think that using acronyms and uncommon words during presentations should be forbidden.

Sometimes this is true BUT -- It's not necessarily a good idea to leave acronyms out of your presentation -- especially when using acronyms makes you look as if you are "in the know" or part of the group. One of the ways that groups of people bond together is through the use of industry-specific or company-specific language and acronyms. Using acronyms to gain rapport is often savvy presenting.

Just remember that you should explain the meaning if a large part of the audience will not know. For example, if you are a sales manager presenting financial information to your sales force you might say, 'I have provided each one of you with our expansion plan detailing our international launch. The package includes financial information we will be giving out. I suggest you look at it to become familiar with it. The accounting principles for next year's business plan use GAAP fundamentals. As you know, GAAP – Generally Accepted Accounting Principles - from the USA are accepted as a standard in many countries overseas. This means our new bankers and stockholders internationally will be familiar with the method we use to project our financials.

Another exception to the acronym rule is commonly used acronyms. USA (as stated above) falls into this category. Other examples of commonly used acronyms are IRS for the Internal Revenue Service, MADD for Mothers Against Drunk Driving, and PC for personal computer.

If you are speaking to a group of people in a common industry and you know precisely how to use specific words appropriate for that group, by all means use words that may be considered uncommon language for the mainstream. In many industries, if the salesperson or presenter cannot use industry jargon or acronyms, the rapport necessary to bond and connect with the audience is diminished. If you are not part of the industry but you **have taken the time** to understand something about the audience, this **extra effort** is often rewarded.

If you have to use acronyms or jargon from your own industry that the audience might not know -- and there is no way around it -- make absolutely certain that you explain your jargon before going any further with your presentation. Educate your audience, if you don't, you will pay a hefty price. Most mediocre presenters make this amateur mistake. This is often why people tell you never to use jargon or acronyms.

For example, “Because you are all in sales, many of you know very little about how my department – customer service – actually operates. Today, I’m going to give you a brief overview of how we do business. We process thousands of telephone inquires from our customers every day. My staff are the people that the customers scream at, swear at, ask for help from, rant at, and generally abuse. I understand that many of you think that my department needs improvement – I agree. When we get a RFP – a Request For Paperwork – from any customer, taking five days to get it out the door is just too long. We understand that you – as salespeople – are picking up a lot of flack for that. We hear you loud and clear. We have come up with some ideas. Let me explain how we think we can improve this situation. At the end of my explanation, I welcome your input for the new process.”

KISS

Now, let's explore some quick and easy ways to create memorable presentations simply by choosing the right words.

The **first rule** is the KISS rule -- **keep it simple and short**.

Instead of saying, "I have made a full analysis of the documentation and my recommendations are inline with those of my colleagues. Vis-a-vis our suggestions – we comprehend that adjustments are in order. We are in agreement that we must compose some timely modifications that need to be implemented before final achievement of the objectives we have delineated within our strategic plan." Instead of that long-winded, confusing babble-talk, simply say, "I looked at the paperwork. It is obvious to me, and others in my team, that some positive changes can be made so that we can get to our goals faster." Nine times out of 10, if you keep your speech at the eighth grade language level, your message will come across clearly and concisely.

Exaggeration

The **second rule** is -- **avoid untruthful or misleading exaggerations**. Exaggeration is what occurs in everyday conversation. It often conveys powerful images. For example, "I was starving." "I was on hold for half the day." "Why is everyone incompetent?" make powerful statements in a listener's mind.

The risk in using exaggeration is that you may appear over-reactive, unbelievable, or not fully based in reality. Your listener may think that you are blowing a simple situation out of proportion to the 'big picture'. This skews the communication of your overall message. The listener's mind seeks truth. If you exaggerate and they think you are untruthful – they will 'switch you off'.

The obvious question here is, "Is it ever okay to use exaggeration as a presentation tool? Can using exaggeration, in fact, sometimes strengthen your presentation? When you use exaggeration with humor it can be extremely powerful. The humor element allows you to exaggerate and therefore strengthen an important point. This works best with careful planning and perfect delivery. If you have to make a statement or get an idea to stick in the audience's mind, only use this technique once or twice during your presentation.

A well-known female executive, dressed to the nines, stepped to the podium. She told a funny story that made the audience roar with laughter as she described how early on in her career she had to go work diligently against the odds of female success in a male-dominated industry. She told the audience that the thing that helped her most in her rise through the corporate ranks was her sense of humor. After one particularly grueling day, as she was leaving the building, she stood in the entrance and looked back on all the petty nonsense and laughed and laughed and laughed.

She said, "I couldn't stop laughing – people were stopping and staring – which of course only made me laugh harder and harder. After ten minutes, my sides were killing me. The worst thing was, I laughed so hard I thoroughly soaked my shoes and had to splash all the way back to my car!" This vivid image was hysterically funny because of the woman who said it. She used her style to poke fun at herself, her Fortune 100 Corporation and to make light of a bad situation. Her highly imaginative use of exaggeration and humor combined with her overall classy image made the audience roar with laughter. Warning: She established high rapport with the audience. If she had not been able to deliver her story humorously, it might have seemed crude.

Creating Word Images

The third rule for great presentations is -- **understand how words are structured and how words form images in people's minds.**

Let's look at some language usage that can be thought of as theatrical props during presentations. These techniques turn rookies into pros – and make boring presentations come alive!

Repetition

One of the fundamental principles of learning is that people learn best through **repetition**. Repeating phrases, words or whole sentences can work very effectively in presentations. Repetition can hammer a point home and make it stick in people's minds. This repetitive learning tool in a presentation is even more effective if you repeat groups of words in an identical rhythm or in a similar tempo. Using this technique draws attention to the phrases. This tool has often been used as the basis for complete speeches. In Martin Luther King's "I have a dream" speech, Dr. King repeated the phrase "I have a dream" throughout his memorable presentation. People might not remember the rest of the words in that speech but, they know exactly who delivered the "I have a dream" speech and the fundamental message Dr. King delivered. It sticks in people's minds because of the repetition technique he chose to use.

Repetition can be used to dramatically create emotional impact or to make an important point. Repetition can be used to establish you as an expert in your field and to make you memorable when compared to other presenters.

The Rule of Three

Another powerful presentation tool is -- **the rule of three.**

The rule of three is the technique of grouping three words, sentences or phrases together. In behavioral science, studies have shown that grouping three ideas, things or thoughts together usually can create a powerful impact on the human mind. Some examples of the rule of three include:

I came. I saw. I conquered. From Julius Caesar

"... Government **of the people, by the people, for the people**..." from Abraham Lincoln

Advertisers often use the rule of three. Some recent examples are -- "**no hype, no hassle, no problems**!" or "So, if you're ready to have fun, relax, and make money -- join us."

Listen to this business example from a speech given by Dr. Robert McAfee at his inaugural address as president of the American Medical Association:

"Since 1990, we've said this 1,000 times in 1,000 forums -- the message is simple -- you can boil it down to three words: voice, choice, and coverage. The physician's voice, the patient's choice, and universal coverage. This is your agenda. This is my agenda. This is what we all stand for, and we will not stand for anything less."

Dr. McAfee's speech used repetition and the rule of three to deliver his passionate message. His presentation resulted in a standing ovation.

How can you effectively use the rule of three? Just take a minute or two to think about your subject. If your subject is quality service -- you might use these three phrases -- **customer focus, superior products, and commitment**.

If your presentation is about effective management – try tying these three words together: **listen, analyze, and act decisively**.

Allusion

Allusion is often used by excellent presenters. This technique is using a particular word -- the allusion word - as a **direct or indirect** reference to something. When you **allude** to a person, thing, or event; you are using the technique of allusion. In general conversation, the allusion technique is usually used by referencing words with historical, cultural, religious or literary significance. The allusion reference works best when the majority of the audience is able to make the connection between the things you are describing and the reference you have chosen to use. There are many wonderful examples you can effectively allude to that are known by the majority of the population from great literary works, mythology, the Bible, and current events. If you are in a corporate setting, it is usually advised to refrain from using religiously based allusion examples.

You might use an allusion from mythology as with this example, "Dorothy, by dropping that bomb shell in our next management meeting, you will be opening a Pandora's box of problems." In mythology, Pandora's box was sent as a gift from the gods to a woman (Epimetheus) who was forbidden to open it. When she did, because she could not control her curiosity, she let loose a swarm of evils and plagues upon mankind. Pandora's box is associated with big trouble. Some other examples of allusion are: from modern culture -- "living and working in the rat race", and another from mythology is "making a Herculean effort".

Alliteration

If you plan your presentations well, you can use another literary technique called **alliteration**. Alliteration is using words that begin with the same sound used close to each other. Think of - Peter Piper picked a peck of pickled peppers and Sally sold seashells at the seashore.

Rhyming

To remember phrases, we have used the technique of rhyming since we were small children. "An apple a day keeps the doctor away."

Many slogans and branding campaigns use this technique to help consumers remember products. The benefit of rhyming is that it has 'stickiness'. It stays in our head long after non-rhyming phases depart. Taster's Choice coffee uses "Your day. Your way." A headline for a story about public speaking from the Reader's Digest magazine: "Faking when you're shaking."

Metaphors

A metaphor is a story that is used as a way to link an abstract concept to a more concrete image in the listeners mind. It forms a relationship between something that is known to the audience to help them understand a new or unique concept. A good example is computers. To people who are unfamiliar with computers, we can explain computers as having senses and a memory just like a brain.

When used correctly, metaphors can create the perfect image for an audience. They can solicit emotional involvement from a group. Unfortunately, too often, presenters fail to deliver the metaphor correctly and its impact is severely diminished, if not destroyed completely. Sometimes, a presenter might even mix up metaphors. When this happens a presenter runs the risk of looking like a fool or appearing ill prepared. A mixed-up metaphor can turn a serious moment into a comedy of errors.

Examples of mixed-up metaphors actually delivered during presentations are:

I want to be sure I'm not killing a dead horse.
We need to compare apples to peaches.
He is his own best friend.
These are the kind of things that drive me out of a tree.
We've come 180, and gone around full circle.
I'm afraid we are killing the chicken that lays the golden eggs.
We're where the balls stop.
We're going to knock their air right out of the water.
Like shooting pickles in a barrel.
We'll burn that bridge when we come to it.
It will be a dark day when you see the light at the end of the tunnel.
We've got to seize the bull by the tail and look him in the eyes.

Techniques using the Influencing Process & Language Patterns

A well-written letter will set you apart from the crowd and impress the person you are attempting to influence.

There are certain things to bear in mind when writing letters or correspondence.

1. **Time is valuable**. People do not want to spend valuable business time reading unnecessary and/or irrelevant information. Keep letters to less than one page.

2. **Spell-check** all correspondence.

3. **Check all syntax and punctuation** - spell-checking software will not pick up syntax errors, punctuation mistakes, ambiguities, some grammatical errors, or incorrectly used words.

4. When you have corrected any errors and **read it again**, (if possible) hand it to another person to read. This is especially important for critical correspondence. Make certain there are no errors because it will jeopardize your chances to make a good impression. It may actually deter your chances of getting the business, landing the position for which you are applying, getting a promotion, moving your influencing goal forward, etc.

5. Understand this fact - there is **no room for error** in professional correspondence. Assume that perfection is your only alternative. Make no mistakes; if you send out sloppy correspondence you will hurt your reputation.

6. Do not send anything out in a rushed, hurried manner. This is when errors occur. **Take extra time** to ensure that everything is perfect before it is sent.

7. **Confirm information** - the correct mailing address, fax number, correct spelling of the person's name you are addressing and ask if there are any titles, designations, or special manner in which the person prefers to be addressed (especially with Miss, Ms., Mrs. or Dr.). Address the person using their corporate position or title in all correspondence. Try to get a business card if possible. Confirm the correct department for delivery and spelling of the department name with appropriate capitalization.

8. If you discover an error and the document is already in transit or has arrived, **send another CORRECT document** as quickly as possible. If possible call the person directly or the assistant to stop the delivery and explain that the corrected version is on the way. I know of a person who discovered that they had misspelled the addressee's name incorrectly and tracked down the Federal Express driver in transit through their radio dispatch operator. They asked that the package not be delivered until a new cover letter was included with the person's name correctly spelled.

CHECK, CHECK and Double Check!

PACING AND LEADING LETTER WRITING TECHNIQUES

In the art of letter writing, the most powerful way to attain your desired outcome is to use the combination of pacing and leading in the following potent formula.

PACE PACE PACE LEAD
PACE PACE LEAD
PACE LEAD
LEAD LEAD LEAD ....Always LEAD to your specific outcome!

Pacing is the art of gaining and maintaining rapport for a period of time by interacting with another person. You can pace ideas, beliefs and behaviors. Whenever we use PACING, we have to ensure that we talk about or do something that is ***verifiably true*** in our prospect's world and is within their realm of experience.

Leading is doing something ***different*** than what your prospect is doing. When you successfully LEAD your prospect, you steer him/her towards your planned outcome.

For letters:

Ascertain your influencing goal (the final outcome of the total influencing process)[16] and write it down. This will make certain you stay on track and always lead toward your goal. Then write down the specific goal for this correspondence. Make certain you write down at least three commands that you will weave into the text of your leading statements that: 1. Move the influencing process further toward your goal and 2. Promote action.

Write down a series of a minimum of three pacing thoughts or sentences. Make certain the series has logical sequence and flow.
Follow your pacing series with your first leading thought.
Next use two more pacing thoughts followed by another lead towards your outcome.
Finish with your last pacing statement, followed by as many leads as you desire.

[16] The letter you are currently writing might only be a small step in the overall influencing process.

Recap for Letter Writing

Always write down your specific outcome (influencing goal) **BEFORE you write your letter**.

Always keep your influencing goal FOREMOST in your thoughts as you write the letter to your client.

Your letters will be extremely powerful if you use appropriate embedded commands that relate directly to your SPECIFIC OUTCOME.

After you have written down your outcome, write down some embedded commands that you feel will be appropriate in your letter to your client.

Follow the PACE/LEAD formula for writing your letter or facsimile correspondence.

SAMPLE COVER LETTER For Product Sale

Exercise

What is the overall influencing goal?

____

____

____

What is the specific goal of this correspondence?

____

____

____

November 5, 2002

Dr. Dorothy Bell
Executive Vice President
Global Sales and Marketing
123 South Street
Anyplace, NY 19999

Dear Dorothy,

(pace) During our meeting yesterday, ***(pace***) we had briefly discussed the fact that your company (employee and client) size has increased. You said you were worried because the increase in staff is causing a backlog in the availability of the photocopying machine – especially for critical tasks. You also said that your department would require a new photocopier immediately for two reasons. The first is to meet your increased correspondence needs to clients in your sales and marketing department. Secondly, you also told me that you had been promoted and had taken on two new departments, one of which was assigned the task sending out all Board correspondence. Congratulations! ***(pace)*** When I returned to my office after lunch, ***(lead)*** I decided to send you further details on our product line, so you could review the options that may meet your criteria for purchasing such an integral component for your office.

(pace) We briefly discussed various ways to decrease copying costs, while increasing efficiency - as your employees find an escalated usage of the copier because your sales are increasing and to meet the rush of client (and Board Member) requests for information prior to the Board Meeting. ***(pace)*** As you already realized (and we very briefly discussed), there are ways to ensure that your client's needs are met without your company undertaking excessive overhead costs. ***(lead)***

Before I left the luncheon, ***(pace)*** you said that you wanted a solution for the current productivity problem. Every day you see too many people hanging around, doing nothing productive while waiting for a big job to finish – when they just had a page or two to copy. ***(lead)*** Because you and I had so little time to chat and your timeline is so short, I would like to set up two meetings. The first one by telephone to specifically discuss the problems you are currently faced with for your photocopying requirements and the second – after I have analyzed your options – so we can meet in person and I can deliver my recommendations. ***(lead)*** I will be in your area next week on Tuesday and Thursday for the second appointment and can meet with you in either the morning or the afternoon. ***(lead)*** I will telephone you in a day or two to confirm the receipt of this material and answer any questions you might have. **(lead)** Feel free to contact me in the interim.

Very truly yours,

Gregory Small

SAMPLE COVER LETTER

February 25, 2002

Mr. Harold Cohen
National Director
Sample Company
777 First Street
Hometown, PA 19000

Dear Harold,

(pace) During our meeting yesterday, ***(pace***) we had briefly discussed the fact that your company size has increased enough to establish a regional office here in Philadelphia. ***(pace)*** When I returned to my office after lunch, ***(lead)*** I decided to send you further details regarding my experience in starting three regional offices for my previous company.

(pace) We briefly discussed various ways to lessen your risk as you enter the Philadelphia marketplace. ***(pace)*** As you already realized and we discussed, there are limited ways to ensure your success. ***(lead)*** In my opinion, the best way to ensure success is to fill the Regional Director position with a candidate who is familiar with both the products you market and the Philadelphia/New Jersey area.

(pace) As you know, Bill and I are meeting next Wednesday to go over my resume and my qualifications for the position. ***(lead)*** I would appreciate you telephoning Bill to let him know the views we shared during our interview. ***(lead)*** I would also like to forward a copy of the enclosed matter to Bill for his perusal. ***(lead)*** I will telephone your secretary before the weekend to obtain Bill's mailing address. **(lead)** We will meet in Bill's office at three o'clock on November 16th. ***(lead)*** I will telephone you on Friday to confirm the receipt of this material and answer any questions you might have. **(lead)** Feel free to contact me in the interim.

Very truly yours,

Gregory Small

Exercise

What is the overall influencing goal?

____

____

____

What is the specific goal of this correspondence?

____

____

____

Sample Letter to Prospect Met Through Networking

May 5, 2002

Gordon Harley
National Sales Director
ABC Corp.
3002 22nd Avenue, Suite 304
Washington, D.C. 20001

Dear Gordon:

(pace) I enjoyed meeting you at our technical update seminar last week and spending time with you over dinner ***(pace).*** During the meeting we discussed your plans to expand the company by entering the Baltimore market. ***(pace)*** As I said, our discussion stimulated my interest in relocating to the East Coast. ***(lead)***

(pace) You mentioned that the new position will be extremely challenging and the growth potential for the operation is exciting. ***(pace)*** You said that the reason you invited me to the dinner was that you thought I would be an excellent candidate for the position, so I am enclosing my updated resume for your perusal. ***(lead)***. My experience in setting up new offices, keeping within budget, bringing projects in on schedule and leading and building a new team is extensive.

(pace) I have also enclosed a brief history of the last two projects I managed. ***(lead)*** I will be back in my office on Tuesday. **(lead)** I will call you to arrange a meeting to discuss the opportunity your company is offering in the Baltimore area. ***(lead)*** My schedule would allow for me to come to Washington for an appointment with you and Mr. Clark on Wednesday, May 17th or Monday, the 22nd. ***(lead)*** Please advise which day would suit both you and Mr. Clark best. ***(lead)*** Feel free to contact me in the interim through my assistant, Janet, at (415) 555-5555.

Very truly yours,

Desmond Smythe

Exercise

What is the overall influencing goal?

____
____
____

What is the specific goal of this correspondence?

____
____
____

Cover letters to "TARGET" companies

GUIDELINES

Paragraph # 1

This paragraph should answer the question of 'Why' you are writing:

- Why should the person receiving the letter read it?
- Why are you writing?
- What is in it for the reader?

Start with a **compliment** about the company to which you are writing.

- "Your company has established a good reputation in....."
- "I was impressed with the recent news of your earnings."
- "Your plans to construct a new facility are impressive."

State that you know that progressive companies are always seeking quality people to hire or to do business with. (Which is true.)

Then say that you feel that your background (or product or service) may be of interest.

Paragraph # 2

This is your QUALIFICATION paragraph.

- Why are you an exciting candidate?
- What is it about your service or product that they might need?
- What it is about you that would be of interest to the hiring manger, executive, or purchasing agent to whom you are writing?

Begin with a few brief statements about your experience (or the benefits of your service or product)
Features: How can doing business with you benefit them?

- Length of experience: Use words such as: extensive, broad, diverse, varied, etc.
- Accomplishments: Mention one or two of your recent and major accomplishments.
- Skills: Summarize in one **short** sentence your best abilities or skills.

Paragraph #3

State that you think it would be to your mutual benefit to meet and talk. Also, say you will contact him/her within a few days to arrange a meeting. (**Avoid using the words "interview" and "appointment".**)

Remember to **CALL when you promised you would** in the correspondence!

Sample Target Letter

Date

Addressee/Title
Address

Dear Sir/Madam:

(pace) I note with great interest your advertisement in the New York Times for the technical advisor position. ***(pace)*** I realize that your company has made major technological innovations in the semiconductor industry. ***(pace)*** I have enclosed my resume as requested along with my salary history. ***(lead)*** My extensive and varied experience with ABC Laboratories has enabled me to complete ISO Certification for my division and to understand current techniques and applications within our industry.

(pace) As you can see from my resume, I have been able to utilize my skills to solve analytical, process development and circuit design problems including:

- Developing and managing implementation of a new customer database resulting in saving the company over $1 million in consulting fees and beat the deadline for achievement by more than one year.

- Establishing statistical quality control procedures for multiple location measurement and process variability.

As you are no doubt aware ***(pace)***, the design team I worked with at ABC Laboratories has been a leader in the field for the past decade. I have noted the requirements for the position you are advertising and I am certain you will agree my qualifications are an excellent match for the position ***(lead)***.

You also required a salary history statement. Please find it attached ***(pace)***. I will contact your office next week ***(lead)*** to ensure receipt of this letter ***(lead)*** and to discuss your availability for a meeting ***(lead)***. Please feel free to contact me in the interim with any questions you may have.

Very sincerely yours,

Xxxxxx Xxxxxxxxx

> Exercise
>
> What is the overall influencing goal?
>
> ____
>
> ____
>
> ____
>
> What is the specific goal of this correspondence?
>
> ____
>
> ____
>
> ____

Sample Letter to a Headhunter/Recruiter

Date

Addressee/Title
Address

Dear Mr./Ms. Smith:

Enclosed please find my resume for your consideration ***(pace)***. As I mentioned on the phone yesterday ***(pace)***, I am particularly proud of the leadership role I played in obtaining ISO certification with XYZ Corporation. As you can see ***(pace)***, I have had key management responsibilities in a wide spectrum of the graphic arts industry ***(lead)***.

Highlighted in my summary statement ***(pace)*** are my primary strengths and my management and leadership experience in a customer focused environment adhering to bottom line results. Also shown in the experience section ***(pace)*** are the technical applications I have dealt with; Heatset, non-Heatset web printing, sheet-fed printing, full web and half webs. For the past twelve years ***(lead)***, facilities under my direction have improved profits every year.

As we discussed ***(pace)***, my preference would be to locate to the Philadelphia area ***(lead)***. My next preference would be the East Coast ***(lead).*** My last salary was $xx,xxx with an annual performance bonus that ranged from 5-10%***(lead)***.

After you have had a chance to review my resume, I will contact you to discuss employment opportunities.

Sincerely,

Xxxxxxx Xxxxxxxxxx

Exercise

What is the overall influencing goal?

____

____

____

What is the specific goal of this correspondence?

____

____

____

Writing Fax Correspondence

Always include the following on your fax cover sheet when using facsimile correspondence.

1. Your name, fax number, and telephone number.

2. Details of the person to whom you are corresponding: their full name, title, and department.

3. If the fax is urgent state the delivery urgency on the cover sheet.

4. If you would like confirmation of delivery and receipt of your complete document, state this request.

5. Always use this type of information for business faxes:

This facsimile is intended only for the use of the individual or entity for which it is addressed and may contain information that is privileged, confidential, and exempt from disclosure. If the reader of this facsimile is not the intended recipient, you are hereby notified that any review, disclosure, dissemination, distribution or copying of the communication is strictly prohibited. If you have received this communication in error, please notify the sender immediately at the telephone number above, and destroy the original or return it to us at the above address by US Mail and we will reimburse the cost. Thank you for your cooperation.

Use the following pacing and leading formula when sending faxes:

PACE PACE LEAD
PACE LEAD
LEAD LEAD

Note: Fax correspondences should be shorter than the final letter.

For facsimile correspondence:

- Start with the goal and write it down.
- Write down a series of two pacing thoughts or sentences.
- Follow your series with your first leading thought.
- Next use one more pacing thought followed by another lead towards your outcome.
- Follow with as many leads as you desire.
- What actions do you want from your fax?
- Is the action easily understood by the receiver?

Sample Fax Correspondence

Sample 1

(pace) As we discussed by telephone today, ***(pace)*** I am faxing you a copy of my resume. ***(lead)*** Please look it over. ***(pace)*** As you can see, I have extensive knowledge of the telecommunication industry, especially in statistical forecasting for sales. ***(lead)*** Please forward my resume to Bob Johnson. ***(lead)*** Let him know that I will telephone him on Monday to ***(lead)*** set up an appointment. ***(lead)*** I will call this afternoon to confirm receipt of this transmittal. Thank you for your assistance in this matter.

Sample 2

(pace) Thank you for the time you spent talking with me on the phone yesterday describing your plans for the Intellectual Property Group. ***(pace)*** I am faxing you my resume as requested. ***(lead)*** I think you will find that I possess the skill set and experience necessary to hit the ground running in your operation.

(pace) As we discussed, I will be available for a meeting to further discuss your requirements early next week. ***(lead)*** I will contact you tomorrow to set up a convenient time for us to get together ***(lead)*** Please contact me at (610) 555-5555 if you have any questions.

NOTE: Study this technique and use it in all of your future correspondence. Combine letter writing with pacing and leading for maximum impact.

Writing Email Correspondence

Always include the following in your email when using the Internet for correspondence.

1. Your name, telephone number, fax number and email address.

2. Details of the person to whom you are corresponding: their full name, title, and department.

3. If the email is urgent state the delivery "urgency" in the subject line.

4. If you would like confirmation of delivery, state this request.

5. Be certain that you have filled in the subject line, multiple cc's and blind cc's correctly.

6. Always use this type of information for business emails:

> This email is intended only for the use of the individual or entity for which it is addressed and may contain information that is privileged, confidential, and exempt from disclosure. If the reader of this email is not the intended recipient, you are hereby notified that any review, disclosure, dissemination, distribution or copying of the communication is strictly prohibited. If you have received this communication in error, please notify the sender immediately by email or at the telephone number above, and delete or destroy the original. Thank you for your cooperation.

Use the following pacing and leading formula when sending emails:

PACE PACE LEAD
PACE LEAD
LEAD LEAD

Note: Email correspondences should be shorter than the final letter.

For email correspondence:

- Start with the goal and write it down.
- Write down a series of two pacing thoughts or sentences.
- Follow your series with your first leading thought.
- Next use one more pacing thought followed by another lead towards your outcome.
- Follow with as many leads as you desire.
- What actions do you want from your email?
- Is the action easily understood by the receiver?

Sample Email Correspondence

Sample 1
(pace) As we discussed by telephone today, ***(pace)*** I am emailing you a copy of my resume. ***(lead)*** Please look it over. ***(pace)*** As you can see, I have extensive knowledge of the telecommunication industry, especially in statistical forecasting for sales. ***(lead)*** Please forward my resume to Bob Johnson. ***(lead)*** Let him know that I will telephone him on Monday to ***(lead)*** set up an appointment. ***(lead)*** I will call this afternoon to confirm receipt of this email. Thank you for your assistance in this matter.

Sample 2
(pace) Thank you for the time you spent talking with me on the phone yesterday describing your plans for the Intellectual Property Group. ***(pace)*** I am emailing you my resume as requested. ***(lead)*** I think you will find that I possess the skill set and experience necessary to hit the ground running in your operation.

(pace) As we discussed, I will be available for a meeting to further discuss your requirements early next week. ***(lead)*** I will contact you tomorrow to set up a convenient time for us to get together ***(lead)*** Please contact me at (610) 555-5555 or email me if you have any questions.

NOTE: Study this technique and use it in all of your future correspondence. Combine letter writing with pacing and leading for maximum impact.

EMBEDDED COMMANDS that Work Effectively for Correspondence

Since childhood, we have learned to obey orders and direct commands or suffer the consequences. We have been programmed to obey short commanding sentences. At school, teachers and authority figures told us how to behave and what to do to conform and/or 'fit in'. **Embedded commands** are commands that fit into the normal structure of a sentence (they are hidden between the other words) without drawing attention to their existence.

Examples of Embedded Commands

Call me to make an appointment
Set an appointment
Get together to go over my qualifications
Get together to discuss the position
Refer to my recent letter
Contact me with any questions
Expect a call from me on Friday
Read my resume
Read the enclosed resume/materials
Refer me to your human resources department
Consider my application
Look over my resume
Remember me
Schedule an appointment
Consider me as a candidate
Forward my name and resume to your department head
Set up a telephone appointment
Expect my call on Tuesday
Set a date for a future meeting
Answer my past letter
Forward my resume to the appropriate person
Forward my fax to the appropriate person
Check/review on my qualifications
Read the last section of my resume
Check my references
Reply to my request
Feel happy
Trust me
Feel contented
Believe me
Get excited
Be interested
Take my word
Be open
Make a decision
Get sold on the idea
Get together soon
Make an appointment
Sit down together
Discuss openly
Be receptive
Feel confident
Move quickly
Feel relieved
Do it now
Convince yourself that it's right
Get it
Buy into the idea
Feel good inside
Put in a good word for me
File my resume for perusal (in January when you hire personnel for your Washington, D.C. office)
See that this is an excellent match for your requirements/position
Consider my abilities (as a team player in your new department/for the position)

Transitional Time Line™

The psychological model affecting people working through change.

The goals *Shorten the time period from notification to achievement* ***AND***
Lessen the negative emotional impact and heighten the positive.

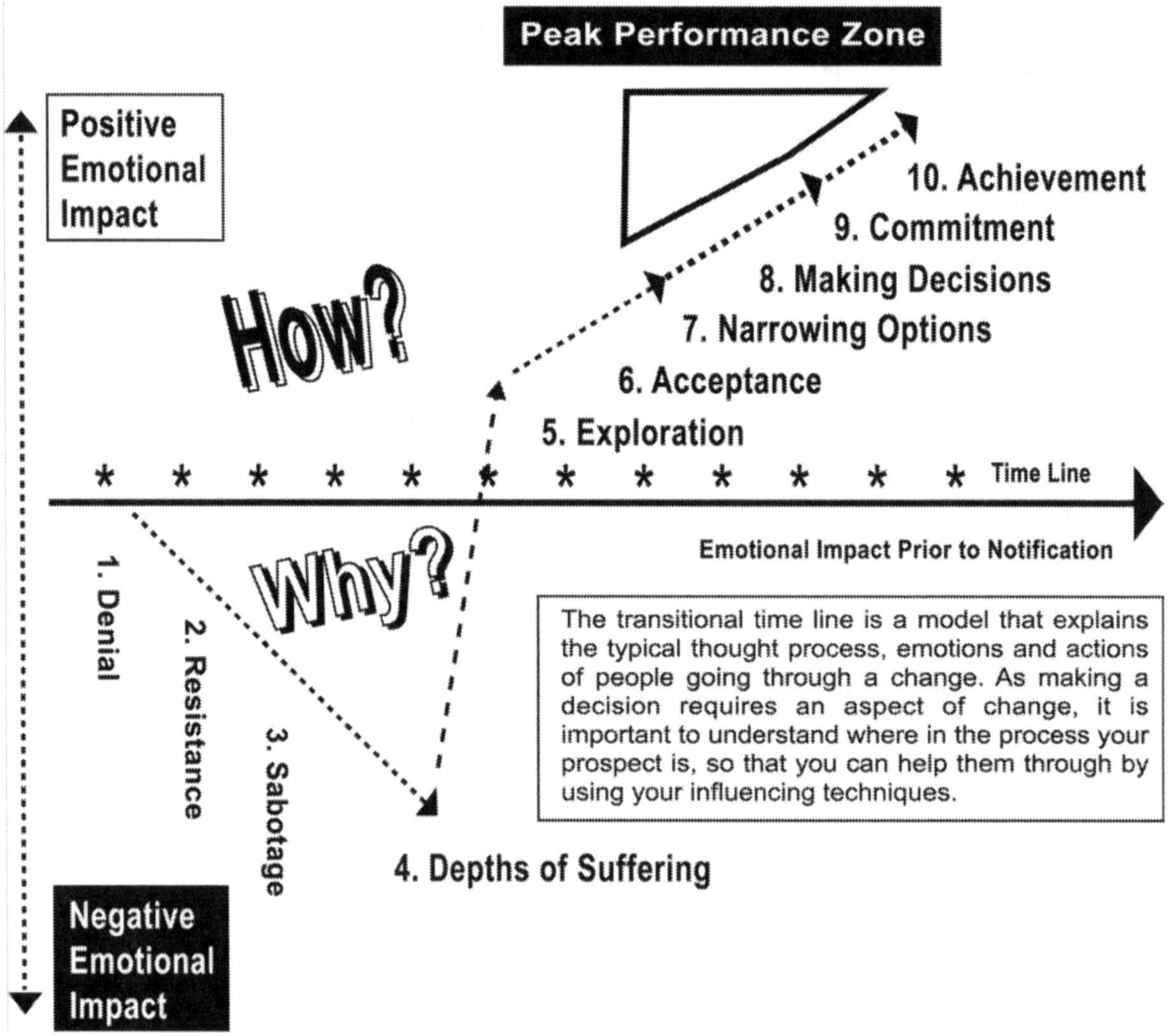
Peak Performance Zone
Positive Emotional Impact
How?
10. Achievement
9. Commitment
8. Making Decisions
7. Narrowing Options
6. Acceptance
5. Exploration
Time Line
Emotional Impact Prior to Notification
Why?
1. Denial
2. Resistance
3. Sabotage
4. Depths of Suffering
Negative Emotional Impact
The transitional time line is a model that explains the typical thought process, emotions and actions of people going through a change. As making a decision requires an aspect of change, it is important to understand where in the process your prospect is, so that you can help them through by using your influencing techniques.

TRANSITIONAL TIMELINE – LANGUAGE PATTERN USAGE

You've got to go through the negative before you can get to the positive.
WIL BURSON

Use Language Patterns to Move People Forward through the 10 Psychological Phases of the Transitional Time Line

The language patterns listed under each phase of the transitional timeline are suggested influencing approaches to use for moving people through each phase as quickly as possible. The less time it takes people to move through the transitional time line (because you successfully helped them to see your perspective) the more quickly you can reach your goal! The first 4 stages are often the hardest stages to move through and beyond as they are the "negative" stages of the timeline (unless you have created and maintained a high level of rapport). It is also important to move people through the exploration and narrowing options phases as quickly as is appropriate in order to shorten the time it takes to achieve your influencing goals.

1. **Denial**
   - Cause and effect (direct and implied)
   - Embedded quotes
   - Embedded questions
   - Single binds (towards abundance, e.g. "The better you X, the more you Y")

2. **Resistance**
   - Cause and effect (direct and implied)
   - Embedded quotes
   - Embedded questions
   - Effective use of 'but'
   - Single binds (away from abundance, e.g. "The more you X, the less you Y")
   - Suggestion pattern #1a ("Have you found...?")
   - Suggestion pattern #2 ("Would it be fair...?")
   - Suggestion pattern #4 ("Just suppose...")

3. **Sabotage**
   - Effective use of 'but'
   - Single binds (away from abundance, e.g. "The more you X, the less you Y")
   - Double binds (choice A or choice B...?) Same outcome. (Direct or hidden)

4. **Depths of Suffering**
   - Effective use of 'but'
   - Double binds (choice A or choice B...?) Same outcome. (Direct or hidden)
   - Suggestion pattern #3 ("What would happen if... [combined with double bind] ...because...?")
   - Suggestion pattern #4 ("Just suppose... [combined with hidden double bind]...?")

5. **Exploration (& Brain Storming Sessions)**
    - Cause and effect (direct and implied)
    - Embedded quotes
    - Embedded questions
    - Effective use of 'but'
    - Single binds (towards more abundance, e.g. "The more you X, the more you Y")
    - Double binds (choice A or choice B...?) Same outcome. (Direct or hidden)
    - Suggestion pattern #1a ("Have you found...?")
    - Suggestion pattern #2 ("Would it be fair...?")
    - Suggestion pattern #3 ("What would happen if...because...?")
    - Suggestion pattern #4 ("Just suppose...")

6. **Acceptance**
    - Cause and effect (direct and implied)
    - Embedded quotes
    - Embedded questions
    - Single binds (away from abundance, e.g. "The more you X, the less you Y")
    - Suggestion pattern #1a ("Have you found...?")
    - Suggestion pattern #2 ("Would it be fair...?")

7. **Narrowing Options**
    - Embedded questions
    - Effective use of 'but'
    - Single binds
        a) away from abundance, e.g. "The more you X, the less you Y". Use this to eliminate an undesirable option for your stakeholder.
        b) towards abundance, e.g. "The more you X, the more you Y". Use this to promote the most desirable option for your outcome.
    - Suggestion pattern #1a ("Have you found...?")
    - Suggestion pattern #2 ("Would it be fair...?")
    - Suggestion pattern #3 ("What would happen if...because...?")
    - Suggestion pattern #4 ("Just suppose...")

8. **Making Decisions**
    - Cause and effect (direct and implied)
    - Embedded commands (hidden within positive structured sentences)
    - Embedded quotes (with third party endorsements)
    - Embedded questions
    - Double binds (choice A or choice B...?) Same outcome. (Direct or hidden)
    - Suggestion pattern #3 ("What would happen if...because...?")
    - Suggestion pattern #4 ("Just suppose...")

9. Commitment

- Embedded quotes
- Embedded questions
- Single binds (towards more abundance, e.g. "The more you X, the more you Y and the more you Z.")
- Suggestion pattern #1a ("Have you found...?")
- Suggestion pattern #2 ("Would it be fair...?")
- Suggestion pattern #4 ("Just suppose...")
- Future Pacing

10. Achievement

- Cause and effect (direct and implied)
- Embedded commands
- Embedded quotes
- Single binds (towards more abundance, e.g. "The more you X, the more you Y and the more you Z.")
- Suggestion pattern #4 ("Just suppose...")
- Prospecting information & referrals

PUTTING IT ALL TOGETHER – SCRIPTS THAT GET RESULTS

Take a page from Eastern philosophies. The Chinese symbol for crisis is a combination of the symbols that depict opportunity and danger. If you use the tactic of moving proactively, well ahead of the stressful situation, the opportunity side of crisis will be far greater than the dangerous side.

Individuals who keep a clear head, use effective words and phrases, and strategize with regard to their influencing messages continually outperform those who do not.

Using the Influencing Process

Planning communication in advance (as much as possible) and using positive, proactive words works exceptionally well when offering reasons (excuses) when deadlines go awry. Understand that obtaining more time is often just a matter of choosing the right words during stressful times.

What to say when you have to re-negotiate a deadline

When deadlines are missed, either someone has broken a promise to you or you have broken a promise to them. Tension and emotional levels usually run high when deadlines are not met. When you break a promise to customers, the corporation runs the risk of losing their business. When slippage occurs between departments, employee relationships suffer.

Broken promises break down relationships and trust. Broken promises result in anger, feelings of betrayal, reduced trust and other negative emotions from the person who expected you to keep your word. The damage caused has to be repaired and the negative fallout has to be kept to a minimum.

Remember, getting more time is usually negotiable when things don't go as planned – especially if you warn people of potential slippage well in advance. Use strong negotiating words during chaotic situations. Studies have shown that the best negotiators consistently use powerful words designed to put them in charge. Most often, the most effective influencer is the person who is perceived as the one who is least stressed.

In today's hectic environment many variables often result in time slippage and deadlines not being met when promised. Extensions often have to be negotiated between employees. The key is to keep trust high and negative emotions low. The goal is to keep the situation in a purely business context first, then in a context that deals effectively with emotional involvement. Dealing with emotions as a secondary focus will often diffuse unnecessary tension. In an ideal world, the third person perceptual prism should be the starting point for all parties. But, most often people begin the dialog with emotional involvement so that the other person will understand that you empathize with their situation.

Let's take a look at a script that attempts to do this effectively.

Eric: John, this is really bad for us. How am I supposed to tell my boss that this is not going to be completed on time? This is a nightmare! Listen, I just can't allow your team to get away with this. You are going to have to put the pressure on and get this work out! I'm deadly serious about this deadline.

John: Eric, I knew you would be unhappy. I was serious about that deadline, too. We have been able to complete the first three phases successfully. In fact, we've come in on time and under budget on all three.

Looking forward, I have to give you a heads-up. The next two phases have the potential of being late. Our engineers are reporting that phase four will consume more time than we budgeted for. I think you will agree with them when you see the reasons. They also said that this is not the stage to start cutting corners.

I know you are caught in the middle, but I wanted you to be aware of what's happening. That's precisely why I'm calling you now to talk about it. We still have three weeks before that initial deadline comes up. Right now, we have enough time to strategize about the best way to rethink dates, alter schedules and adjust the completion date for the entire project. If we manage this **methodically and investigate our options** we can expedite product delivery to the client without severely impacting our resources.

We can take care of this and deliver without any mistakes. If we move forward with haste, with only a short-term view, without modifying the time line, we run the risk of alienating the client in the long-term. This would cost our corporation millions in future revenue. (*Business reason in the 3rd perceptual position for renegotiating the timeline)*

Eric: John, why don't you give me some more details? I have to tell you, I'm not happy.

John: I'm not happy either, Eric. But, we have to focus on the big picture—on what's best for client and our company and its employees. (3rd perceptual position) I've had a hard time putting my emotions aside about this deadline, but I know that it's the right thing to do. I just got off the line with Tony in operations and the deadline is off because we had three unforeseen liability issues. Tony thought we should get our parties in alignment as soon as possible and re-schedule the deadline until these issues are resolved.

I have to tell you that my blood was boiling when he called but **what he said made sense from a business standpoint** *(agreement from 3rd perceptual position)*. We can't put the company in this potentially risky situation with the customer. Let's sit down as soon as possible to figure out how we can deal with this now that we've established why we have to re-schedule.

Eric: I was not aware that the company was at risk.

John: I realize that you probably were in the dark as much as I was until 30 minutes ago. I just wanted to give you a heads up as soon as possible so that we can stay on top of the issue. I have two more calls to make to gather some more information. Let's get together this afternoon and hammer out a strategy and a new time line.

Eric: I'm in a meeting until 1:30 p.m. I'll meet you in the conference room at 1:45.

Exercise — Negotiating a Deadline

What strategies were used in the story above?

How effective were they?

What can you use from this script?

How to influence a client to allow you to budget adequate time for project (when the client wants it yesterday!)

Mrs. McConnell: My attorney said that I have to get this financial plan to his offices by Friday. When Rick referred you he said that you did great work—fast.

Susan (financial planner): Mrs. McConnell, I realize that your attorney needs this by Friday. Our process usually takes ten business days. In order to meet your deadline, we would have to rush delivery of your plan and complete it in 48 hours.

In my experience, mistakes occur when things are not planned appropriately and thought out fully. This is especially true when dealing with financial matters.

In order to complete the process efficiently and effectively, my offices have to consult with all of your advisors and it is imperative to gather all information before proceeding. This process takes time. If we skip any of the integral components, the effectiveness of the plan suffers.

We have a choice here—we can rush it out and cleanup any oversights later or we can reduce our time line slightly and do it right the first time. Give us seven days and I can promise to deliver the superior quality we are renowned for. I'd rather you were 100% satisfied instead of 75% happy and 25% unsatisfied. Delivery of quality financial planning is usually more important in the long run than losing a couple of days in the short run.

Your attorney has had several months to complete his side of the planning process. I'm sure he'll understand why we would prefer to do it correctly the first time; rather than alter our work after we discover more details that didn't surface until after the project was complete.

Let's see if we can renegotiate Friday's deadline or at least comply with some of the information and analysis he needs by Friday. I'm sure we can resolve this time issue to everyone's satisfaction.

Mrs. O'Connell: My attorney was quite adamant about Friday but I can see your point. Why don't you give me an idea of when you can complete the project and I'll phone my attorney about his deadline?

EXERCISE — NEGOTIATING A DEADLINE

What strategies were used in the story above?

How effective were they?

What can you use from this script that will help you to influence others?

Answers to the Exercises

Examples of Absolute and Generalities

Absolutes	Generalities
Absolutely	Generally
Whole	Part/partial/ Just about
All the time	Sometimes
Every time	Pretty much Sometimes
Complete	Incomplete
Definite	Part/partial/ Just about Maybe
Finite, wholly	Part/partial/ Just about Infinite, undefined
All	Pretty much Mostly numerous
Only	Some Just about
Entire	Some Part/partial/ Just about
Never	Once in a blue moon Sometimes At times Occasionally
Every one	Some people A few
No one	Some people A few
None	Some Part/partial/
Always	Pretty much Sometimes Rarely On occasion
Nobody	Some people A few
Everybody	Most people A few Several people

Absolutes	Generalities
People/someone's name Everyone No one	Some people A few Several people
Exact percentages	Approximately some/most/many several/few some/few/most Between
Last/last one/final the end/final/close out	Near the end Drawing to a close
First/foremost/first one/one of a kind (innovative)	One of the first One of several
Couple	Some Few
I am certain	I predict, project, participate, expect, forecast
Impossible	Could be possible
Certain	Probably, likely, unclear, some
I know	I think, I suppose
All	Some/part/partial
Nobody	Somebody
All	Approximately/most (high)/few (low)/a good percentage (low, medium, or high)
Everyone	Few/several
Highest	Higher
Lowest	Lower
Deepest	Deeper
Truth, fact	Ambiguity, ambiguous

Expectations for movement 'towards' or 'away from'

People move 'towards' or 'away from' because they have expectations about what will happen if they take a course of action.

You must uncover their expectations to determine if the person's expectations are in line with what your product, service, and or influencing goal will deliver.

Here is a list of phrases the person might say:

Toward (Pleasure and Goal attainment)	Away (Pain and Avoidance)
Attain financial security	Fear of losing people's respect (losing reputation)
Make more money	Avoid embarrassment
Satisfy hunger	Steer clear of troublesome individuals
Be liked (be popular)	Avoid physical pain
Attract a mate	Dodge sensitive issues
Assuage curiosity	Sidestep criticism
Be in a position to take advantage of opportunities	Steer clear of dangerous situations (Politically and physically)
Get rewarded for efforts	Stay away from extremes
Be praised	Avoid conflict
Save time	Prevent exclusion from a group or team
Save resources	Shun complications
Conserve energy	Stop losing money or assets
Be comfortable	Avoid risks
Make life simpler	Keep away from change
Achieve work/life balance	Stay away from disputes
Live in beautiful surroundings	Avoid feeling excluded
Stay warm	Steer clear of feelings of inadequacy
Be part of the team	
Feel included	
Have the respect of friends, peers and family	
Be involved in the community	
Become 'the go to guy' – an expert	
Have freedom of choice	

EXAMPLES	LANGUAGE PATTERNS TO USE TO MOVE PEOPLE

DENIAL:

Client: We don't need to discuss options now, the rate increase is not for another month.

Cause & Effect:
If we get started now, any change that may occur will be easier for your employees.

Embedded Quote:
You know I had a similar situation with ABC Company. Last month, after we did this, Joe said "I'm glad that I started the process early because all my employees had their ID cards before the effective date."

Embedded Questions: If you don't do this now, what will the impact be on your employees if a change needs to be made?

RESISTANCE:

Client: I don't need to look at any options; I know you'll be able to reduce this rate action.

Suggestion Pattern #4:
Just suppose, I am unable to do that and reducing the rate action any further isn't an option; what types of benefit alternatives might you and Sarah accept so that we can sign off on them and get this complete before the month end?

Suggestion Pattern #2:
Would if be fair to say that if we come up with an acceptable alternative plan (at a better price) that you would stay with this plan?

Negative Single Bind:
The longer we wait to look at alternatives, the more unhappy your employees will probably be when having to make the change anyway.

SABOTAGE:

Client: I am sure that Alexis Company will be able to provide me the same benefits at the current rates I am paying.

Effective use of 'but':
Yes but; Alexis Company does not have the national network access that you need.

Single Binds:
The more you review Alexis Company QPOS benefits; the more you will realize that they are more restrictive than our PPO benefits.

Double Binds:
You can look at some alternatives with us or go through the aggravation of changing carriers and then find the network is not what the president is insisting on. You might have to change back to us anyway, and you know how much people hate change.

DEPTHS OF SUFFERING:

Client: How am I going to explain the rate increase to my CEO?

Double Binds:
You can present two options to the CEO. Either keep the benefits the same and switch to Direct Access or keep your PPO with some co-pay and deductible changes that will alleviate the burden of increasing the rates.

Suggestion Pattern #3:
What would happen if you offer the HMO plan to your employees and have them "buy up" the current PPO plan?

Suggestion Pattern #4:
Just suppose that we could show the CEO all the alternatives available; would that help?

EXPLORATION:

Client: I don't know if Direct Access would work for my employees since the network is different than the PPO.

Suggestion pattern #3:
What would happen if we do some research and we find out that most of your employees were already using the Direct Access physicians out of preference anyway?

Embedded quotes:
When ABC Company was making the same decision; Joe said, "Most of my employees were using Direct Access physicians anyway when I surveyed them".

Suggestion pattern #2:
Would it be fair to say that as your employees are spread around the country having the nationwide access is more important and the fact that the network does not change with the switch to Direct Access is secondary?

ACCEPTANCE:

Client: How do I know that Direct Access will work for my employees?

Embedded Quotes:
When we made the change at ABC Company; Joe said, "My employees were really happy with the new plan."

Suggestion Pattern #1a:
Have you found that your employees prefer to keep deductions to a minimum or not change benefits and share more of the cost?

Suggestion Pattern #2:
Would it be fair to say that your employees would be happy with the fact that they won't need to obtain referrals anymore and that nationwide access is something they enjoy on the PPO?

NARROWING OPTIONS:

Client: We still want to get more quotes

Suggestion pattern #4:
Just suppose that you got more quotes, and spent lots of time on this. From my experience, most plans are similar in cost but the service you'll receive is what you should make your choice based on. Also, the more you look, the more you'll realize that the other plans will not give you the open access and nationwide network that you are looking for.

Single Bind:
The longer you wait; the more you risk our rates going up.

Suggestion Pattern #1a:
Have you found that when you have too many options in front of you it becomes more confusing and difficult to make a choice?

MAKING DECISIONS:

Client: I need to bring this to the CEO, I don't know what he will want to do.

Double Bind:
Do you think he would prefer to keep the PPO with co-pay and deductible changes or change to the Direct Access with the same plan design?

Suggestion Pattern #3:
What would happen if you focus your spreadsheet on Blue Cross Blue Shield of NJ options; because, then you would not have to think about the hassle of changing carriers?

COMMITMENT:

Client: We are not ready to schedule enrollment meetings.

Single Bind:
The longer you wait, the more service issues your HR people have to deal with.

Suggestion Pattern #4:
Let's look at best-case scenario. Just suppose, we schedule the enrollment meeting and had all the applications back in two weeks from today. I am confident that we could deliver the ID cards back to your office prior to the effective date. Wouldn't that make your employees happy?

Embedded Quotes:
I just got a call from Sally at ABC Company and she said "I am so happy that we were able to complete enrollment early, it is amazing how smooth it went. I didn't get any phone calls from my employees at all!"

ACHIEVEMENT:

Client: I'm sorry the accountant's out, we can't give you a check.

Cause and Effect:
That is unfortunate since we cannot begin processing the paperwork until we receive a check. Is there anyone else authorized to do his job in his absence?

Embedded Commands:
Doesn't the CEO have check writing ability? Why don't we ask the CEO to write the check?

Suggestion Pattern #4:
Just suppose I come by at 9:00 am tomorrow and pick up the check, we can get the group processed by the end of the week.

Language Pattern Cheat Sheet

Language Pattern	Definition	Formula	Examples
Commands			
Embedded Command	Command inside a sentence	Opening phrase + COMMAND + closing phrase	Let's sit down together and set a date to meet with your investment agent.
Embedded Quote	A command hidden in a quotation within a sentence. Instead of telling the person directly what they should do, an embedded quotation suggests the action that should be taken based upon what another person in a similar scenario said or did.	Beginning of Sentence + Quotation + end of sentence	Just last week, another client, Mr. Jones, said to me, "I like this product. It will fit my current needs for security and long-term growth."
Embedded Question	A command hidden in a question within a sentence. This is an especially effective way of softening commands because they allow the receiver of the message to take responsibility for applying the command to him/herself – without requiring the speaker (or sender of the message) to do it. The receiver plays an active role in the application of and answer to the question (command).	Prelude to embedded question + command + question.	I sometimes ask myself, "Why don't you just get on the phone and make appointments, immediately!?" I'm wondering whether.…
Cause & Effect			
Cause and Effect	An explanation for the relationship between action and consequence – based on interdependence of people in the communication loop. Words that suggest a cause and effect relationship: *As, since, invokes, creates, determines, causes, makes, during*	X causes Y If you buy this product you will become more confident, build a better image and get the job of your dreams!	Listening to customers causes you to evaluate your course of action and consider better matches with their buying criteria.
Implied Cause & Effect	A language pattern that requires the receiver of the message to determine the relationship between the action and consequence, based on the implication of the effect/result outcome.	As X, Y Buy this product and see all of your financial and workplace worries disappear! (Sender requires the receiver of message to determine HOW this will happen)	Invariably it is true—as is the inner so always and inevitably will be the outer. RALPH WALDO TRINE You might not want to risk that. (implies a negative outcome)
If… Then	A language pattern that explains how the brain deciphers the relationship between two or more things	If A occurs then B is likely to be the consequence	If you believe you can do a thing, you can do it. CLAUDE M. BRISTOL
Nested If's	A language pattern that helps receiver to gather necessary information and eliminate unnecessary data (when data does not comply brain moves on to next question)	If A occurs then move on to the next if B (to gather more specific info) and so on	If you are a past or present member then… Do you have a fulltime membership? If YES then see next question.

Convincer Strategies			
Single Binds	Two statements that express a cause and effect relationship. Single binds always reflect only one comparison (with no alternatives) of what will occur (the positive and negative consequences inherent in the cause and effect) for the two statements.	The more you X, the more you Y. The more you X, the less you Y. The less you X the more you Y. The less you X, the less you Y. The more you X, the more you Y, & the more you Z. The more you practice, the more you remember. The more you practice, the less you forget. The less you practice, the more you forget. The less you practice, the less you remember. The more you practice, the more you remember, and the better you get.	The harder the conflict, the more glorious the triumph. **THOMAS PAINE** The more your team understands the process, the less confusion will exist
Double Binds	A sentence structure that subtly influences the receiver of the message by giving them the illusion of choice. Two commands are used within a sentence that is formatted to allow the person being influenced to make a decision on which option to choose. Both decisions will yield in the favor of the sender and will propel the influencing process forward.	B choice or C choice Used to provide the illusion of choice	You can justify this proposal on cost savings or consider its merits based on customer services. We must all hang together or assuredly we shall all hang separately. **BENJAMIN FRANKLIN**
Multiple Pattern Double Binds	A series of double binds and hidden double binds (with or without a verbal response from the other person in the communication loop) preplanned to achieve a desired outcome.	Beginning of sentence……B (choice) or C (choice) & repeat pattern Provides a series of choices that moves ever closer to the influencing goal Perception of giving the other person control.	I'm in your area every Tuesday and Thursday. When are you available in the morning or afternoon in order for me to gather your criteria?

Convincer Strategies			
Hidden Double Binds	The structure for a hidden double bind is the same as the structure for a double bind. Instead of completing the thought you continue talking and then ask a question. The double bind is sandwiched between the structure of the sentence and the question at the end.	Beginning of sentence....B (choice) OR C (choice) ....QUESTION? Assumes compliance without the person having to state that they agree.	As you continue to learn to use these patterns, do you think that you will find them useful in your professional life or simply be able to integrate them into your behavior to enable you to be a more efficient businessperson? I have found that speaking indirectly can be more tactful in a sensitive negotiation. Did you know that the Japanese communicate this way?
Installing Ideas and Suggestions with Just and Yet	This language pattern helps the sender of the message to open someone's mind up to prime them for a new idea. It prepares the receiver to be more open for to be influenced during the communication process.	Question with words yet or just within sentence structure. Purpose is to keep the mind open to influence and suggestions.	Can you just imagine what it would be like to live in Florida where the weather is nice all year round? You could drive your convertible down there even in the winter! I know the initial thought of relocating is scary, yet have you considered how much money you will save on living expenses by going down south?

Suggestion Patterns			
Suggestion Pattern #1a	This pattern helps people to see if their current beliefs are aligned with the outcomes of those beliefs. Is what they are getting truly what they want?	Have you found (outcome)?	Have you found that flexible pricing options enables companies to use new and better communication systems?
Suggestion Pattern #1b	Same as above – but word ever increases intensity of the question and requires people to delve deeper into past memories to provide a truthful answer.	Have you EVER found (outcome)?	Have you ever found yourself less than satisfied with your service from XYZ company?
Suggestion Pattern # 2	This pattern encourages the prospect to either agree or disagree with your question according to their beliefs and their understanding of the information you provided. This pattern is used to provide reiteration of the positive aspects of your presentation. The goal is to establish a relationship between the prospect and how your product/idea/service/goal can serve and best benefit them.	Would it be fair to say (outcome)?	Would it be fair to say that when you <u>consider all the alternatives</u> that the best option is often to choose the one sitting right in front of you?
Suggestion Pattern # 3	This pattern helps people to explore the possibilities of what can happen from a different viewpoint. Here you are asking people to prepare themselves for a different outcome (a better outcome perhaps) if they are willing to do/try something new.	"What would happen if__________" (because)	What would happen if you made the commitment to read one new motivational book a month? Do you think it would have a positive impact on you and your family?
Suggestion Pattern # 4	This suggestion pattern is another way to encourage the prospect to entertain an idea that they may not have considered before. You can help them to create a mental picture that suggests that taking a certain action could lead to a certain outcome. You help prepare them for future positive and negative possibilities by looking at them now.	"Just suppose" or "Just Imagine" "Just suppose" is much more subtle than "just imagine". In your prospect's mind you start to build an image without blatantly leading him towards your outcome. Very effective when combined with embedded commands.	Just suppose you <u>use some of our services</u>. Which ones do you think would benefit you and your company most?

ABOUT THE AUTHOR - HELLEN DAVIS, CLU

Overview

For more than two decades, Hellen Davis has been a corporate strategist, executive consultant, and motivational speaker. Hellen Davis is the President & CEO of Indaba Training Specialists, a management consulting and training corporation. Her clients include executives and leaders from dozens of Fortune 100 corporations. Ms. Davis is an entrepreneur and self-made millionaire who has been a guest on many talk shows and has appeared on a large variety of TV and radio stations across the country (CNN, Dateline, EXTRA, etc.). She recently appeared on the cover of Main Line Today and is frequently quoted in national publications. Her books, manuals, and audio-visual materials are widely distributed by bookstores, online, in corporations, and by independent consultants.

Keynote Experience

Hellen has delivered motivational, strategic planning and sales presentations worldwide. Her keynote addresses are described as dynamic, motivating, captivating, and educational. She entered the sales arena in the life insurance industry where she quickly rose to become one of the top producers in a $14 Billion insurance company. Her skills and success in sales result from being a top sales person for a Fortune 100 Company, as well as a general agent for a multi-national insurance company. Hellen says, "The experience I had selling financial products and services as well as my experience in air sports (skydiving, flying, and hang gliding) was the grounding and springboard for the goals I have achieved. This unique combination of experiences forced me to confront fear, overcome adversity, plus it taught me that to a large extent survival depends on achieving a high level of knowledge in the endeavor I am undertaking." In keeping with her love of the life insurance industry, she personally coaches over fifty insurance and investment people annually so that they can attain similar success. Hellen also coaches dozens of CEOs, executives, and management teams in the process of accountability and executing strategic goals. She is well respected for her extensive knowledge of influencing strategies, strategic planning, behavior modification processes, sales and peak performance expertise, and negotiation tactics. Her keynotes and seminars focus on influencing strategies, communication & management development, sales management practices and training techniques.

International Experience

Hellen Davis has an impressive knowledge of the international marketplace and shares her global philosophy with audiences. She lived overseas in Africa and Europe for more than twenty years and is fluent in five languages. She founded, owned and operated an import/export company in South Africa dealing with Europe, the Far East and other African countries, the United States, and Canada. After immigrating to the USA, she and her husband founded 30glycolic.com, a company that has supplied skin care products online throughout North America, Europe, Asia and Africa since 1988.

Publishing & Corporate Products

Several years ago, Indaba Training Specialists, Inc. formed a subsidiary, Indaba Press. With Ms. Davis' leadership, Indaba Press has produced numerous audio cassette series, corporate manuals, support and training materials and workbooks; including several based on the cutting edge techniques in the fields of influence and of neuro linguistics (the language of behavior and brain patterns), specifically designed for sales, marketing, customer service, and management professionals.

Media

Hellen has graced the cover of "**Main Line Today**" magazine, headlining an article entitled, "*Women in Charge*" and "**Philadelphia Magazine**" voted Hellen Davis as one of Philadelphia's "*Women to Watch*" because of her business acumen, her contributions to the area's networking affiliates and women's business organizations, her role in raising consciousness for effective networking and her good standing in the community. She is often quoted in publications and newspapers; including the Philadelphia Inquirer, Philadelphia Daily News, Lancaster New Era, etc. Ms. Davis has been a guest on many talk shows and has appeared on a large variety of TV and radio stations across the country (CNN, Dateline, EXTRA, Philly After Midnight, **ABC**: WPVI-Philadelphia, **ABC**: WHTM-Harrisburg, **CBS**: WHP-Harrisburg, **NBC:** WBRE-Wilkes-Barre, **NBC**: WGAL-Lancaster, **FOX**: WOLF Scranton, **96.5** WWDB-Philadelphia's Talk Station, **1210** WPHT-Talk Radio etc.).

Community Involvement

Hellen Davis is Past President of the Main Line Women's Network, Past President of Women's Capital Funding, a Past Board Member of The Women's Referral Network of Chester County, Past President of the Tri-County Business Alliance, current Board Member of the YMCA Heritage Foundation, and a Charter Member of the National Association of Female Executives.

Education

Ms. Davis was educated in the United States, England, Scotland, France and South Africa. She holds a BS Computer Science, Masters Designation in Neuro Linguistic Programming, and holds a CLU from American College focused on Estate Taxation and Planning, Corporate Taxation, Financial Analysis and Budgeting, and Accounting Practices in Corporations. While in the insurance and investment industry, Hellen successfully completed several NASD securities licenses.

Hobbies & Interests

She resides in the Philadelphia area with her husband, Jack, and their two children, Jazmin and Justin. When she was younger, she modeled overseas and she holds the Mrs. East Coast USA 2002 title. Ms. Davis came to the United States more than 15 years ago from South Africa with next to nothing and is now a self-made millionaire. She is creative and artistic and in her free time enjoys spending time on the beach with her family, reading voraciously, and working with stained glass and mosaics. She has over 6 years experience in the skydiving world and was parachuting instructor. Hellen was a coach and judge for two skydiving World Champion teams. She plays tennis, golf, likes to water ski, and loves entertaining friends.

THE INDABA STORY

Indaba is a Zulu word for the concept of 'seeking knowledge'. Indaba is a process of discovery, analysis, goal setting and self-fulfillment.

The three initial stages of Indaba are:

1. Assessment of your current possession of knowledge.
2. Formulation of goals.
3. Examination and determination the steps necessary to achieve your goals.

The heart of Indaba is discovering your inner strengths and weaknesses and using both to achieve your life's goals. Indaba's power lies in the process of putting ego aside -- allowing acceptance of the fact that you may not currently possess all the knowledge necessary to fulfill your true potential. This acceptance will enable you to go to the next level of growth -- active search of relevant information. The strength of Indaba is proactively seeking out the knowledge you need to achieve peak performance and your ultimate goals.

Throughout African history, the people and warriors of the Zulu nation actively sought the advice of the council of elders. The seeker of knowledge first told the council of their goals and/or of the dilemma/s they faced. Each elder listened intently and gave a synopsis of their view of the path the knowledge seeker should follow to achieve their goals and/or to solve their problem. After all the elders gave their opinion, the warrior then left the council area.

At no time did the elders form joint consensus of the dilemma that faced the seeker of knowledge, nor did they try to impose their will upon the seeker. The council's purpose was to provide accurate, concise, factual information and to exhibit differing viewpoints and strategies. In this manner, the seeker had a highly experienced forum to advise him/her.

The Zulu council comprised of diverse facets of the community; from many disciplines and varying wisdom patterns. Each member offered an extensive breadth and depth of knowledge. At the end of the session, the seeker often asked for one solution to the situation he had described and brought to the council. The answer the council gave was always the same, 'We have given you many wise, well thought-out options. Now, the decision is yours. Go in peace -- this is your Indaba.'

The three final stages of Indaba:

1. Assess and analyze all options, knowledge and council received.
2. Weigh opportunities and analyze potential pitfalls -- closely examine the consequences of each choice.

Choose the best goal path for your individual situation -- follow your destiny with forethought, clarity, motivation and purpose.

About Indaba: The Company

We believe in accountability.
We achieve long-term results.

Organizations are more challenged than ever. Competition is greater. Customers' expectations are higher. Technology is advancing at the speed of light. The bar continues to rise at a resounding rate. Employees and organizations need to work harder and smarter.

Clients look to us because we consistently solve problems and implement solutions.

Corporate leaders find that they benefit from having us come in to provide an objective view. We can help you grow people and develop strong leaders. Indaba consultants have established a track record of success with executives, teams, managers and employees to implement behavioral modification and change. Indaba assists you in reaching goals and quickly creating organizational alignment based on accountability and profitability. How? Our certified consultants and instructors teach psychological models of excellence and we help you put them into action within your company.

Indaba Training Specialists, Inc. focuses on training, consulting, and improving individual and organizational effectiveness. *We specialize in:*

- Teamwork
- Leadership Development
- Change
- Influence and Communication
- Delivering Feedback and Receiving Coaching
- Advanced Communication Skills
- Sales and Negotiation
- Executive Coaching
- Customer Service
- The Accountability Factor: RA^2 Interface
- Customized Executive and Team Retreats

What makes our organization unique?

- We have designed creative and customized training courses for optimum adult learning and employee development.
- We teach advanced psychological models with the goal of behavior modification.
- Indaba has a proven track record of success since 1988.
- We have an extensive network of experienced trainers, coaches and consultants.
- We have worked with a range of industries and many diverse organizations

Books

ISBN:1-58570-160-2
Price: $29.95

ISBN:1-58570-383-4
Price: $29.95

ISBN:1-58570-307-9
Price: $29.95

ISBN:1-58570-063-0
Price: $29.95

ISBN:1-58570-072-X
Price: $19.95

ISBN:1-58570-291-9
Price: $29.95

Seminars, workshops & programs

Indaba Institute Executive Coaching Certification Program (CCE Designation)
The Executive Coaching Certification Program will educate you through our condensed training program on how to become a professional executive coach. The Executive Coaching Certification Program will allow you the ability to work with individuals helping them reach their true and full potential. With your help as a Certified Executive Coach, your clients will have the power to meet today's growing demands to grow profits, cut costs, and maintain productivity and morale. They will also have the support needed to meet business goals. You will be transforming results in corporate communities and organizations. CCE following your name will show that you meet the coaching industry's highest standards, and assure you clients of your competence and professionalism.

Teambuilding -- Cutting Edge Team Dynamics
Develop high-performance teams by improving the behavior of team leaders and team members. An interactive, time-sensitive workshop provides a high-impact learning experience. The team designs and builds a visual reminder for longevity of the lessons learned.

Influence and Communication
This program provides the means to break the communication code wide open. Just imagine if you had the power to understand the exact meaning and intent of communication. Picture being able to decode messages you receive. What if you could transmit the exact meanings necessary to achieve your goals? What potential!

Alignment: The RA² Interface
Marry expectations and metrics - Deploy people with:
1. Clearly defined responsibility.
2. Accountability- benchmark metrics as previously agreed upon
3.Authority factors necessary to complete goals. The goal is to foster intercompany and intradepartmental cooperation and alignment.

The 21 Laws of Influence
The 21 Laws of Influence will help you to clearly understand how people are persuaded and how others affect our beliefs. The course provides the basis for deciding which strategies will be most effective on those you must influence and will educate people to avoid getting caught in a web of influence or roped into a persuasive argument without being aware of the mechanics of persuasion.

Change -- Is Your Organization on Fire?
Employees are taught to deal effectively with the phases of change. The goal is to move your people through change in a manner that stokes creativity and innovation, enhancing corporate goals and visions.

How to Deliver Feedback and Receive Coaching

How do you grow employees if you don't deliver feedback effectively? This course provides the processes on how to reduce the fear associated with delivering feedback and how to receive feedback with an open mind.

Sales Coaching Certification Program

Targeted behavioral changes build superior salespeople. This MBA- like course is specifically designed to drive individuals to reach the next level of sales and best influence customers with their personal style. The goal is to establish long-term client relationships and increase product and service purchases.

PARTIAL LIST OF CLIENT PARTNERSHIPS

Air Products
Allegheny Power
Allstate Insurance
American College of Physicians
Ardmore Alliance
AT&T
Blue Cross Blue Shield of NJ
Businessman's Life of Kansas
Centra Financial Group
CoreStates Bank
Corum Healthcare
Department of Energy
DVFG Financial Group
Eastwood Company
E.F. Hutton
First Capital Holdings
GE Medical
GMAC
Hansch Financial Group
Icon Clinical Research
Leadership Peak

Lee Hecht Harrison
Lincoln Financial Planning
Liberty Life
Lutheran Brotherhood
Massachusetts Mutual Life
Meridian Bank
MetraHealth
Metropolitan Life
MISO – Midwest ISO
National Computer Services
National Assoc. of Female Exec.
National Security Agency
Nationwide Provident Insurance
New England ISO
Northwest Mutual
Pacific Corinthian
Parke-Davis Pharmaceutical
PECO Energy
PennDOT
Pfizer Pharmaceutical
Philadelphia 76ers NBA Franchise

PJM Interconnection, LLC
Prism
Provident Mutual
Prudential Life Insurance
Raytheon
Sears Financial
Corporation
Shop Rite
Supermarket
Spohn Medical – Texas
St. Paul Companies
State Farm Insurance
Sun Corporation
Texas A&M
Ursinus College
US Senators
Verizon
Wakefern Corporation
Warner-Lambert Pharmaceutical
Wharton School of Business

To receive our free eBook, ***"The Complete Influencing Process for Sales & Leadership Professionals",*** and a subscription to our free monthly newsletter, ***"Influence & Inspiration",*** valued at **$189.95** send an email with **'free eBook' in subject line to: eBook@21laws.com.**

Power point presentations, manuals and audio also available for sale on website.

For more information on Train-the-Trainer programs, Executive Coaching Certification programs, consultant programs and training materials, bulk pricing on products, and speaker information please contact our office.

Indaba, Inc.
866-894-1222
info@indaba1.com
www.Indaba1.com
www.21laws.com

www.ingramcontent.com/pod-product-compliance
Lightning Source LLC
LaVergne TN
LVHW080020110826
845148LV00019B/988
* 9 7 8 1 5 8 5 7 0 1 0 1 8 *